THE IMPORTED PIONEERS
Westerners who helped build modern Japan

BY THE SAME AUTHOR

The Shinkansen Train Song and Others (Private printing 1976)
The Golden Age of Yokohama on Postcards (1980)
Yokohama E-hagaki Sho (Yurindo 1980) In Japanese
Yokohama Grafica (Yurindo 1989) In Japanese
The Pedlars of St. Columb Minor 1590-1990 (Four Turnings 1990)

THE IMPORTED PIONEERS

Westerners who helped build modern Japan

Neil Pedlar

Japan Library Ltd
Sandgate, Folkestone, Kent

THE IMPORTED PIONEERS
Westerners who helped build modern Japan

© 1990 Neil Pedlar

First published 1990 by
JAPAN LIBRARY LTD
Knoll House, 35 The Crescent
Sandgate, Folkestone, Kent CT20 3EE

ISBN 0-904404-51-X

British Library Cataloguing in Publication Data
Pedlar, Neil, *1940–*
    The imported pionieers : Westerners who helped build modern
Japan.
    1. Japan. Relations with Western World, history 2.
Western World. Relations with Japan, history
    I. Title
    303. 4825201812

ISBN 0-904404-51-X

Set in Times Roman 10 on 11 point by Visual Typesetting, Harrow, Middlesex.
Printed in Great Britain by BPCC Wheatons Ltd, Exeter

Contents

Acknowledgements

THIS BOOK began in 1977 when, as an alternative to writing letters to *The Japan Times,* I wrote a lengthy article for the magazine *Tokyo* which was edited by Geoff Murray. He accepted the article and appointed me history contributor. However, the ill-fated *Tokyo* lasted for only 10 issues. Some of the unused articles I had prepared were submitted to *The Japan Times* itself, and Mr. Gyo Hani, the managing editor, agreed to publish them on an irregular basis. Some were adapted and published in various magazines and newspapers in Britain.

Most of them were written in my small house at the less affluent end of the Bluff in Yokohama which had a view across to Mount Fuji and the Hakone Hills on those rare clear days. At the time I taught science at the Yokohama International School where Edward Bernard was the Careers and History teacher whose family had lived in Yokohama since the 1870s, and who was part of the history recorded here. His knowledge of the Meiji period ran wide and deep, some of it uniquely a part of his own family heritage, and his advice after reading my articles was invaluable and he often corrected or readjusted my own views.

As my research became more involved, so my circle of friends widened and my *meishi* (name-card) case became thicker. The history office of Yokohama City Council provided photographs, the British Council librarians found where I could borrow rare books, Susan Manakul in the Library of Congress searched through old magazines for me and a host of acquaintances helped me translate sections of Japanese books. A few journalists became interested in my activities and wondered why I was so concerned about the history of Japan, and I could only reply that while living there I was a part of that country and that, anyway, some of the most perceptive books about America were written by Japanese and that many valuable books on the English language came from foreigners for whom English was a second language!

Still, I did feel that the industrialisation of Japan was a vital world topic that had not been explored enough at the popular level. The compartmentalisation of knowledge, coupled with nationalism, seemed to have left a gap in understanding. There was the emergence of science in Europe as a superb quantum leap for man in terms of his control of his environment and as an intellectual achievement to satisfy his inner cravings in Christian Europe. Then there was and is the phenomenon of Japan so far away making use of this knowledge to emerge as a 'superstate' and, according to one commentator, as 'No. 1' in terms of a Utopia where a stable society produces goods of superior quality at unbeatable prices. But what happened in between? The essays attempt to provide an answer. And the answer is merely the lives of a group of men and women of differing characters, ambitions and achievements for whom only a minority can speak. They are an international set — a set which does not fall into the realm of any one nation, except Japan, and Japan would prefer to group them as assistants who were interesting but insignificant. The western nations from whence they came tend to ignore them and regard them as weird eccentrics because their experiences are so far removed from the norm. When I was looking for the monument to Will Adams in Gillingham, none of the citizens I approached in the street could tell me where it was, and even the local librarians had to bring out an expert from their ranks to give me guidance.

But what fantastic catalysts these men were! What expert farmers to sow the seeds of the West in the East and have them grow so healthily. The forces of national politics, as has always been the case, disrupted the growth and created perverse and unhealthy diversions, but the general trend continued and became inseparably entwined with the direction of human events so that Japan can now hold a privileged position in the world, being an intimate part of both western and eastern culture and helping to blur the distinctions and contradictions between the two.

So acknowledgement is due to all those who took part in the great adventure, from Plato to Yukawa, from Galileo to Soichiro Honda and from Rudyard Kipling to Yukio Mishima. But special acknowledgement goes to those personal friends mentioned above, and John Dowdle who helped me correct the proofs.

List of Illustrations
(8pp of plates facing page 128)

1. Games in the Gankiro teahouse (from original print) of 1859
2. No.9 House, Yokohama
3. Girls from No.9 House, Yokohama 1900
4. Early photograph of 1890s pin-up

5. Portrait of Commodore Matthew Perry
6. The Perry monument in Shimoda
7. Memorial to William Adams at Ito
8. Rickshaw puller struggling uphill in Yokohama, c.1900
9. The original Anglican Christchurch in Yokohama, destroyed by the 1923 earthquake

10. The attack on the British legation in Tokyo in 1862, as drawn by Charles Wirgman
11. Laurence Oliphant (1829-88)
12. Henry Dyer (1848-1918)
13. Jonathan Goble (1827-1896)
14. Panoramic view of The Bluff in 1861. (Photo: W. Saunders)

15. 'Life in Japan'. Postcard, c.1900
16. Broadsheet newspaper of 1853 announcing the arrival of Perry's squadron
17. Monument in Yokohama celebrating Japan's first daily newspaper in 1871

18. Yokohama celebrates its fiftieth anniversary in 1909 with parades, speeches, and fireworks
19. The Osaka mint completed in 1870.
20. Granite plaque in Yokohama commemorating the opening of Japan's first telephone service in 1869
21. Replica of Brunton's first iron bridge in Japan erected at the same spot in Yokohama as the original (built 1874)
22. Ernest Fenollosa (1853-1908)
23. William Henry Brunton (1841-1901)
24. T.B. Glover (1838-1911)
25. W.H. Stone (1837-1917)
26. William Eliot Griffis (1843-1928)
27. John Milne (1850-1913)

28. Postcard showing coaling at Nagasaki, c.1900
29. British postcard, early twentieth century, poking fun at a newly 'westernised' Japanese
30. British postcard commemorating the Anglo-Japanese Alliance first signed in 1901
31. Japan's young prince Hirohito (Emperor Showa) with King George V in London during the 1921 visit

Preface

THIS BOOK comprises 42 chapters and five introductory sections on various aspects of the history of Japan which are all related on account of the western 'link' with that country. This 'link' is established through the outstanding (sometimes bizarre) characters that impacted to a greater or lesser extent on Japan's pathway to industrialisation and modernisation. My hope is that the chosen order and organisation of the book, as well as the westerners that have been selected provide a fairly comprehensive picture of how the Japanese were able to emerge from semi-feudal 'Third World' status in the 1850s to become one of the most affluence nation's in the world to the extent that in the 1990s almost every household in the West, and many in poorer countries, are pleased (often with implicit snob value) to possess articles manufactured in Japan. Whatever one's view in the West may be, the fact is that the names of Japanes companies have become household names around the world, such as Mitsubishi, Honda, Seiko, Yamaha, Sony, Toyota, Hitachi, Pioneer, Brother and Atari.

Originally, I intended to explore the way that western science and technology was introduced into Japan, the nuts-and-bolts of the pre-war industrialisation and post-war 'miracle', but it soon became clear that in order to deal with this process fully, politics, the law and even art and religion would have to be considered. So followed a period of intense self-instruction on these related topics which led to fanatical purchasing and borrowing of old books and other documents relating to Japanese-western intercourse in the past.

It seems to have been the aim of some writers of history to give the reader a narrow view of events from the stance of the group of which the writer was a part or with which he or she identified. This is especially true of island states, like Britain and Japan, with easily defined borders, and of those larger countries that place great emphasis on their borders due to the different economic circumstances of the peoples each side of that border, like the United States and Russia. But there is a growing change in attitude among some history writers to view events in both whole-world, or global village, terms and in terms of the struggles of individuals. This book attempts to concentrate on the latter while phenomena are explored. For it was individuals from the West, with

11

their own particular cultural or national bias, who interacted with Japanese individuals with their own bias, expectations and aims, that created the situation whereby Japan could progress so rapidly.

Japan was never colonised by any western nation in the nineteenth century as was every other country in the Far East one way or another. Some believe that Genkis Khan's attempt in the thirteenth century laid the foundation for resistance to this form of exploitation. Despite this, and more probably because of it, Japan is the only country to become independently modernised in the true sense outside of Europe and North America. It was a unique achievement. Such 'progress', however, cannot be totally praised or admired by the less-developed countries (LDCs) of the modern world, for what Japan accomplished was not without intense suffering and devastating agony in human terms, and even today many in Japan ask: Have we really achieved a paradise?

The comfort and convenience of efficient communications and transport systems, of labour-saving and amusement devices (many of which are junked before their useful life is over to be replaced by later models) in a country where all are consumers because of high salaries and a fairly even distribution of wealth, is offset by the unsightly disturbances to the natural environment that such systems produce. In Japan this has been especially noticeable, particularly since the Pacific War; but now, having achieved domestic affluence and a strong economic base, there are strong moves in two directions. The first is towards preserving the natural environment, which often means reintroducing nature in derelict places once ravished by industry, and carefully planning future construction in terms of the human dimension rather than simply for the creation of wealth. The second direction is to move out into Third-World countries with not only products, but with expertise in the shape of individuals. Individuals much like the Britons and Americans who arrived in Japan in the last century. Events have come full circle.

NEIL PEDLAR
Porth, Cornwall
Spring 1990

Introduction

I: KEYHOLE TO THE PAST

WHILE EUROPE came alive with new ideas and inventions during the Renaissance and the Industrial Revolution, Japan deliberately isolated herself from the rest of the world and persisted in a unique kind of feudalism under the Tokugawa regime. Then, suddenly, just after the mid-point of the nineteenth century, the country began to change. It decided to become part of the modern industrial world and the speed of absorption of 300 years' of technological progress that had taken place in the West was extraordinarily rapid. It took a mere 50 years for Japan to change from being a feudal society, where there was virtually no mass-production and where two-sworded samurai warriors strutted through muddy streets and over mountain paths, to become a world power that could hold a major industrial exhibition in London, and defeat a western power in a full-scale modern war. This was a remarkable and unique achievement, unequalled anywhere. But how was it done?

In Japan there had been no Copernicus, no Galileo, no Newton — but the fruits, both bitter and sweet, of the science and technology that such men had helped create were made available by men who came from the West to Japan's shores to sow the seeds of industrialisation there. Who were these men? — these catalysts who showed the way in technology and in other aspects of western culture to a country full of men impatient to learn? Who were these pioneers whose know-how was essential fuel to Japan's industrial revolution? And what problems did they face after they had landed in a strange land where the language, social customs, and even food, were mysteries to them.

There were thousands of them who sailed to Japan, over 3000 working for the government alone, and their stories are full of adventure, comedy and tragedy. Most of them were dedicated men who found ways to overcome the language barrier and the initial discomforts, and a great many of them are still remembered in Japan with affection. But the overall story is not a simple one, as it is sometimes made out to be. It is a story wrought with political intrigues, with terrorist acts, with racism

13

and with misunderstandings of all kinds. There was injustice and over-generosity. There was enlightenment and love. It was not a simple matter of scientists, engineers, journalists and teachers doing the same job as they did in their own country in the West. Unique and unimagined problems arose. But, as is now so evident today, the project was an outstanding success which has brought other problems in its wake.

The early years of the Emperor Meiji's era (1868-1912) must have been exciting and inspiring for the foreigners who went there with more than personal ambitions. Those with a desire, perhaps, to help build a Utopia, for they must have regarded Japan as an empty canvas as far as industrialism was concerned. Those days should be seen in terms of the then current philosophies in the West. The confusion, chaos and misery caused by the decline of dogmatic Christianity upon which much political and legal thought was haphazardly based, the rise of a new science and technology that men with vision saw as a possible solution to all the problems of the human race - in faraway Japan, all this must have crystallised into some new pattern for those *'yatoi'* (government foreign employees) and other westerners who had arrived to put into practice what they had learned. Most of these men were British, and there was great optimism, an excellent salary, a government that supported them, and a chance to flourish and make something of their lives. Those who are remembered did use all their powers and abilities to benefit Japan, and despite the untold hardships of 'culture shock' in all its aspects, they succeeded in their work and helped to get the wheels of industry rolling. Some even delved into a study of Japan's history and traditions in their limited spare time, and became experts on the so-called mysteries of the East. The way that the various man-made languages, laws and religions are used to respond to the needs and desires account for all the differences.

But not all the foreigners from the West became enthused by the possibilities Japan presented, especially those in the business section of the community. Some complained continually about their existence, mainly because the ways of the Japanese were very different from their own and they could not make the effort to understand them, to appreciate their advantages, and adapt to them. Under the unequal treaties and extra-territoriality, whereby each foreign subject was governed by his own consulate and was outside the laws of Japan, they tried to exploit their privileges and regarded their Japanese hosts as merely an awkward set of people with customs that did not conform to their own ideas of 'civilisation,' but who had to be tolerated because they were a means to riches for themselves. Japan for many of them was like a gold-mine. They had to go down into the darkness, remain there for a period, and having grabbed their nuggets, escape back from whence they came. This, at any rate, was the feeling of the German Baron de Hubner when he wrote about his fleeting visit to the Yokohama foreign community in 1871:

'Yokohama is an important place. A great deal of work is done here, but not too much. There is a good deal of activity; but not that exaggerated, feverish activity that characterises the great centres of industry and commerce in America. A new arrival has not been twenty-four hours at Yokohama without finding out that all the world is home-sick. Talk to them of Old England, and a cloud at once passes over their faces. They are always looking for some happiness in the future instead of seizing what is granted to them in the present. Life in these distant countries fosters this disposition. Those who have become really rich (and they are the exceptions) leave with joy the exile where they have passed the best years of their lives. They decide to go home — they are *homeward bound*. What music in those two words! But I fancy the happiest moment for these favoured mortals is the passage. Hardly have they arrived in their own country, with its leaden-grey sky and murky fogs, than they begin to regret the loss of the bright Japanese sun, the beautiful cedars which shaded their house, the quantities of servants, the work, the animation — in fact, all the surroundings of their Yokohama existence. There, at any rate, they were *somebody*. In England they find themselves — *nobody*!'

A few years afterwards, the American missionary teacher, W. E. Griffis, made some critical remarks about Englishmen in Japan and offered an explanation:

'Perhaps most of the Englishmen are fair representatives of England's best fruits; but a grievously large number, removed from the higher social pressure which was above them, and which kept them at their true level in England, find themselves without that social pressure in the East; and they are apt to become offensively vaporous in their pretensions. They are most radical and finical concerning every idea, custom, ceremony, or social despotism of any kind supposed to be English. They are the foreigners who believe it their solemn duty, and who make it their regular practice, to train up their servant "boys" in the way they should go by systematic whippings, beatings, and applications of the boot. In this species of brutality we believe the vulgar John Bulls to be sinners above all the foreigners in the East ... Be it remembered that in these remarks we do not refer to that large body of educated, refined, and true-hearted Englishmen who have been such a potent influence in the civilisation of Japan.'

Griffis, however, was not without intolerance in his Christian zeal, as on the occasions he jumped up upon sacred statues in Japanese temples and preached impromptu sermons to all around him! Arriving back to Yokohama after a year's residence as the only foreigner in the country town of Fukui, he remarked:

'My year's residence has given me the ken of a native. My eyes have not altered their angle, yet I see as the Japanese see. The "hairy" foreigners are ugly. These proud fellows with red beards and hair look hideous. What outrageous clothes, so different from uniform black! How ugly those blue eyes! How deathly pale many of them look! How proud, how overbearing and swaggering, many of them appear, as if Japan were their own!'

Yet, for all his strange prejudices which stemmed from his intense loneliness, Griffis does describe many of the dangers that faced foreigners in Japan at this time, and gives an idea of the state of the country. Of course, the filth, disease and dangers present in all European countries at the same time must not be forgotten.

'I have escaped many dangers since I first left home, more than a year ago. No steamer on the Pacific had burned, as the *America* did, foundered, wrecked, broken machinery, or blown up, as one did on Lake Biwa, with me on board. No stray gun-shot from bird shooters in the rice-fields has hit me. No ronin's (masterless samurai) sword has slit my back or cloven my head. No red-capped, small-pox baby has accidentally rubbed its pustules or shed its floating scales on me. A horse has kicked, but not killed me. No fever has burned my veins. No kago (palanquin) has capsized over a precipice, or come to pieces while crossing a log bridge over a torrent. No earthquakes have engulfed me, or squashed my house upon me, nor flood overwhelmed me, nor typhoon whirled or banged me to pieces, nor fires burned me. No jin-rik-sha has smashed me. I have not been poisoned to death by fresh lacquer. No charcoal fumes have asphyxiated me (alas poor Bates!). I have not been seethed to death in hot water by jumping unwittingly into the boiling baths so often prepared for me. No centipedes or scorpions have bitten me, neither have the fleas in mountain inns, though they have taken more than Shylock's portion, utterly devoured me. No drunken soldier has quarrelled with me, nor skewered me with his sabre.'

II: WHO COPIES WHOM?

The technological and industrial achievements of Japan are unprecedented. No other country outside of Europe and North America has achieved so much in so little time with so few resources. Many countries, with stronger ties to Europe in the nineteenth century, and with greater resources, have had ample opportunity to follow a similar course to Japan, but still persist in systems of slow feudalism. What made Japan different from these other places?

No single, simple answer to this question is, of course, possible, but there are factors in many aspects of the Japanese way of life that indicate explanations. The old prejudiced accusation that the Japanese merely borrowed, copied and adapted from discoveries made in other countries is naturally true, but which particular country could at any time claim that all its technological activities originated exclusively within its boundaries? It is a meaningless accusation based on jealousy and fear, for the evolution of science and technology has known no national boundaries. It has taken place world-wide, and great advances have taken place when and where the environment was right; sometimes in the secure peace of a university, in the back room of a working-class home or in government establishments at the height of war. So once the principles of scientific investigation were established in Japanese colleges, then Japanese researchers were to be found in the forefront of advances. Hideki Yukawa, for example, was awarded the Nobel Prize for physics in 1949 for his theoretical work on forces within the nuclei of atoms which led to the prediction of mesons. His work, carried out at the University of Kyoto in the early 1930s, was substantiated in 1937 when experimental discovery confirmed the existence of mesons. Previous to this, Ishiwara had published a scientific paper in 1915 on the quantisation of periodic motion, but found that Niels Bohr had been doing similar work in Europe and had taken the credit for this particular break-through in the understanding of the atom.

One British journalist who visited a Honda car factory in Japan in 1981 commented that if that factory had been a straight copy of a British factory, then the British car industry would have nothing to worry about! Such an observation seems to crush the misconception that Japanese manufacturers merely copy. In almost every modern industry in Japan, newly created developments and original ideas have led to more efficient techniques and better products, and this has often left the West scratching its head in wonder. It is at such times that nationalistic politicians have made meaningless accusations about imitation and copying, and in doing so have spread hatred, to cover their own incompetence and mismanagement. The genius of the Japanese in the field of innovation rests with an extraordinary ability to interface products with human beings, not only physically in relation to the body but aesthetically as well, for the old pre-industrial arts have not been allowed to die in Japan. In this way, the customer becomes an integral and important part of the product. One small, but classic, example is the famous Japanese tooth-pick!

Other commentators regard Japan's traditional social system, which has been largely retained from feudal times and which has evolved with the ethics of Confucianism and a complex honorific language, as perfect for the activities of a super-industrial nation. But this is a rather simplistic view and presupposes many things. But the fact remains that the Japanese did manage to adapt their old life-styles and philosophies to the new order as industrialism grew, and made an excellent job of it. The evolution was at first fairly smooth and controlled. But during the period 1895-1945, that control was slowly lost when the military faction gained more and more power, and when fascism was rife world-wide, the country was pushed into a World War. Since 1945, however, the earlier values have been restored to their important place in national life.

All industrial countries, of course, had to adapt and change their traditions of the agricultural and feudal past as the industrial landscape came into being. New laws concerning the new activities had to be made and enforced, but these were based upon the old feudal legal system and their effectiveness in relieving misery and providing solutions to new problems to the satisfaction of all was a reflection of the quality of life under the old feudal order. Nevertheless, the old order was eroded away and disrupted, and the rearrangement of the social order that industrialisation demanded caused many hardships. Economic necessity forced a great many to leave the countryside and seek an entirely different kind of employment in the cities; contact was lost with their families and with nature as they became mere cogs in the new economy. The profit motive caused much unnecessary misery amongst the thousands of unskilled and uneducated workers. Religious leaders in the West, sponsored by the government, were given power to counsel the unfortunate to bear with the system, not to indulge in the escape of alcohol, and to believe in a better time after death. In this way, an adapted, perhaps twisted, Christian ethic proved a useful force to control the work force during the early advance of industrialism. Thousands of impressive new churches were built from the new wealth in the industrial cities to provide visual proof that God was indeed present. Such a situation naturally led to the rise of atheistic communism, and to various blends of socialism.

Japan had two distinct advantages when industry came to her shores. First, she knew to a certain extent what to expect. For there *was* contact with the West through Dutch traders who were allowed to operate on Deshima Island in Nagasaki harbour, despite the policy of isolationism. The basic ideas about industrialism and an industrial society were known in outline, and the most suitable methods could be considered in advance for adoption in Japan. Thus Japan did not have to feel her way in the dark so much, as happened in Europe where it all started. Also the westerners who came to Japan with direct experience of industry, and all its pitfalls, were invaluable and played a vital role. The ones who were contracted to work for the government, and who were permitted to stay in Japan for many years, were adaptable men without dogmatism. Those who saw their function as merely to create and imitate the institutions of their own countries on the shores of Japan were soon sent back home, but those who saw their function to create these institutions in Japan, in a Japanese way, with the cooperation of all around them, and in a way suitable for use by a people with entirely different customs, language and culture, were appreciated and honoured. That many of this group decided to remain in Japan, marry into a Japanese family, and spend the rest of their lives in a country that they visited primarily to do some job, shows that they preferred Japan to their own country of birth. After all, was not Japan partly their own creation?

There were many reasons for this preference to remain in Japan, and obviously most were personal, but studies of records indicate that these would involve the higher status they enjoyed in Japan compared to that which they would (or would not) have in their own country, their greater earning power, and the gentler climate. Other factors may have involved the desire to escape from communities where life and conversation revolved around what they perceived as hypocritical Victorian Christian ethics, so revolting to intelligent minds of the time. The Christian God was specified as a personal, protecting force to those who conformed; whereas the Oriental gods were impersonal, frightening and destructive — and the latter view would seem to be nearer to the reality of human existence, especially in a land of earthquakes, volcanoes and typhoons. It is interesting to note the difficulties in translating the word 'God' into Japanese. 'Kami,' the usual term used (as in 'kamikaze' — 'god of wind'), refers more to an *essence* in some object or creature that makes it superior, and was not the meaning that Christian missionaries required. When the Jesuits during their evangelical drive in Japan about 1600 decided to use the original Latin word 'Deus,' for they could find no suitable Japanese equivalent, it was pronounced as 'deusu' because of Japanese conventions of pronunciation. But this sounded much like 'daiuso,' meaning 'a great lie'!

Be this as it may, the main reason why many of the foreign experts chose to remain in Japan — for money, status and a kind climate would be no compensation for being discontented — must have been that they were happier within Japanese society and found the customs, food and way of life closer to their desires as human beings on earth. The environment for them in Japan certainly did allow them to excel in their work. One British doctor, Henry Faulds, while working with Japanese students in a mission hospital in Tokyo in the 1870s, made a startling discovery. He found that finger-prints were unique for each person and they did not change during their lifetime! He even suggested that the police might use his discovery in the detection of criminals. But Scotland Yard rejected the idea until 1901.

Another foreign expert from Scotland was Henry Dyer who was the principal and a professor of Engineering at Imperial College, Tokyo, during 1873-1880. In his book *Dai Nippon — A study in National Evolution,* he wrote: 'Great Britain should not be above learning a few lessons from Japan.' And he went on to point out that 'in many respects engineering education in Great Britain was very defective,' but for this he was criticised by some of the foreign residents and even by some of his colleagues. Yet it took many years for 'practically all of the improvements which we had adopted in the Imperial College of Engineering, Japan, to be found in almost all the colleges in Britain.' It is amazing to realise that even before 1880, just twelve years after the Meiji Restoration, Japan had an engineering laboratory more advanced than any in Britain. Dyer informs us that 'when Lord Kelvin was inaugurating the James Watt engineering laboratory in Glasgow University, he reminded his audience that 'the Imperial College, Japan, was the first educational institution which had a laboratory of this kind. The experimental and graphical methods introduced into every department of its course are now common in all the colleges of Britain. The method of combining theory and practice in the training of engineers which I introduced into Japan is now being strongly recommended under the name of the "sandwich" system of apprenticeship.'

Towards the end of his book, Dyer explained how national unity
was maintained in Japan, and criticised British policy of the day, and
at the same time made a startling prediction:

'Is it not rather true that we (British) have no real national policy,
and that our statesmen drift according to their own whims or to what
may be called accidental circumstances? Our greatest need is a conscious
national aim to which all our efforts would be constantly directed, and
to which the latest developments of science would be efficiently applied.
In this connection, however, science must not be used in its limited
sense, but include all that is essential to individual and national welfare.

'The days of crooked diplomacy, gunboat policy, veiled threats and
monstrous indemnities must be looked upon as past, and all questions
must be discussed and settled on a basis of international equity. If the
bogey of the "Yellow Peril" ever becomes a reality, it will be on account
of the conduct of some of the militarists. Neither Japan nor China has
shown the slightest signs of aggression, they simply ask to be treated
with justice and to be allowed to develop on their own lines.'

Dyer's final statement, made over eighty years ago, summarises his
ideas:

'The engineer has shrunk the world into small dimensions, and the
social and economic conditions of the various countries are closely
connected. Statesmen must therefore study what may be called the
dynamics of politics if they wish to carry on their work in a rational
manner. We have been told very often recently that we must think
"Imperially." I would rather put it that we must think "Internationally,"
and I am convinced that the greatest real successes will fall to those
statesmen who are international in their conceptions and not insular and
individual.'

The second advantage that Japan had at the outset of her
industrialisation, and which accounts for much of Japanese ingenuity
and creativity in it, stems from that period of isolation that lasted 222
years (1636-1858). Some historians regard these years of isolation as a
strange retrogressive step in the history of the nation that caused it to
be 'backward' when the country was reopened. Ignorant of the details
of industrial processes it may have been, but certainly not 'backward.'
Any collector of pre-industrial Japanese swords, carved ivory or
woodblock prints will confirm this. Their achievements in feudal arts
and crafts were never equalled anywhere in the West.

But this period of isolation (*sakoku*), when the building of ocean-
going ships was forbidden to prevent any Japanese going abroad and
coming into contact with other cultures, and when shipwrecked sailors
from other countries were put to death if they landed in Japan, is seen
as preventing Japan from coming into contact with developments in
science and technology taking place so rapidly in the West. And this is
pefectly true, although it is not the whole story. There is a positive side

to 'sakoku' that is vitally important and is a factor in Japan's current economic successes.

By regarding the Japanese archipelago, its population and entire ecosystem as an isolated system, with the population about twice that of Britain's, with a small percentage of usable land and with little energy resources, it seems a miracle that the Japanese could survive as a unified nation for so long under such conditions. With virtually no imports or exports over this 222-year period, Japan was not only self-sufficient but developed in many different fields. This fantastic achievement was due to several factors. First, there was the ingenious political system devised by the Tokugawa family that ensured political stability and unity, whereby the daimyo (feudal lords) of each han (fief) were obliged to make annual visits to the capital city, Edo (Tokyo), bringing their families and bearing expensive gifts for presentation to the Tokugawa Shogun. Each daimyo, therefore, needed to keep a house in Edo which ensured that the city remained rich and with full employment, and the gifts — a primitive form of taxation — ensured that wealth and power did not build up in any one han to challenge the leadership. The production of these gifts meant that each han had to grow a surplus of agricultural products, usually rice, while in the rich city a sophisticated commercial economy evolved so that when industrialisation arrived at the end of the period, there was in Japan an extremely clever business community. On returning to their han, many daimyo were obliged to leave their wives in the Edo house as a kind of security for good political behaviour.

But no less responsible for the achievement of maintaining an isolated, self-sufficient society was the ingenious use of energy resources, including food, by anonymous Japanese citizens. As regards food, the Japanese are renowned for their culinary arts and skills in preparing for human consumption almost every creature that swims, crawls or grows in the sea, or walks on land. The preparation of each dish (and creature) is today the result of an approach to preparing food that has developed over centuries. Octopus, sea-cucumber, snake, fish of all species, the different shellfish — each have their own unique method of preparation and tradition of consumption. The average westerner is still amused, confused and often irrationally revolted by the resourceful exploitation by the Japanese of their protein supplies! But to the Japanese such variety of culinary artistry that makes their eating times pleasant and interesting, is taken for granted, and many are equally revolted by the generally bland foods elsewhere!

In terms of the use of heat energy from wood or fossil fuels, the Japanese tradition has again shown genius. The economic use of energy in the Japanese bath is famous, though rarely used in the West, and the 'hori kotatsu' (low table with a long, heavy cloth heated from underneath) used for keeping the human body warm in the winter without heating the whole room is another energy-efficient device unique to Japan. All this is very significant in a world now having problems with energy resources and food supplies.

III: INTERACTIONS — STRANGE AND FAMILIAR

The introduction of western science and technology into Japan, with all the spectacular results it has produced, followed a familiar track in one respect. As in Europe and America before and since, each scientific discovery or technical innovation was first of all considered by the government for its military implications. Young students are not taught this sad fact in their science classes. But as Sugimoto and Swain proclaim in *Science and Culture in Traditional Japan*: 'We are just beginning to realise how complex a historical process modernisation has been, and still is. The norm has been to think of "modern civilisation" — a conglomerate of industrial technology, modern science, and whatever values and institutions happen to be conventional in Europe or the United States at a given time — as a force which replaces "backwardness" with the ineluctability of a gas rushing in to fill a vacuum.' So care is needed to avoid general statements when trying to explain sweeping historical movements.

In the turbulent decade before 1868, strange political manoeuvres took place. The original unequal treaties had been signed between western nations and the Shogun, and they had been forced upon the Japanese people virtually at the end of a gun: the guns on the bristling steam warships that had sailed into Tokyo Bay. Japanese resentment was generally kept under control, although there were a few tragic incidents, for there was a real threat of invasion by one or other of the more colonial-minded western powers. The leaders of Japan fully realised that their military power was insignificant compared with that of the western nations. The unfair treaties, nevertheless, had caused much misery among many Japanese, and a rallying cry of 'Expel the Barbarians!' was heard from anti-Shogun men who supported the Emperor and the old Japanese ways.

As this movement gained strength because more and more daimyo found they were losing their wealth, and the Emperor was indeed restored to a position of prominence in governmental affairs, there began a great fear among the foreign settlers that they would all be slaughtered or driven away. For now there were no treaties signed between the foreign powers and the new Imperial government, and the foreigners had no legal rights or privileges. However, the Emperor soon accepted the old treaties, but a movement was begun to change them. Within a short time, the rallying cry of the Imperial government had been changed to 'Western techniques, Oriental morality!'

There followed a period of intoxication with western ideas. Sometimes it went to extremes. Associations were formed to promote the use of Roman letters in the writing of Japanese and to abandon the kanji and kana characters. Suggestions were made that the kimono be abolished along with many Japanese foods. One man, Yoshio Takahashi, even published a book, *The Improvement of the Japanese Race,* in which he claimed that the Japanese were physically and mentally inferior to westerners, and he recommended that all Japanese males divorce their wives and marry western women who would bear children with superior characteristics, and so improve the Japanese stock! A song composed in 1878 for children as they played with a ball, called the *Civilisation Ball Song,* was designed to impress on their young minds how superior western technology was. At each bounce of the ball, they had to recite the names of ten objects that would improve their country: 'Gas lamps, steam engines, horse-drawn carriages, cameras, telegrams, lightning conductors, newspapers, schools, letter post and steamships.'

In practical terms, the technique used to actually get the wheels of industry rolling in Japan so that all these products could be made, was in theory simple and sensible. But there were complications. The Imperial government found out which country was most advanced in a particular field, and requested the country concerned to send some experts to Japan on contract for a few years to apply their knowledge and teach Japanese students about it. The Japanese students were willing to work long hours to learn the language of the expert before he arrived so that there would no no communication barrier. Then the experts were to return to their country of origin, often with a life pension and honours bestowed by the Emperor, and the Japanese they had taught would continue in that field. That was the theory, but it did not operate in exactly that way. As Basil Hall Chamberlain, who was professor of Japanese and philology at Imperial University, Tokyo, recorded in his book *Things Japanese:*

'To the Japanese government belongs the credit of conceiving the idea (of industrialisation) and admitting the necessity of the great change, furnishing the wherewithal, engaging the men, and profiting by their labours, resembling in this a wise patient who calls in the best available physician and assists him by every means in his power. The foreign employees have been the physician, to whom belongs the credit of working the marvellous cure which we all see. One set of Englishmen — indeed at first a single Englishman — took the navy in hand, and transformed junk manners and methods into those of a modern man-of-war. Another undertook the mint, with the result that oriental confusion made way for a uniform coinage equal to any in the world. No less a feat than the reform of the entire educational system was chiefly the work of a handful of Americans. A Frenchman has codified Japanese law, Germans have for years directed the whole higher medical instruction of the country, and the large steamers of the principal steamship company are still (1891) commanded by foreign captains of various nationalities. The posts, the telegraphs, the railways, the army, the trigonometrical survey, improved mining methods, prison reform, sanitary reform, cotton and paper mills, chemical laboratories, water-works and harbour works — all are the creation of the foreign employees of the Japanese government. Nor must it be supposed that foreigners have been mere supervisors. It can be a case of coats off, of actual manual work, of example as well as precept. Technical men have shown their Japanese employers how to do technical things, the name of *chef de bureau,* captain, foreman, or what not, being indeed generally painted on a Japanese figurehead, but the real power behind each little throne being the foreign adviser or practical man.

'It is hard to see how it could have been otherwise, for it takes longer to get a Japanese educated abroad than to engage a foreigner ready made.'

Chamberlain had arrived in Japan in 1873 and remained there through most of the Meiji era, observing, writing and translating, and he personally knew many of the other foreign employees. His metaphor about the patient and physician may not stand up to strict analysis, but his remarks about non-expert Japanese taking the credit for the achievements of the foreigners seem to be confirmed by Francis Henry Trevithick, grandson of the great Cornish inventor, when he wrote that his brother, Richard Francis, had built the first steam locomotive in Japan, yet all the credit went to the Japanese man overseeing the project.

Despite these arguments, Japan's sensible and practical method of effecting the transition from feudalism to industrialism was disrupted by certain diplomats who were greedy for their own nations. Underhand political intrigues took place through the whole period, with each European embassy vying with the others for contracts with Japan in the various spheres of industrial development. Some vague notion of national influence must have guided them as well as a desire to create more wealth for their own nation, but in fact what they were doing was to put their own short-sighted national interests before a desire to see Japan evolve and develop in the most efficient and effective way. Britain excelled in such tactics, Sir Harry Parkes being a prime protagonist.

Probably none of the foreigners who went to Japan in the Meiji era to introduce his own special knowledge or skills would have considered himself to be a hero, yet in overcoming so many problems each one must have shown heroic resolve. The reason why hardly any of them are well-known in the West and only partly appreciated in Japan, except to a few history students, is that their lives had little nationalistic significance. The heroes who are publicised and popularised in various countries are those who took part in destructive activities abroad. Those who crossed national barriers to perform constructive tasks tended to be ignored because their own leaders did not want their people to admire a person whose education was more advanced in some field, who had a strange appearance and ways, for it could have been taken as a reflection of that country's incompetence and inferiority. The country of emigration, delighted on the one hand that one of its subjects may influence another people, on the other hand ignores and distrusts such men in case they bring back new and and 'foreign' ideas to upset the status quo. Key questions at interviews for men seeking government posts concern their parentage, as well as their contact with foreigners. The armed forces are particularly sensitive about this incestuous mentality.

But if any kind of permanent solutions are to be found to world peace, to the energy and food problems, then the lives of such men and women who have faced and solved problems within other cultures will have to be examined in detail from all angles. The concept of nationalism will have to disappear, and the 'global village' concept replace it. National flags will have to be hauled down, or at least lose their feudal and tribal connotations. The computer age will usher in a time when even technological discoveries will be made and come to fruition through a programme made by a few men. Men of the future, very much like those foreign experts who went to Japan a century ago. Perhaps even the word 'foreign' will become an antiquated curiosity!

IV: INTERNATIONAL MARRIAGES AND THE LAW

A further complication of this sensible method of introducing industry into Japan concerned the relationships of foreign employees with the opposite sex. The legal attitude of the Japanese government in this field is interesting. Four possible options were open to the heterosexual foreign males. To remain continent and alone, to court and marry a foreign woman who was living in Japan, to court and marry a Japanese woman, or to resort to the facilities of the Yoshiwara. Although all four routes were followed, the first two were difficult and uninteresting.

The pleasure quarters, or Yoshiwara, in the Treaty Ports of Japan were well controlled and regulated by the authorities. Such areas had existed for centuries and their traditions were an accepted part of society. A great authority on the Tokyo Yoshiwara was the English lawyer, J.E. de Becker, who wrote a classic study of it in 1899. One possible purpose in publishing such a detailed survey, in which he described the procedures for checking and controlling V.D., and how all participants in the 'mizu shobai' (lit. businesses that flowed like water) were kept in order, was Becker's concern for the terrible conditions in Britain at that time. Perhaps he thought that Britain could learn from Japanese methods in this area if he presented it in great detail. In Europe at the time, especially in London, the situation in equivalent pleasure quarters was chaotic, poorly controlled and full of violence and fraud. This may have been because prostitution was not accepted as an integral part of society, and so it was largely ignored by the authorities.

In the Yoshiwara, wherever they were, special facilities were provided for the newly-arrived foreigners who cared to visit the establishments, most of whom were pleasantly surprised with the sophisticated Japanese attitudes towards the whole question of sexuality. Their attitude was far more practical and healthy than in the West. Many foreigners remarked on the innocent way country people in Japan bathed naked in public, the larger communal baths accommodating both sexes at the same time, while in Britain and much of Europe, strict taboos kept all women covered from neck to ankles in thick, heavy clothes at all times when in public. But despite the taboos and the lack of effective official regulation of the seething 'red-light districts' of Britain, there were some surprisingly close parallels with Japan.

Wealthy men of Victorian Britain had kept mistresses, for example, and to be such a mistress was the ambition of every intelligent prostitute. 'Competition to be in the top flight of prostitutes was fierce,' wrote researcher Ronald Pearsall in *The Worm in the Bud — The World of Victorian Sexuality*. 'Few of the aspirants had the qualities to make it. The successful not only had to perform well, but had to look well, talk intelligently, and if possible possess additional talents; a good singing voice was highly prized.' Such a description could be equally applied to a high-class Japanese geisha.

On another level, it was declared with a sense of outrage by many foreigners who visited Japan in the Meiji era that the selling of young, unwanted daughters to pleasure houses in the Yoshiwara by poor country farmers was inhumane and uncivilised. Yet in Europe at the time, exactly the same situation occurrred. Brussels was the main centre of child prostitution, and in 1880 a Mrs Josephine Butler reported:

'In some houses in Belgium there are immured little children, English girls of some twelve to fifteen years, lovely creatures (for they do not care to take any who are not beautiful), innocent creatures who, stolen, kidnapped, betrayed, got from English country villages by artifice are sold to these human shambles... The secret is known to none except the wealthy *debauches* who can pay large sums of money for the sacrifice of these innocents.'

The other option open to a male foreign resident living in Japan for several years and at the height of his powers, was marriage with a Japanese lady; this involved strange legal complications that still need attention by international lawyers. It was not until 1873, almost twenty years after the first treaty was signed with Commodore Perry, that Japanese were permitted under the law to marry foreigners. The oriental concept of marriage as an institution differed from that in the West, and still does. As Chamberlain pointed out in 1891: 'Marriage among the Japanese is less of a personal and more of a family affair than it is in western lands. Religion has no say in the matter, and the law regards it from a different point of view ...A Japanese wife is not only supposed to obey her husband, but actually does so. The husband, if well enough off, probably has a concubine besides and makes no secret of it, indeed he often keeps her in the same house with his wife.'

The one or more concubines that the rich husband maintained had certain rights, and any children born to them were usually accepted into his family. All that was required was for him to declare that he was the father, and their names would be entered on his family register as equals to his legitimate children. In contrast, children born out of wedlock in Britain were termed 'illegitimate' — illegal entries into the world — and were so handicapped through their lives. If he admitted paternity, the man involved was punished, to quote the official jargon, 'For Unlawful Carnal Knowledge'— the shorthand for which caused lawyers to bring a new four-lettered word into the English language.

In Japan, under the New Criminal Code of 1870, illicit sex outside the Yoshiwara did become a crime and was punishable by 70 strokes with a stick. This law was opposed by many elder statesmen in the Japanese parliament, for the new law would create hardships for both the concubine and her child because no man would admit paternity under threat of such punishment. But the new politicians, under the influence of puritanic thought from the West, passed the law. Foreigners came under the terms of extra-territoriality until it ended in 1898, and so none of them was ever subjected to the 70 strokes for illicit sex.

In 1918 Becker gave a realistic summary of the legal position of foreigners who desired to marry Japanese, indicating that it still remained different from western law:

'The family law of Japan...differs from the other parts (of the Civil Code) in being mainly of native origin. They are founded upon and adapted to the peculiar conditions of society in Japan. (It) has for the most part, exempted foreigners from the operation of its peculiar family law and left them to be governed by the laws of their own nationalities.'

This meant, and still does mean, that a Japanese woman marrying a foreigner became an outsider, and an embarrassment to the system. Her children could not take Japanese nationality, and thus had no rights in education and employment in Japan. When the strain of this situation led to a break-up of the marriage, as it sometimes did, or the father died, the position of the children became many times worse. Now they were foreigners in their country of birth, with very bleak prospects for education and employment. Unfortunately, the legislators who created these laws could find no way to integrate them. This failure still persists today, and it has led to an important contradiction between the Japanese Constitution and the Nationality Laws. Under section 1 of Article 14 of the Japanese Constitution, it is stated that: 'All Japanese nationals are equal under the law and there shall be no political, economic or social discrimination based on belief, *sex*, social status or lineage.' Yet the Nationality Laws state that for a Japanese woman married to a foreigner, their children must take the nationality of the father even if the children are born in Japan, and they may not be granted dual nationality. Whereas for a Japanese man married to a foreign woman, their children are automatically granted Japanese nationality no matter where they are born. Similar laws operated in the Meiji era, and the children of the foreign experts who decided to marry Japanese girls and stay in Japan, were therefore of foreign nationality. This obliged them to register annually with an Immigration Office and a Ward Office, requesting further leave to remain in their country of birth. Such laws were obviously intended to exclude foreigners from Japanese society, and it is one of the reasons why International Committees frequently publish studies and documents that declare Japan remains a 'closed society.'*

Many of the foreign experts were not deterred by the laws, and did marry Japanese girls, and settled in their newly-adopted country. After a certain number of years' residence, the law allowed them and their children to apply for Japanese naturalisation. In being accepted they were obliged to change their names to Japanese ones, and usually they took their wife's family name. Thus they became more or less absorbed into Japanese society, and were identified with it to a certain extent.

So in Japan there came into existence three overlapping groups: the indigenous Japanese, the foreign residents with working permits, and the descendants of the Meiji era foreign experts and other foreigners who came later. Of course, it should be mentioned that there still exist genes in Japanese society from the original inhabitants of the Japanese archipelago, the proto-Caucasoid Ainu people, and even genes from Will Adams and the other English, Dutch, Spanish and Portuguese settlers of the early seventeenth century, many of whom married Japanese and had offspring. But all traces of the latter have long since been absorbed within the Japanese population, and no records tracing these roots or origins can be found, yet the genetic material must still be in existence. So whatever man-made laws are passed, or however names have to be changed, the foreigners from all eras will always remain a real part of Japanese society. The nature of human intercourse during man's two million-year existence on earth has always gone along similar lines everywhere.

*New legislation in Japan (1984) has now altered this situation making it less sexist and racist. How it is implemented remains to be seen.

V: EDUCATION AND THE COMPUTER REVOLUTION

Education of the populace is an essential requirement for a country if it is to organise itself on industrial lines. But in the stage before this, in feudal times, general education was regarded as a serious threat to the status quo for it could create clever, popular and persuasive rebels who were able to see through the lies that governments traditionally used to keep their country functioning in agricultural and military affairs. There was a danger of the whole structure of society collapsing if there were too many educated élite. So education was limited to the selected few, and kept by and large in the mainstream of certain powerful families. This probably was sensible from a biological point of view, for it may be that eldest sons in families, taken over a large sample, are more able and adaptable than others born afterwards when the mother's body has been strained. However, in agricultural, feudal and early industrial societies in the West, education was not universal and this maintained a helpless, obedient populace whose affairs were monitored by the local priest, who was supported by the government, and who was obliged to perform any writing tasks required by individuals in their illiterate flock. Such a system, though unjust and cruel in retrospect, did provide general stability most of the time. Its main fault was that it did not allow all individuals to develop mentally to their full extent.

In the traditions of the Orient, though the same fears existed, a practical system to exclude this fault was adopted. The master in any field could accept any promising student into his own family and educate him. The master-student relationship was a special and honoured one whereby the master slowly revealed his knowledge as he became more and more sure of the allegiance and obedience of his students. There was a kind of symbiosis as the master depended economically on the efforts of his students, and the students depended upon the master revealing his knowledge. This system is probably responsible for the fact that Japanese achievements, in art and craft, during the feudal era were far more advanced than anywhere else.

But with the restoration of the Emperor Meiji in 1868, an Imperial rescript declared: 'The acquiring of knowledge is essential to a successful life...It is intended henceforth that education shall be so widespread that there shall be no house in any village, no person in any house, without learning.'

This was a wise and forward-looking move, for the Japanese leaders knew that without education no foreign expert could teach his Japanese students. Without general and universal education, industry could not survive and develop in Japan. At that time about 50% of all boys and 15% of all girls received formal education outside the home. By 1908 all children in Japan attended school until the age of 14 years. Whereas in Britain it was not until 1922 that a law was passed to make formal education compulsory until the age of 14 years, and this was not totally implemented until 1961. In Japan at present over 90% of students seek further education beyond the compulsory age, and twelve times more than the pre-war level are enrolled in colleges and universities. Education in Japan is not free for students, unless the student's financial position is exceptionally difficult.

Schools, colleges and universities have to develop and expand rapidly when a country moves from a feudal to an industrial stage. However, such institutions tend at first to be organised on feudal lines, involving the rank concept as found in military organisations. Again, this is not conducive to the full intellectual and mental development of students, for they become involved with the power politics of the system to the neglect of their studies. The larger the institution becomes, the more this occurs.

But it is a fact of human life that education is necessary if the next generation is to understand anything at all. No child can even learn to read and write without a teacher, no student will understand the simplest mathematics or the most obvious law of science without guidance. No independent group of people, no modern nation, can progress without an efficient education programme, and increasingly such a programme requires the use of expensive equipment. By denying the teacher his aids to teaching, he cannot undertake his profession, just as a surgeon cannot save life without adequate instruments. The patient will die or remain diseased, the country the same. The Japanese realise this and take delight in leaping ahead in this field, devising all kinds of apparatus to try in and outside the classroom, for their industries are geared to it. Because of the affluence of the country, micro-computers and many other devices using the micro-chip can be purchased by every school student. The electronics market at Akihabara, just north of Tokyo Station, teems every weekend with students of all ages seeking all manner of components with which to carry out their projects. No Mecca of modern gadgetry of such size exists anywhere else in the industrialised world. It is also a fact that many British, European and American workers consider, with good reason, that the computer will replace them and remove their livelihood, and they are opposed to the new technology and endeavour to slow down its introduction. Whereas Japanese workers view the computer as an exciting and valuable tool which will bring further prosperity and increase the quality of life. They have no fear of it, for their industries have been carefully integrated to society. They are not bothered either by religious qualms, which in the West preaches the joys of poverty and self-denial, and which regards materialism as a sin.

So when the 'third wave' of automatic control has flooded across the industrial world, Japan will be well prepared to handle the new order. It will no doubt be carefully embedded in society, as was 'second wave' industry, to improve the quality of life. Will Britain and her western partners then still be too proud to learn from Japan? Will the dogmatic feudal power structure still force the successors of the Luddites to keep disrupting achievements and slowing progress? Or will thousands of Japanese experts have to be invited to the West to teach about these advances, just as those thousands of western experts were invited to Japan in the last century?

PART I

Discovery of Japan and Early Adventurers

GROUPS OF HUMAN BEINGS spread across the earth in the millennia before and after the agricultural revolution, mostly maintaining themselves in fairly isolated communities. These were broadly separated by oceans and mountain ranges which were furnished with terrible gods and given sacred characteristics, and men feared them because of the stories about the power of the elements and the mythical monsters there. Then, in Europe in the fifteenth century, confident in their large, armed ocean-going ships, men began to range restlessly around the globe. What was the purpose of such adventures?

Opinions vary, but the quest for gold by each national unit in Europe so as to become richer and more powerful than its neighbour was a major factor. Also there was an increasing awareness of the benefits to be obtained from trading, and of the value of an external reserve of natural resources. Coupled with this was the inflexible sense of the righteousness of their ideas throughout the world by the Christian leaders in Europe, who were then also the political leaders, many of whom had a genuine desire to obtain new knowledge about more remote places, while others craved to plant their national flag amongst different peoples and control affairs there.

Marco Polo's second-hand account of 'Zipangu' (Japan), which he heard from itinerant travellers who had been there, mentioned: 'They have gold in great store...the King's house is covered with gold...gilded windows and floors of gold.' These words were circulated through Europe in about 1300, and must have inspired the building of larger ships and the fitting out of expeditions to discover this Eldorado. One result was the discovery of America by Columbus who was searching for a route to Zipangu. However, it was exactly half a century later that Japan was first discovered by Europeans, and then purely by chance.

31

Chapter 1

Hirado Island

HIRADO is a small island just off the north-western tip of Kyushu. Wild and washed by the currents of the Tsushima Straits at the southern end of the Japan Sea, its population is sparse but it provides on its leeward side a sheltered anchorage. In recent years, a steel bridge of box-construction has been built across to it where the motorist is charged an extortionate toll to pass, but this may help increase the tourism in this isolated spot that holds so much history. The main village is dominated by an ornate Catholic church of polished marble and effigies of dubious artistic merit, and around the shore and on the cliffs are the relics and plaques that celebrate its past: the alleged grave of William Adams — the first Englishman to visit Japan, the site of the English factory and a white statue of a Japanese girl who represents the many such girls who gave birth to children fathered by the Europeans.

As in the old days, small Japanese children still follow the foreigner around as he tours the sights, and yelp with excitement if their remarks are countered with a phrase in Japanese! The sleepy shopkeepers are glad to serve the tourist who has made the long journey to his island as the slow pace of life continues from day to day. But Hirado has known hectic activity, and was once the focus of foreign intercourse when some of the world's famous merchant-adventurers lived and worked there. At present, however the clear, restless sea laps over the solid stone steps built by the Dutch nearly four centuries ago which fishermen still use to come ashore and dry their nets on, while their wives arrange the tiny *aji* fish on racks in the sun just above.

In 1281, Hirado was one of the first places where the Mongols landed in their second unsuccessful invasion of Japan. But 60 years later, after the demise of Kublai Khan, it became a centre of trade with China, and raw silk, gold, swords and copper were exported while imports were silk fabrics, velvet, porcelain and musk. Two centuries were to pass before Europeans discovered Japan — in 1542 three Portugese sailors led by Mendez Pinto on their way to Macao were blown off course and landed — and new factors caused radical changes in the nature of foreign trade.

One year after Christopher Columbus rediscovered the American continent in an attempt to sail west to Japan after hearing the fabulous reports of Marco Polo, the Pope proclaimed that he had the authority of Almighty God on how the earth was to be exploited commercially. A line shall be imagined, the Papal Bull of 1493 announced, running from the south to the north poles through Rome, and all pagan lands discovered east of this line will belong to the Portuguese and those to the west of it to the Spanish.

By 1549, Portuguese traders had set up trading posts around the coast of Japan, including Hirado, and had penetrated inland as far as Kyoto. Glowing reports about Japan had been sent back to Portugal. Soon afterwards Francis Xavier, a Jesuit priest, disillusioned with his lack of success at conversion in India, arrived at Kagoshima with a Japanese criminal called Anjiro to act as interpreter. His party was welcomed by the Satsuma daimyo (feudal lord), who expected lucrative trade with the Portuguese to follow, and he gave them freedom to preach their new doctrine. When trade did not come, and after his Buddhist priests had complained of Xavier's 'aggressive intolerance,' the daimyo issued an edict in 1550 outlawing Christianity. Xavier moved hurriedly to Hirado, where guns of Portuguese ships signalled his arrival.

The daimyo of Hirado, Matsuura, was by now enjoying the fruits of the new commerce, and noting the reverence shown by the traders to Xavier, he issued orders that all his vassals should listen to the Catholic propaganda. Within 10 days Xavier was able to boast over 100 converts. But as historian, F. Binkley, wrote: 'Sermons preachèd in Portuguese or Latin to a Japanese audience on the island of Hirado in 1550 can scarcely have attracted intelligent interest.'

Xavier, of course, realised the influence that the daimyo's orders had had on his 'success,' and soon set off on foot for Kyoto to seek favour with the Emperor himself, hoping to convert the whole country at one stroke. But neither the Emperor nor the Shogun would receive him because of internecine strife in the capital city, and Xavier and his companion, Fernandez, were reduced to street-preaching. Anjiro had been left behind, and as neither man could speak Japanese fluently, they experienced great difficulty in communicating with the people. After this Xavier decided he would travel to China to preach, for, he concluded 'if the Chinese adopt the Christian religion, the Japanese also will abandon the religions that have been introduced from China.'

Over the next decades Hirado saw the outcomes of a *Menage à trois* — the Portuguese traders, the Jesuit priests and Japanese officialdom. In 1577, visiting priests organised a spectacle when they 'sent brothers to parade the streets, ringing bells and chanting litanies; they caused the converts, and even children, to flagellate themselves at a model of Mount Calvary, and they worked miracles healing the sick by contact.' This caused a landed lord nearby to destroy Buddhist temples and overturn idols: retalation resulted in the desecration of the Christian cemetery, street riots and the burning of buildings. The Jesuits left quickly, but similar violence from similar causes was to follow all around Japan. This was complicated further by rivalry for Portuguese trade between the daimyo, and in 1562 the Hirado daimyo tried to burn several merchant ships because they had supplied foreign goods to his neighbour, Sumitada. The latter, however, continued to be supplied whereupon he became a stalwart Christian and tried to stamp out Buddhism in his territory by strong-arm methods. The revolts and problems that this caused, when the Christian town in Hirado was entirely destroyed, were solved by his building a church at the fishing village of Nagasaki so that Portuguese traders along with their attendant priests could have a focus and safe asylum. By 1572 Nagasaki had grown to 30,000 inhabitants and Sumitada was one of the richest daimyo in Japan.

*   *   *

In 1590, Portuguese missionary work came under the leadership of Alessandro Valignano, and he encouraged his priests to adjust to Japanese ways to avoid some of the conflicts. But a change in policy by the Pope had allowed Spanish friars to work in Japan, which Valignano opposed, and a new rivalry was born. The King of Spain intensified the jealousy and distrust by decreeing that Spaniards could trade with Japan. The common Christian cause was thus weakened by this Spanish intrusion, the tolerance of the Japanese was strained and a crisis seemed imminent. However, the situation was saved by the appearance of the heretical Dutch who had rebelled successfully against Spanish rule in 1594, and had begun trading with their own ships in the Far East. After several fruitless attempts to find the northern passage around Russia, the Dutch began sending ships around Cape Horn. On a small fleet of five ships sent in 1598 were three Englishmen, among whom was William Adams, the chief pilot of the expedition. They had ignored the Papal Bull, for in 1534 King Henry VIII had repudiated papal authority and set up the less aggressive Anglican Church. Adams nevertheless appreciated the pioneer work of the Portuguese Magellan who had discovered the passage around the Horn — and even this was contrary to the edict of the Pope.

Only one of the five ships, the *Liefde* (Charity), survived the voyage to the Far East after being attacked by natives in Chile, threatened by Spanish warships, battered by storms and running short of food. Only six of the 24 survivors were able to stand when Japan was finally sighted on 19 April 1600. On reaching shore in Bungo Province, Japanese doctors made efforts to save the lives of the exhausted and starving seamen, while fishermen and others thoroughly looted the *Liefde*. Six of them soon died and the rest were imprisoned in much the same way as described by James Clavell in his book *Shogun*. Immediately Portuguese Jesuits were summoned to assess the new arrivals and words of condemnation flowed from their Christian lips, for the priests saw their monopoly over trade and religious propaganda threatened. Death was insisted upon, for the arms cache in the *Liefde*, argued the priests, surely showed that piracy was the intention of the intruders. Jacob Quaeckernaeck, the Dutch commander, was too sick to defend his crew against such arguments, but William Adams, who spoke some Portuguese, demanded that he should explain the situation to a high authority before any hasty decision was reached. After one month, it was arranged that Adams should have audience with the most powerful administrator in Japan, the Shogun, Ieyasu Tokugawa. The Tokugawa family had, after centuries of civil strife, finally managed to unite Japan. Ieyasu had set up a system whereby he was easily approached; it was an absolute, integrated but flexible system that lasted for over two centuries.

Adams has often, but incorrectly, been described as a rough English seaman. But the facts are that he could read and write his native English well and with style, which was no mean feat during the Shakespearean age, and also he had a command of spoken Portuguese and probably Dutch. Within a short time he was to become fluent in Japanese, and he became a personal tutor of the Shogun, teaching him mathematics, astronomy, history and geography. He was born in Gillingham, Kent, on the Thames estuary where a large memorial to him was unveiled in 1934. After a shipbuilding apprenticeship, he went to sea and by the age of 24 achieved the rank of captain. His education was to prove its worth as, coupled with sound diplomacy, he negotiated with Ieyasu in person. Soon a close personal relationship developed, and later he was requested to become the court interpreter, replacing the Portuguese, Tcuzzu. One of his most remembered achievements was the building of 100-ton European-style ships for Ieyasu, and as a reward he was given an extensive estate at Hemi, near Yokosuka, with about 90 retainers.

Through Adams, the Dutch were spared despite the intrigues of the Jesuits, but they were not allowed to leave Japan. Adams accepted his confinement with pragmatism, married a Japanese girl (even though he already had a wife in England) and began a trading business. He bought a house in Tokyo near Nihonbashi in an area later named in his honour as 'Anjin Cho' (Pilot Street), and soon was a man of wealth and influence. This upset the Portuguese, for they feared he would now try to ruin them in revenge for their evil attitude when he had first arrived, and they tried to persuade him to leave. However, it was not in Adams' character to bear malice, indeed in business affairs he cooperated with them, and he delighted in debating with them on religious doctrine. On one occasion in 1614 at Uraga, a young friar in a fit of religious fervour, proclaimed that miracles do happen if sufficient faith existed. In the heat of debate he offered to prove his claim by walking on the sea. Adams insisted on a demonstration, and a time and place was set for the 'miraculous event.' The news was spread amongst the Japanese citizens and a huge crowd appeared. The friar arrived on the beach dragging a large wooden cross which he clasped to his body as he waded into the water, but when he attempted to stand on the cross and walk

on the sea's surface, he capsized and went under. A Dutch spectator
rapidly put out in a boat and just saved the friar from drowning.
Afterwards Adams was blamed for the failure because of his lack of faith.

*   *   *

Ieyasu, in 1605, gave permission to Captain Quaeckernaeck and his
shipmate, van Santvoort, to leave Japan and look for the Dutch colony
in the East Indies. They took a letter from the Shogun inviting the Dutch
leaders in Holland to trade with Japan. Four long years later two Dutch
trading ships put into Hirado. Adams greeted the seamen and offered
to help. He arranged to travel with a delegation to the Shogun to seek
trading rights and to ask permission to establish a 'factory' or trading
post at Hirado. All went well, and Jacques Specx, a Dutchman from
one of the ships, remained behind to supervise the venture. But over a
year passed before more supplies arrived, and Specx himself had to sail
to the Dutch colony at Patani to fetch some goods to sell. A renewal
of the trading agreement was needed, so again a Dutch party visited
Ieyasu with Adams as interpreter. This time more generous terms were
granted, and they could trade without any supervision by Japanese
officials. But by now, in 1611, they had competition with Spanish traders
who operated from Acapulco, Mexico, and the Philippines to Uraga on
the Miura peninsula. Uraga was close to Adams' estate at Hemi, and
it was Adams who had also arranged the Spanish venture when he went
on a diplomatic mission for Ieyasu to the Philippines in 1608.

Adams was now moving into a tricky and delicate position, for he
had assisted and become friendly with the Dutch, Spanish and
Portuguese, and each was now at loggerheads. There was a danger that
each national faction would come to blows with the other — and the
English were yet to arrive. The situation could become extremely
embarrassing for Adams in the eyes of the Japanese authorities if this
was to occur. The arrogant and overbearing manner of the Spaniard,
Vizcaino, caused him special concern. This man, fresh from the Spanish
colony in Mexico, extended his domineering attitude even to Ieyasu,
and he demanded that the Dutch and English be expelled from Japan
for rebelling against their lawful ruler, the King of Spain. Adams
afterwards moderated by explaining that Catholics, especially the
Spanish, had intentions of conquering the whole world. First they sent
in religious missionaries to each country to convert as many people as
possible, and followed this up by sending in armed troops to overthrow
the government with the help of these Christian converts. It was a neat
exaggeration that gave the Shogun cause for alarm, and in 1614 he
ordered that all missionaries leave Japan and all churches be closed.
His orders, however, were not enforced.

The English, with a virgin Queen who had been excommunicated
by the Pope, and defending their shores against Spanish invasion, were
determined to survive as a nation despite these hardships. Adams had

sent many letters to England, including a few to his first wife, Mary, detailing the excellent trade prospects in Japan and explaining with his technical knowledge of navigation how to get there. With one letter he enclosed a map he had made of Japan during his earlier voyages around the coast. On 12 June 1613, the English vessel *Clove* arrived at Hirado under Captain John Saris.

. The *Clove* belonged to the new East India Company, and Saris' instructions were to find Adams and ask his advice as to 'what course should be held' in the matter of forging diplomatic relationships. Adams was at Shizuoka, and a messenger was sent to him by Matsuura, the Hirado daimyo, who had befriended Saris. Saris enjoyed several sensual days in Matsuura's convivial company while waiting for Adams, and he acquired some Japanese pornographic prints as souvenirs for his private collection. Saris had then been persuaded to lease a property in Hirado as headquarters for the English company. For Matsuura, foreseeing even greater income for himself if other foreigners operated in his territory, had convinced Saris that the remote island was an ideal trading centre. How wrong this proved to be!

* * *

Adams had resided in Japan for 13 years before he saw another Englishman. The first English vessel, the *Clove,* under Captain Saris had arrived in Hirado, and Adams, who was proficient in Japanese, had been sent for to help his compatriots.

When Adams finally arrived he was welcomed by the firing of the *Clove's* cannons, and was shown the greatest deference. He was guest of honour at a dinner that Saris had arranged, and his opinions sought on the setting-up of the English 'factory.' Saris, however, became annoyed by Adams' other interests and sympathies, and complained that he behaved like a 'naturalised Japanner.' And when Adams began a series of leave-taking incidents in order to complete business with his Dutch, Spanish and Portuguese associates, Saris' opinion became more jaded. Still, they did visit Ieyasu, the Shogun, together, delivered a letter from King James of England, and obtained generous trading privileges. During these meetings Adams again asked the Shogun if he could have permission to leave Japan and return to England. To his astonishment, Ieyasu agreed and the overjoyed Adams made plans to leave on the *Clove*. However, as the days passed he assessed his situation — his large estate, his wife and children in Japan, his honoured status — and finally decided to stay.

He was then, after an argument about salaries, made an employee of the East India Company. Richard Cocks, a London merchant, was put in charge of the operation. Saris, before he left, insisted that Hirado should be the headquarters for trade in Japan but Adams strongly disagreed, pointing out the proximity of Dutch competition, with the Portuguese not far away at Nagasaki. Adams suggested Uraga which was close to Tokyo, Kyoto and other major centres where little competition existed, but Saris suspected that Adams would attend more to his own personal business at nearby Hemi if Uraga was the base. So isolated Hirado was chosen against Adams' better judgement, and its poor location was the main reason why the English 'factory' was to fail.

Before Saris sailed back to England on the *Clove*, he left written orders for Cocks not to entrust Adams with any company money, not to allow him to travel alone from Hirado to the Shogun's court and to monitor his activities with the Dutch and Spanish. These insinuations against Adams were all without foundation, but with Saris himself it was a different tale. When the *Clove* arrived back in England in 1614, it was found that Saris had used the ship to transport a great quantity of goods for his own private trading. An examination of the accounts proved he had personally profited from such activities on a huge scale. His cabin was searched and the pornography discovered. A scandal ensued and the offensive materials publicly burned, and Saris was fired from the company. For the rest of his life he lived quite comfortably in Fulham, London, on the profits from his illegitimate trading.

Chapter 2

The English 'Factory'

The 47-year-old Cocks, with the six men under him, had £5000-worth of goods to trade. He kept a detailed diary during his 10-year stay in Japan, most of which survives today, and he wrote long letters to friends in England. Some of these were read by King James I who remarked, after hearing about some aspects of Japanese culture, that Cocks was the 'loudest liar.' Cocks' attention to company records, however, was not so thorough.

Cocks soon established branch agencies in Tokyo, Shizuoka, Osaka, Sakai, Kyoto and Nagasaki, all with the help of Adams. The Tokyo agent, Wickham, was a haughty and overbearing character who tended to look down on Adams as a low-class seaman, and to reject his advice. Arguments followed, and Cocks had to mediate to keep the peace. Wickham died in 1618, leaving £6000, which proved he, too, had been trading on his own behalf. By this time aggressive English haughtiness was renowned worldwide after the defeat of the Spanish armada. Queen Elizabeth in 1576 had, in official defiance of the Papal Bull, granted rights to her subjects to conquer and trade anywhere, and to 'make laws, imprison and levy fines.'

Nothing went smoothly for the English factory in Japan, and Cocks was plagued with bad luck. His unfounded suspicions of Adams, who did his utmost to forward the aims of the venture, overshadowed the selfish and thoughtless activities of his subordinates whose real indiscretions went unnoticed. Cocks' overall plan was sound: to set up a triangular traffic of trade between China, Japan and England. To exchange cloth and manufactured goods from England for silk in China, and then sell the silk in Japan for gold and silver which would go back to England. The weak link was with China, and Cocks endeavoured to cultivate the cooperation of a certain 'Chinese Captain' who promised, in return for monetary favours, to obtain permission from the Chinese Emperor for the English to trade directly with China. This never materialised, and the company lost over £1000 in useless bribes.

Meanwhile, Adams was hard at work in Hirado preparing a junk for a voyage to Thailand 3000 miles away. This craft, the *Sea Adventure*, set off in December 1614, but a storm damaged it and they put into Naha, Okinawa, for repairs. The slowness of the natives in getting materials for repairs caused problems: the Japanese crew made trouble ashore, stealing and running up debts, and Wickham and Adams almost came to blows. The junk eventually had to limp back to Hirado, making a loss for the company. Adams did, however, buy a quantity of a new root vegetable which Cocks planted in his garden. Thus the sweet potato was introduced into Japan, now a popular 'traditional' food.

Adams did successfully navigate *Sea Adventure* to Thailand in 1616, and a large profit was made for the company. The East India Company failed to regularly supply goods to their Hirado factory, and often goods were damaged when they arrived, but in that same year, the ship *Advice* arrived and soon afterwards further pilgrimages to the Shogun were undertaken. By now Ieyasu had died and his son, Hidetada, was the supremo. Hidetada's attitude towards foreigners, and Adams in particular, was not as liberal as his father's, and diplomatic conflicts followed. One reason was that Hidetada was jealous of Adams' influence over his father, and another was that Adams' wife had sheltered illegal Catholic priests at Hemi, and now Adams was kept waiting daily at the Shogun's palace for many weeks before the now-restricted trading rights were renewed. All the branch agencies had to close, and English activities confined to Hirado. Adams' status was obviously in decline, for shortly afterwards he was assaulted twice by irate Japanese, and no justice meted out for these. In the first attack, the 53-year-old Adams had his arm violently twisted by relatives of the Hirado daimyo because he had refused to give them an extortionate share of the cargo he had brought back from Thailand. A few months later, 15 Japanese seamen, who had sailed to England with Saris, returned and demanded extra payments from the company. Adams refused to support their fictional claims, and in retaliation they entered his house and tried to throttle him. Happily, they were driven off by others in the house.

But worse was to follow. On 8 August 1618, two Dutch ships put into Hirado bringing an English merchant vessel they had fought and captured. Angrily, Cocks protested strongly to Specx, calling the Dutch 'common thieves and robbers.' At that moment, Adams was at the Shogun's court with his Dutch associates requesting a renewal of their trading rights. So Cocks sent an urgent letter to him demanding he, as a loyal Englishman, leave the Dutch delegation. Adams refused. Cocks, furious, wrote that Adams was 'completely Hollandised.' He then, with lavish gifts for the Shogun, rode to Tokyo and met Adams on the way back, and he persuaded him to return to court to complain about the Dutch act of piracy. Adams agreed, but was kept waiting for two months, till finally the answer came that because the piracy took place outside Japanese waters no measures could be taken.

The next year Adams fell ill, and in May 1620 he died after providing in his will for both his wives. His Dutch, English and Japanese colleagues also benefited, while his estate at Hemi was inherited by his son Joseph.

Hostilities had risen to fever pitch at Hirado since the piracy, for although the Dutch had returned the ship, it was devoid of cargo. Bloody fights involving murder flared up regularly. Meanwhile, in Europe an allied Dutch-English 'Fleet of Defence' had been formed to attack Spanish and Portuguese ships in the Far East. When the fleet anchored at Hirado, after a voyage of piracy and robbery, the two factions argued over the division of the spoils, and more violence and murder erupted. In the brothels and bars ashore, there were many cases of rape, robbery and violence by the English and Dutch seamen against the Japanese, and the authorities were forced to take strong action.

*   *   *

Relationships between the two business communities in Hirado finally stabilised, yet still the seamen caused trouble when they arrived. In 1622, the English, with their headquarters in Batavia (Djakarta), decided to withdraw from the 'Fleet of Defence' and also to close down the factory in Hirado. The company complained of the lack of profits, and of the behaviour of their personnel who were 'so miserably given over to voluptuousness!' For Cocks and his men, from puritan England, had led lives of sensual pleasure in Hirado. Each had Japanese 'wives,' who were frequently changed, and there were rounds of drunken parties where special 'dancing girls' entertained. Cocks, naturally, was reluctant to leave and procrastinated, sending a message to his superiors that many affairs in the factory were not in order. How true this was!

Then in December 1623, angry at this disobedience, the company sent the vessel *Bull* to Hirado to force the Englishmen to leave. Many of the Japanese nobility owed the company money but, knowing the factory was being closed, refused to pay their debts, and this spelt more trouble for Cocks. But time was short, and after asking the Dutch chief to receive any outstanding debts on behalf of the company, and after a final round of wild farewell parties, they all sailed away from Japan to face the wrath of their superiors. Cocks, fortunately perhaps, died on the voyage back to England, and so was spared the trial of explaining how his mismanagement had caused the English factory to fail.

The Dutch remained at Hirado until 1641, importing such modern goods as microscopes, telescopes, alarm clocks, lead pencils, various chemicals and 'unicorn horns.' This latter was in fact the long, pointed tusk of the narwhal for which the Japanese paid high prices because of its 'life-prolonging and memory-building' properties. They were then forced to move to Deshima, a small island in Nagasaki harbour, and there could only sell their goods to approved government agents. This move followed the construction at Hirado of a new stone warehouse, which had carved on the gables the date '1640.' But these figures, referring to the Christian calender, offended a recent anti-Christian law and they were ordered to destroy the building. They obeyed, for anti-foreign feeling in Japan was now so bad that they would have all been slaughtered for refusing. New harsh restrictions followed: no observance of the Sabbath, no carrying of firearms, no foreigner to be accompanied by a Japanese servant outside their house and all imports to be sold, no matter how low the price, within one year.

By this time, the Dutch were the only foreigners, apart from a carefully regulated Chinese community, allowed to remain in Japan. The Spanish and Portuguese had all been expelled, and those who had stayed had been killed in a massive anti-Christian campaign. The Dutch were only permitted to stay because in 1638, under orders from the Hirado daimyo which could have meant death for disobedience, they had helped government forces annihilate 37,000 Christians during the Shimbara Rebellion. This was an uprising by the poor of Kyushu against desperate economic conditions, in which the Christian religion was used to provide unity of purpose.

There followed in Japan a period of over two centuries of virtual isolation when no Japanese could travel abroad, and any that returned from abroad were immediately executed. The Dutch, almost imprisoned on Deshima, provided the only tenuous contact with events and inventions in the outside world.

Chapter 3

Chichijima

THE BONIN ISLANDS and Ogasawara Gunto are the same group of islands in the Pacific Ocean a thousand kilometres south-east of Tokyo, and Peel Island is the main island in the group. Port Lloyd was once the name of the main village although it is now known as Omura. A similar confusion concerning the names of the inhabitants also applies; for example, we find that families directly descended from Messrs Savory, Webb, Gilley and Washington are nowadays known by different names.

One of the first documented visitors was the Spanish explorer, Don Ruy Tropez de Villalobas who landed there briefly in 1543. Fifty years later it was the turn of the Japanese warrior, Sadayori Ogasawara, who declared that the island was 'bunin' — meaning 'empty of men' — from which the name 'Bonin' is derived.

However, the island remained uninhabited until 1827 when a British naval ship *HMS Blossom* under Captain F.W. Beechey, 'discovered' the island again. He nailed a bronze sign to a tree claiming the whole group of islands in the name of King George IV. After this he sailed to Honolulu and informed the British consul there. Action was taken in 1830 when the consul appointed Martteo Mazarro, an Italian, as British governor of the islands (in all about 100 sq km.) which were to be named: Peel, Parry, Beechey, Volcano and Marcus.

Mazarro took the first 'community' out there — a band of thirty people of various nationalities who started a new life there. The ship sailed by way of the Sandwich Islands where the crew seized about twenty of the native women to keep them company. Primitive huts were soon built and wild pigs and goats were captured and fattened. They even set up a liquor still and a weird kind of alcoholic beverage seared the throats of these tough pioneers.

An American negro called Washington was delighted with the island and not so happy with his work as a cabin-boy on a whaling ship when he arrived in 1843. He jumped ship, hiding in the trees until his boat sailed, and settled down there with one of the native women, and so another island family began that still remains today.

Governor Mazarro was the one who most appreciated the home-brewed liquor and was perpetually drunk and unable to govern his domain. It was Nathaniel Savory, an American from Massachusetts, who did most of the organising and who was well respected by the others for his sober judgement and hard work. He began to question the validity of Britain's claim to the islands, on account of the fact that the first decade of occupation passed without a single supply ship calling in or for that matter any official endorsement from Britain. He also knew that in 1823, four years before Beechey's visit, Captain Reuben Coffin in the American whaler *Transit* out of Nantucket, had stopped over at Port Lloyd and explored the islands. So perhaps the United States of America had a legitimate claim to the islands, thought Savory. He awaited his chance which came in 1854 when Commodore Matthew Perry's flagship *Susquehanna* and the rest of the famous 'Black Ships' fleet dropped their anchors in the calm waters of Port Lloyd.

*   *   *

Perry came ashore and met Savory. They discussed setting up a coaling depot somewhere on the islands so that American ships would have a staging point when trade with Japan was established. Perry also reckoned that an American station so close to Japan would increase the influence of America on Japan. He purchased a sizeable plot of land on the sea-front of Port Lloyd with $50 of his own money, no doubt hoping to make a profit for himself if the US government bought land for the intended coaling depot.

Perry's entire crew also came ashore at Peel Island and one of them described the visit:

'A man by the name of Horton who was discharged from the *Plymouth* is the one who generally pilots vessels in. He generally has a number of fine turtle. He has a pen made in the water so you always have them fresh. At the head of the bay on the left hand side facing up is a fine place for hauling the seine. There are a number of sharks here and also whales, both kind frequently coming by the ship. There is a fine watering place about NE from Castle Rock. Wood can also be got but you have to cut it. There is a good number of vegetables to be got but not enough for a number of vessels coming in there at one time.

'Now to give a description of my walk on the island. After walking on a level place where some houses were I came to a mountain up whose steep sides I climbed. It was covered with tropical verdure of all kinds and small trees in which thousands of birds were singing and the air was perfumed with the sweet smell of a beautiful white flower. Now and then we would come across sugar cane.

'After descending into the plain I beheld signs of cultivation: water melons and cantelopes vines being all around, also corn growing and all vegetables common to gardens. I then proceeded along the beach picking up a variety of shells. There was a number of turtle lying on their backs waiting for a boat to carry them off to our ship where they would be made into soup, a very fine way of disposing of them.'

On this visit, Perry arranged that Savory should be elected the chief magistrate of the islands, for by this time Mazarro had died of drink. Perry also increased Savory's status by appointing him the Island Agent for the US squadron. So Nathaniel Savory, adventurer and pioneer, became a civilian working for the US Navy on an isolated Pacific island that was officially a British possession.

*   *   *

In the summer of 1861 a large Japanese junk arrived at Peel Island and more than one hundred men disembarked under the eyes of the settlers. They came quietly ashore, speaking a strange language and carrying strange tools and equipment. The inhabitants were puzzled. It was not a raiding party that had come to steal, it was not a drunken crew from some whaling ship that wanted to rape the women before they sailed back to their base, it was not a shipwrecked crew who had lost their ship and needed food and medical care. What did they want? It became even more puzzling when the junk immediately sailed away over the horizon.

It took a few days for the two parties to communicate, but then the islanders realised that they wanted some land so that they could start living there. What could Savory do? He could not drive them out because they had no boat. He could not kill them for that was against his Christian principles; he was a peace-loving man who loved the sun, the sea and the life he was living. So he made arrangments for them to stay because they were not aggressive, in fact they were extremely polite and courteous. After a few weeks, in which the original settlers offered as much help and advice as they could, the newcomers had settled down and had been very industrious in building themselves shelters and in beginning to cultivate the land they had been given. It took several months before they became completely independent of Savory and his people. Then it became apparent that these intruders were not as they had at first seemed.

It came to light that amongst these hundred men who had arrived so mysteriously, six of them were samurai warriors and one was a government agent from the ruling party of Japan. This was revealed one sunny day and the agent firmly informed Savory that *he* was the governor, for the islands had been discovered first by the Japanese warrior, Ogasawara, almost three hundred years before. Furthermore, this officious official declared that the name of Peel Island shall be changed to Chichijima and the group of islands shall henceforth be known as 'Ogasawara Gunto.' Savory was naturally flabbergasted and a trifle nonplussed. He appealed to the American and British governments for help and advice. Nothing happened and he was forced to accept the situation.

*   *   *

For a little more than a decade, the two groups existed peacefully. The routine of living and working proceeded, with Savory still being the real leader because of his superior knowledge and experience of living on the island and dealing with the elements and all the quirks of nature there. In 1874, old Nathaniel Savory died and the Japanese agent took control. But the next year another large Japanese junk arrived and the first group was replaced by a second that took over the running of the affairs of the islands. There was nothing official about the situation, no government had shown any interest in owning the islands and helping the inhabitants up to this time. Then in 1877 the Japanese government formally claimed the islands in the name of the Meiji emperor, and no other country protested.

So the Savorys, the Webbs, the Washingtons and the Gilleys and all the other families found themselves living in Japan, although they were not Japanese citizens. At that time the governments of the western nations had come to an agreement with Japan that any of their subjects living in Japan were not subject to the laws of Japan. They had what were called 'extra-territorial rights,' which meant that they were ruled by one of their own leaders. So a Savory, the old man's son, was back in charge of the affairs of his friends, just as the British consul was in charge of the affairs of the British people living in Tokyo, Yokohama and Kobe at that time.

Extra-territoriality ceased in 1894 after such figures as the English lawyer, Dr de Becker, had slowly helped to mould the laws of Japan so that they were more or less in line with those of other western countries. All foreigners, including the settlers in Ogasawara, came under Japanese law. Some of the settlers left, but the majority remained and intermarried with the colonists. An international community, in which the blood and wisdom of at least three races flowed in the veins of most of the inhabitants, had evolved and for them nationalistic feelings seemed quaint and meaningless.

During the years after 1894, the community was terrorised by the arrival of strong-arm agents from the gangster organisations of the Yoshiwara (prostitute quarters) of Tokyo. They came to 'recruit' young girls who had traces of western looks in their faces and bodies. It was such creatures who had the power of arousing rich Japanese businessmen and getting them to part with their money. Many a simple island girl was whisked away by these agents to become a working member of the 'mizu-shobai' in the cities. The position of women in Japan at this time was very low, and the status of women with foreign blood was even lower.

*　　*　　*

During World War II the American forces saw the islands as vital 'stepping stones to Tokyo'. The climax came on 19 February 1945 when the neighbouring heavily guarded island of Iwo Jima was finally occupied by American marines after a loss of 27,000 lives from both sides. Curiously enough, although occupied by the Japanese military, Chichijima was never invaded but it was bombed almost daily during the Pacific War.

Before World War II, 6400 inhabitants of Chichijima were evacuated to Tokyo and many remain there to this day. In 1946, when the US Navy was administering the Bonin Islands, 135 descendants of the original settlers were allowed to return. They found their island war-scarred and riddled with tunnels and gun-emplacements; the rusting hull of the *Hinko Maru*, which had been deliberately beached as a form of defence, was around the headland from Futami Bay near Omura. Just above the graveyard where their ancestors were buried, the navy had constructed a weather station and jeeps and trucks roared around the mud roads. On the shore at Omura, an open-air movie theatre had appeared.

A large proportion of them found work with the navy and all of them enjoyed the free medical care and the children went to school along with the sons and daughters of navy men. Several of the island girls married men from the occupying forces and later left the island. Every week or so a Grumman HU-16D seaplane would fly in from Guam bringing supplies and personnel, and heavier supplies arrived by a Landing Ship Tank which returned to Guam with fish that the islanders had caught — including the famous Wahoo fish.

In 1968, the Japanese government resumed control of the Bonin
Islands and the US Navy moved out which caused complications for the
young people who had been educated only in English. The Americans
had been there for twenty-three years, and all those under thirty years
old had to get a first-grade 'Kanji Primer' and begin to learn how to
write their own language. What is more, the inhabitants now found that
they were part of Tokyo City and controlled by the Metropolitan
government. Land speculators arrived by the shipload, and there was a
danger that the character of the island would be lost. This unsatisfactory
situation lasted ten years, then in 1978 the Governor of Tokyo, Ryokichi
Minobe, visited the island and informed 100 residents gathered at a
meeting that in April 1979 the Ogasawara Isles would become
autonomous. Cheers rang out. Once more they would be independent.
A new regional development plan was suggested by Yoshio Sakurauchi,
director-general of the National Land Agency, and a further page of
history was turned on the volcanic island in the sun.

Chapter 4

Dr von Siebold, Illegal German Immigrant in the 1820s

THE DOCTOR TREMBLED with fear when they arrested him. The crime
that he had committed two years before had at last caught up with him.
Still, he had had a good run, and got away with many illegal acts in his
lust to satisfy himself. But on Deshima island in Nagasaki harbour with
Japanese guards watching him closely, he was full of fearful uncertainty.
He was a German and should not have been there at all, for only the
Dutch were allowed in Japan. He remembered the fate of other illegal
immigrants that had preceded him, like the Italian priest John Baptist
Sidotti whose Christian evangelism had brought him to Japan in 1708
against the laws of the Tokugawa shogunate, but, he thought, under
the guidance of God Almighty who would protect him in his
righteousness. Sidotti was immediately arrested, and a year later taken
to Edo (Tokyo) where he was imprisoned. But still he had persisted in
trying to make converts to the prohibited faith of Christianity. Even the

two old servants that the authorities had so kindly provided to look after him were subjected to his fanatical evangelism, so that finally he was placed in a covered pit less than two meters deep, and fed through a small hole in the lid until he died in the winter cold of December 1715.

But now it was 1828, and Dr Philipp Franz Balthasar von Siebold hoped that times had changed. For he had only a scientific interest in Japan and did not want to gain power through religious propaganda. True, he was there to find out all he could about Japan for the Dutch government so that trading could be strengthened, but that was a pragmatic and useful ambition that would bring mutual advantages. His was no vague, angels-in-the-sky-after-death venture, his feet were firmly on the earth. He had brought his medical instruments and his scientific education to Japan with him in 1823, and since then had effectively cured many sick who had come to him.

Before he left the Dutch headquarters in Batavia (now Djakarta), Siebold had heard that smallpox was rife in Japan. He therefore packed a supply of the vaccine, prepared from cows' lymph, that the British physician, Edward Jenner, had perfected in 1798. Unfortunately, his batch lost its potency during the long journey, but, despite repeated requests, the Japanese authorities would not allow him to obtain any more as they thought that the introduction of cowpox into the human body was dangerous. The principle of vaccination against smallpox had, in fact, been originally discovered in China during the Sung era (960 - 1279) in which scabs from victims of the disease were powdered and taken by inhalation through the nose by patients seeking protection. However, excessive doses had too often induced the disease itself, and this method had not been used widely in Japan.

It annoyed Siebold to be forbidden to prepare fresh vaccine, for smallpox was reaching epidemic proportions. But his knowledge in curing other diseases and his success in surgery caused this 27-year-old doctor to be an attraction for many young and ambitious Japanese who were studying medicine. They learned a vast amount about western methods and science from Siebold, but it is unknown if he revealed to them the political state of Europe and the reason for his presence in Japan. The French had conquered Holland during the Napoleonic Wars, and the British then occupied all Dutch colonies overseas. Deshima was not a colony but a concession given by Japan to the Dutch for trading purposes, and when the British moved into Batavia in 1811, Deshima was the only place on the earth where the Dutch flag was raised!

It was not until 1816 that Holland regained independence after the end of the wars in Europe, and soon Java was returned to the Dutch. By this time the Dutch-Japanese trade, once so profitable, was almost non-existent, mainly because of Britain's increasing influence in the Far East. From 1809 to 1817 no Dutch ships had brought goods to Deshima, and during these years the Dutch traders, with no resources, were supported only by the generosity of the governor of Nagasaki. The Dutch government desparately wanted new, up-to-date information on

Japan in order to revive the trade. When Dr Siebold had made it known that he had studied all available information on Japan in Europe, and was keen to go there, the Dutch, disregarding the agreement that only Dutch could reside in Japan, had sent the German doctor as part of a fact-finding expedition. So Siebold's life ambition had materialised, and was financed by the Dutch.

*   *   *

The enthusiasm that Siebold showed for Japan, and his willingness to teach any interested Japanese medical doctor about western clinical methods, resulted in the authorities granting him unprecedented privileges. He was allowed to purchase a large house on the outskirts of Nagasaki, in Narutaki, where he lectured his students and demonstrated practical clinical procedures on the Japanese patients who came to him. It was also arranged that a mistress, Taki, should live with him in the house.

Such direct instruction in medicine provided his students of 'rangaku' (Dutch learning) with a real breakthrough in their understanding. Previously, all their work had centred around studying and translating books, a slow process riddled with errors and misunderstandings. Now they had direct contact with an expert teacher, and received systematic instruction with the opportunity to ask questions; Siebold's fame soon spread to Edo and other rangaku centres.

But in his classes the learning was not all one way. Like all efficient teachers, Siebold learned from his students. He assigned essays, to be written in Dutch, as exercises for his students but also designed to reveal information about Japan. 'Description of diseases in Japan,' 'Insects in Japan,' 'Whales in Kii province,' 'Cultivation of tea and its use' — these were a few of the titles he suggested, and later Siebold published many of them in western journals.

The annual visit of the leaders of the Dutch post at Deshima to Edo, as demanded by the first Tokugawa shogun, Ieyasu, in 1609, was reduced to once every two years in 1764, then once every five years in 1790. Such visits, where the Dutch were obliged to bring fine gifts for the shogun (there were reported occasions when the Dutch visitors were even required to grovel at the shogun's feet and to dance and sing) had always been used as occasions to glean information by both the Japanese and Dutch. But when Siebold accompanied the Dutch mission in 1826, he took his energetic and systematic quest for data to extremes. He collected specimens of plant and animal life on the journey, used a compass and plumb-line to survey the Straits of Shimonoseki, used a sextant and chronometer to determine the exact positions of all the large cities they passed, and all the while he used gifts as bribes to obtain all kinds of information and objects. All his surveying activities were, of course, completely illegal, and much of the information he received was supposed to be secret.

In Edo many admirers from all walks of life were eager to meet him. One of these was Kageyasu Takahashi, head of the shogun's library and founding director of the Translation Office of the Bureau of Astronomy. Siebold persuaded Takahashi to exchange two maps of Japan for nine maps of the Dutch East Indies along with a book on travel. This, too, was highly illegal, and absolutely forbidden by the military-minded shogunate. Trouble was bound to follow if the transaction was discovered.

Meanwhile, Siebold lectured in Edo, giving demonstrations of western surgery and therapy, and received in exchange gifts and information of every description. He was admired and almost adored, indeed he became something of a cult figure. Even women in those chauvinistic times insisted on being introduced to him, and as he wrote, 'although no women could lawfully be admitted to us, the concourse of our fair visitors was greater here than anywhere else. One gentleman would sometimes bring with him six ladies, especially in an evening, on which occasions our large stock of confectionery and liqueurs suffered prodigious reductions.' Then he went on to complain, presumably after much of the liqueur had been consumed, that: 'At these visits the ladies often unpacked our trunks of clothes, expressing much wonder at the form of the garments, as well as curiosity concerning the mode of wearing them. We were thus obliged to present them with some of the more valuable articles.' Then, revealing the true idolisation of the foreigners: 'At all events, something as a remembrance they must have, were it but a couple of Dutch words written upon their fans.' The analogy with modern autograph-hunting fans of pop musicians is intriguing.

*   *   *

When the Dutch delegation left Edo to return to the confines of their island in Nagasaki harbour, the procedure was elaborate and filled with emotion. The visit of the 'Hollanders' had brought excitement and new ideas, had created a sense of progress and had provided an interest outside the normal grind of life. The men of power had made them dance like fools, the men of intellect had picked their brains, while the ordinary folk had glimpsed exotic human forms dressed in strange clothes. It was not easy to get away. Departure was not sudden and decisive like entering a taxi or train and roaring off, for 'we were obliged upon coming into the street, to close our "norimon" (palanquin) against the great concourse of people, who, notwithstanding the harsh means employed by the guard escorting us to keep them off, jostled each other to get a sight of the Hollanders.' As they passed each palace or large house, they had to get out and communicate with the noble personage who lived there, giving and receiving presents as they went. At the Emperor's palace in Miyako (Kyoto), they were received with great formality by a grand judge, but the Emperor himself would not see them for 'the "Sun of Heaven" probably esteemed himself a personage too holy to be lawfully known to, or even thought of, by Christian foreigners.'

But Siebold was unperturbed, for he had his secret maps, documents, measurements and specimens on top of his norimon, and a mass of new information in his head. In legal terms he was a potentially dangerous spy, but he regarded himself as a mere investigator determined to increase human knowledge and understanding. Just as religion created a dilemma for investigators in Galileo's time, nationalism created a dilemma for men thirsting for new data in the industrial era.

From Kyoto the party travelled by boat down the river to Osaka. Here they were shown the town and attended several theatrical performances, but as there was no translation of any play extant, they could only record their impressions of drama in Japan. In Osaka, too, they took the opportunity to buy a quantity of charcoal, because it was much cheaper there than in Deshima.

On the last night of their journey before they reached Deshima, at Yagami, the interpreters and friends travelled out to meet them. Here all their trunks and baggage were examined by officials, but as one commentator remarked, 'the investigation is conducted with a forbearance that allows the prohibited wares they are well known to contain to pass undisturbed.' No doubt a few coins exchanged hands again.

Returning to his house, Siebold began preserving and classifying his specimens, writing down the new information systematically, and studying his prohibited maps. His medical work and instruction continued for two more years, then he decided to return to Europe for a while. His packed trunks, containing all the scientific materials he had collected, were taken to a ship in Nagasaki harbour. But a sudden typhoon grounded the ship, and as his trunks were being unloaded they were inspected, and some illegal articles exposed. The goods were all impounded, and Siebold put under house arrest on Deshima. He stayed in this situation for several months, but he was not idle. He copied the forbidden maps before being ordered to hand over the originals, and persuaded his friends to secretly replace many of the specimens that had been taken away. All through this activity, Siebold became more worried as the long months passed, for he knew he was guilty of espionage. But finally, in 1829, he was simply told to leave Japan for ever, and he sailed to Europe. The fate of his accomplices in the 'map affair' was not so kind. Takahashi was imprisoned and died before being sentenced. His two sons were exiled to a faraway island, and others were punished in various ways, including life imprisonment.

Back in his native Germany, Siebold established himself as Europe's greatest authority on Japan. He published several books dealing with all aspects of Japanese life and the country, arranged his scientific collections in museums at Leyden, Munich and Wurzburg, and propagated many species of plants that he had brought back. Thus European gardens were introduced to Japanese lilies, peonies, camellias, chrysanthemums and scores of others.

*   *   *

After his departure, the influence of Siebold on the direction and increase in pace of western medicine in Japan was enormous. His Nagasaki students spread knowledge throughout the country, not only by teaching more students but also by translating and writing new books that were more accurate. The understanding of physiology, especially, improved. Previously this field, so central in western medicine, was for 'rangaku' students merely a collection of vague notions, for a direct translation into Japanese of the concepts involved was not possible. But Siebold's teaching had brought it into focus, and by 1832 his student, Choei Takano, published 'Igen Suyo' (Principles of Physiology) in 12 volumes.

However, the traditionalists became even more opposed to 'rangaku' despite, or perhaps because of, its success in the medical sphere. Political intrigues raised their ugly heads to obstruct its progress. Takano was one to suffer. He had joined a group of intellectuals in Edo called the 'Bansha' (Barbarian Circle) that discussed the destiny of Japan in terms of the West and western learning. Often they criticised the government's actions, as when soldiers bombarded the American ship *Morrison* as she approached the coast of Japan to return some shipwrecked Japanese sailors. Takano's critical polemic on this incident caused him to be arrested in 1839, and sentenced to life imprisonment. In 1844 the prison burned down, and he was released for three days but failed to surrender himself at the end. He wandered around the country as a fugitive for several years, then returned in disguise to Edo where he resumed translating and practising medicine. The police eventually arrested him in 1850, whereupon he committed suicide.

So there was no smooth path in Japan for the fruits of western discoveries, even after Siebold had demonstrated the methods in medicine, and explained wider implications of other fields of knowledge. In fact, in their thirst for knowledge both Siebold and Takano were, in one sense, responsible for the success of political opposition to further progress because of their indiscretions. Academics of the old school did not need to attack the new ideas, they needed only to criticise the criminal nature of their exponents. This ancient political trick worked, for in 1840 all western studies were banned except medicine, and in 1842 the translation of western books came under central government control. Such laws, however, could never be strictly enforced.

Some years later, after Japan had been forced to reopen her doors to Americans and Europeans, due to the efforts of Commodore Perry, Siebold sought an opportunity to return. In 1859, now 63 years old, he arranged a passage back through the Dutch authorities in a semi-official position. But he was no smooth diplomat, and he embarrassed the Dutch consul-general on numerous occasions during those sensitive times. He was asked to leave, and did in 1862. Four years later he died.

PART II

Westerners in the Treaty Ports of Japan

BY THE EARLY 1850s the factories of Europe and America were mass-producing all manner of goods as demonstrated by the Great Exhibition at Crystal Palace, London, in 1851. The exponential exploitation of the earth's natural resources had become a fact of life in human society, and was generally blindly accepted, although there were a few isolated prophets, like Malthus, who could foresee great dangers. Raw materials needed to produce these goods and markets in which to sell them, involved more and more the searching for both throughout the world and the setting up of more sophisticated trading operations, and the establishment of supply stations for the transporter ships.

The piece of land westerners called 'Japan', after Marco Polo's nomenclature, but 'Nippon' by those resident there, was seen as a valuable location for refuelling and supplying American merchant ships running between the West Coast ports of America and Chinese ports. By this time, western trade was well established in China and many parts of Indonesia. After many attempts by British, Russian and American missions, using a variety of strategies, to obtain an agreement with the leaders of the unknown country, it took the careful balance of diplomacy and show of military force as exercised by American Commodore Matthew Calbraith Perry in 1853-54 to successfully negotiate the first international treaty with Japan.

Perry sailed into Tokyo Bay with a squadron of huge black steamships bristling with cannon and a crew of well-disciplined marines, presented his documents and the treaty, then steamed away with the promise that he would return the next year for the signing ceremony. This he did and in February 1854 with a fleet of ten armed vessels, and on 31 March the Treaty of Kanagawa was signed which allowed American ships to be supplied with water, food and fuel at the so-called Treaty Ports of Kanagawa, Shimoda and Hakodate.

A further agreement allowed Americans to live and trade in these ports but not to travel elsewhere without special permission. This arrangement came into effect in 1858 by which time other nations, including Britain, had signed similar treaties with Japan. They stated that foreigners would not come under Japanese law but would be governed by their own consuls in each port, and the trading procedures were much to their benefit and to the detriment of Japan. Later other ports, notably Kobe and Nagasaki, were opened but the unequal treaties were always an embarrassment to the Japanese.

Rapidly western-style institutions and buildings arose in these ports — business houses, churches, schools, hospitals and cemeteries. For birth, education, disease, activity and death still existed in all places, as did the conservative desire to maintain the unique customs of the individual's own culture. However, immediately the customs and ways of the West were interacting with those of Japan with unique results. And the Japanese government was to provide some controversial surprises for the westerners.

This section deals with events during this early period.

Chapter 5

Yokohama City

'YOKOHAMA' conjures up images of paper lanterns, obliging almond-eyed girls, crowded and bustling streets, silks and exotic lacquerware, green tea and business tycoons — a romantic, yet vigorous image — but the actual meaning of the name is simply 'beach across by the side.' All the images mentioned existed and still do exist, but so much has happened so quickly in the 120 years of the city's existence that one often wonders if the place is real or not!

Four generations ago Yokohama was a collection of fishermen's huts, rarely marked on maps of Japan, yet now it is a major industrial city and one of the world's busiest ports, while its land ranks amongst the most expensive on earth. Such a young city, yet crammed full of history, and where archaeological digs have taken place on the buried foundations of buildings erected less than 100 years ago. A city completely razed to the ground three times, yet rapidly rebuilt on the original pattern by conservatives with only a century of tradition, seemingly without a thought for the future or for the logistics of human habitation. A city regarded by some foreigners and some Japanese as not being part of 'real Japan.' Yet a city appreciated by resident foreigners with their special privileges there, and loved by the Japanese if the crowds that pour in every weekend are anything to go by.

It was near the fishing village of Yokohama that the Treaty of Kanagawa was signed, and it was Yokohama itself that was later to develop into a city where the trading, and afterwards the manufacturing of goods, was to take place and flourish. During Perry's five-month visit his seamen were allowed to explore some of the neighbouring countryside and communities and they also began to fraternise with the local Japanese girls. According to Preble, who kept a diary during this historic visit, the girls were not endeared by the Americans' beards and whiskers, and soon it was found that 'a man's morals could be judged by the length of his moustache.'

* * *

In the treaties signed between Japan and the various countries of the West, it was stated that one of the Treaty Ports would be Kanagawa which was a small village on Tokyo Bay. There was no mention of Yokohama, which was much smaller with only 101 families. Between the time that the treaties were signed and the beginning of actual trading two issues had been debated. First, the Japanese authorities were fearful of security and decided that Kanagawa was too close to the main Tokaido highway along which princely daimyo, soldiers and others travelled. This would allow the foreigners to observe and communicate with these travellers, assess the internal political situation and perhaps take advantage during a time of instability. Japan desperately wished to retain her own identity and not become a colony of some western power as had happened elsewhere, but she realised that this could happen because of the superiority of western arms. Therefore, to the Japanese, Yokohama — across a wide river and away from the Tokaido — was a better choice of location.

The second issue concerned the topographical nature of Kanagawa. It was on the coast but the water was shallow. Large trading vessels would not be able to get in close, and this would require extra men and additional costs for the loading and unloading of ships. The first merchants arrived illegally before the diplomats, and they were not impressed by Kanagawa at all. But when shown Yokohama with its deep water running in close to the shore, they were delighted. Predicting this delight, the Japanese authorities had already built wooden houses and storerooms for them to use at Yokohama. The merchants immediately moved in and commenced business.

On their arrival, the diplomats were not at all pleased. They found a situation remarkably like that of the old Dutch trading post on Deshima Island in Nagasaki. The foreign settlement was completely surrounded by water and narrow, well-guarded bridges were used to check and control their movements, and to vet whom they could meet from 'mainland' Japan. The spying would be all one-sided! The diplomats protested time and again that Kanagawa, as the treaties stated, be developed as the treaty port, but all to no avail. Eventually, the consulates were built on the waterfront, or Bund, at Yokohama. The western diplomats had had to step down and lose face.

Almost immediately conflicts began. Many-sided conflicts involving the greed and arrogance of the Europeans, the child-like curiosity and ignorance of the Japanese of Western business and industrial methods, the evangelistic enthusiasm of American missionaries trying to please God by conversion of 'pagans' and to find an escape from the Civil War, the silent manoeuvring of Confucian Chinese carefully gaining positions of power and the hustling of a host of stateless drifters with a smattering of business and technology all trying to make a living. All were males. All were enclosed in a small, prison-like 'foreign concession.' Fist-fights, knifings, swindling, thieving, and drunkenness were prevalent. Add to this primitive conditions such as the lack of proper drains, sewers, water supply, lighting and road surfaces — and the tensions, frustrations and the existence of continuous conflicts can be understood. The complexities of the legal aspects of extra-territoriality did not ameliorate the situation. It is small wonder the Japanese coined the term 'hairy barbarian' and tried to contain all the foreigners in one small area!

The construction of the Gankiro Teahouse and other pleasure houses in Yokohama may have been the first positive step towards peace. But when Englishman Michael Moss shot a Japanese policeman in 1860 the tension mounted again. Two years later a pig-headed, colonial-type Englishman from China named Richardson was murdered by the guards of an important daimyo for a stupid, but trivial, act of bravado. The retribution of one *harakiri* and thousands of pieces of gold seemed to spell justice. In 1864, two British soldiers were slaughtered by *ronin* (masterless samurai) at Kamakura and so British and French troops were stationed at the sea-end of the bluff in Yokohama to protect the foreigners. They saw no action, but made great displays of marching with their bands around the settlement, muskets at the ready. Many succumbed to cholera and typhoid and were buried in the foreign cemetery with the others. All this activity was carefully recorded by Japanese artists on wood-block prints, and by journalist John Black in his book *Young Japan*.

In 1866 there was a major fire which virtually destroyed the entire town and foreign quarters. Many lost their hope of gaining a quick fortune, but the Japanese were used to such disasters and cheerfully started to rebuild. With the restoration of the Emperor in 1868, internal stability within Japan seemed assured. Now real progress could be made. Other countries could invest large amounts of money without fear of losing it to some temporary leader, for Japan had decided now to become an industrial, manufacturing nation herself and many of the old conflicts disappeared.

*   *   *

With the coming of money, there came the foreign experts. The two went together as far as the investors from the West were concerned. Bankers, engineers, lawyers, teachers — Trevithick, Brunton, Stone, Kinder, Griffis — the list is a very long one. In fact, over 3000 *yatoi* (government hired foreign experts) arrived at Yokohama over the next 50 years to help Japan catch up with the West after over 200 years of isolation. Another list of men would include Black, Beato, Bernard, Wirgman — who came to work for private companies or to set up their own businesses. Each one made an impression, and many decided to remain and live in Japan. A law passed in 1874 permitted foreigners to marry Japanese, but, as is still the case today, men had to adopt a Japanese name if they wished to become naturalised. Rules such as this, along with other factors, tended to keep the foreigners and Japanese in two distinct groups.

From the early days, Dr Hepburn and his wife had been established in a shrine on the site of the present Yokohama Immigration Office and he, with his unique gifts of scholarship, had made the Japanese language clear to foreigners. His comprehensive dictionary and grammar, and system of phonics are still used today. This was achieved on top of his duties as a medical doctor. On 24 September 1875, a visitor of his called Clara Whitney, showed that religious or idealistic conflicts also existed, as she observed: 'Young men here (in Yokohama) are wicked and depraved, and insult the gentle Japanese as often as they can. Merchants — married men — keep native women in their houses without marriage. Sailors are even worse still, and it is pitiful to see the poor little half-caste children running around uncared for, as the Japanese regard them as unclean and their fathers don't care.' A few years later, Clara was to marry Umetaro Kaji and bear him six 'unclean half-caste children'! Unfortunately, she lived before genetic scientists investigated the human species and found that 'mankind has always been a mongrel lot' and before Benito Mussolini explained that 'race is a feeling, not a reality.'

But this was the start of a period of ecstatic expansion for both Japanese and westerners. Intense enthusiasm was shown by Japan for the technological achievements of the West, causing internal arguments about which country was more advanced in a particular field and should therefore be followed, while many westerners found in Japan a unique gold mine of art unequalled anywhere, and the literature published about it flourished. Yokohama was the first melting-pot for this two-way enthusiasm and saw many westerners become resident in Japan and many Japanese leave to get closer to the core of science and technology in the West.

By the beginning of the twentieth century the circle had been completed. Japan's cities all contained western-style hotels, shops, law-courts, police stations, schools, as well as means of communication and transportation. More often people wore western clothes and ate western food. The economy was strong and Japan's military forces were now capable of facing up to any 'Black Ships.' But as local resources were poor, and as Japan had largely been led and influenced by Britain, she began to undertake various military adventures. In retrospect, the results of these seem strange. After waging a successful war against Russia in 1904-5, Japan welcomed many white Russian refugees during the 1917 Red Revolution. Many of these Russians found a niche in Yokohama. After supporting Britain in World War I (an outcome of the Anglo-Japanese Alliance, 1902-1922), expecting to take over German possessions in the Far East, Japan found herself accepting many German refugees, some of whom settled in Yokohama and introduced their expertise in bread and sausage-making. So, just as many of the yatoi had previously contributed to basic municipal installations in Yokohama by teaching the techniques of road-making, street-lighting and drainage. these newcomers revealed techniques in more luxurious fields. The culture of Japan thus became wider and deeper in much the same way as had occurred in different countries in Europe as the result of military struggles.

The Great Earthquake of 1 September 1923, however, created an unexpected disruption of such steady and natural development. This disaster may have made Japan begin to lose confidence in science and logic, and retract into a shell of self-pity and look more towards her older values, such as her notion of destiny. Yokohama took some time to rebuild but was never the same, and the feeling created by the disaster might well have played a part in the chosen path that led Japan into war. World War II finally ended with two explicit and devastating jolts that once again demonstrated the power of science to Japan. Yokohama was one of the first A-bomb targets considered by the American strategists, but eventually it was Hiroshima and Nagasaki where the 'Black Rain' fell.

*   *   *

During 1944-45, concentrated conventional bombing left Yokohama once again devastated. Rebuilding commenced quickly after the Americans had staked out areas to contain their Occupation forces. Interned foreigners reclaimed their properties and life returned almost to normal.

As the twenty-first century approaches, the old order in Yokohama is crumbling away. Still the majority of the foreign community sees themselves as just that — a separate entity — and those of 'mixed blood,' the descendants of the western experts or of the Occupation forces, find it difficult to identify with either group, although for economic reasons they tend to be more associated with the Japanese sector.

Moreover, with the staggering economic 'miracle' of Japan over the last few decades the old system of privileged apartheid for the westerners is coming to an end. The one remaining foreign hospital, the two sports clubs and certain schools that in the past have admitted westerners exclusively, are now inevitably changing their policies. The hospital is now integrated into the Japanese system of medical care; the sports clubs now accept Japanese members under special conditions, and the schools, contrary to Japanese law, freely admit Japanese students who, for a variety of reasons, are not prepared to go through the Japanese educational system. These changes in Yokohama are a direct result of Japan's present economic status.

The reasons for the lack of integration in the past are numerous. The one-sided treaties were replaced by lop-sided Japanese laws that discriminated against the outsider; the differences in income between Japanese and foreigners of equal standing provided another barrier as well as the perennial hurdles of the language barrier, religious differences and indoctrinated racist feelings. Sometimes all these man-made barriers seemed to be insurmountable, but encouraging changes can be detected at the present time.

Resident foreigners, many of whom are subject to annual 'residents and city tax,' have had no control over municipal affairs. They paid their taxes but had to bear a host of discomforts that need not exist in an affluent city. The frequent sewage smells that drifted into their homes because, to save money, the rainwater drains were connected to sewage disposal drains; the slow, dangerous and chaotic traffic system that, in order to save money, lacked simple automation; the illogical house addressing method that lacked the universal logic of sequential numbering which caused many to suffer tragically through the failure of the fire service to locate them in time. Still, rational changes have occurred to reciprocate the contribution of the foreign community and to improve the quality of life in the city.

A free, monthly English-language newspaper, the *Yokohama Echo* informs foreign residents of recent developments and cultural events as well as topics dealing with Japan's developing welfare system. The new conference centre, with facilities for simultaneous interpretation, encourages people of all nationalities to give presentations and express their views, and the Kanagawa International Association also provides a forum and offers Japanese language lessons at low cost. The new Yokohama Archives of History, located in the old British Consulate building, contain several libraries and collections of materials accumulated by westerners, and the regular exhibitions held there often highlight the past contributions to the city that foreigners have made.

It is all very indicative of a positive attitude towards integration in a city where East has met West very intimately.

Chapter 6

Games at the Gankiro Teahouse

MANY OF THE BEAUTIFUL Ukiyoe prints from the beginning of the Meiji era illustrate the appearance, life and activities of the first foreigners to arrive in Japan. Prints of this type are in a class of their own and are usually referred to as 'Yokohama Ukiyoe.' Several of them depict the interior and exterior of an establishment known as the 'Gankiro Teahouse' which was world-famous during its brief existence; equally famous was 'Number 9' which was built afterwards.

The Gankiro Teahouse, which is referred to by both Pat Barr and H.S. Williams in their books dealing with this period, was sponsored by the government and like their modern equivalents, probably had a mysterious symbiotic relationship with the local police force. However, it must be made clear that the real protagonists in the story, the courtesans or *'musume'* (daughters), are considered to have had a miserable life, having been sold by their families into their profession, while suicides amongst them were not infrequent.

To give the story historical perspective, we should start in the 1850s with Commodore Perry and his Black Ships forcing in the wedge to open up Japan to western trade and commerce. We should also mention the arrival of the first American consul, Townsend Harris, at Shimoda in 1856 and his subsequent journey to Yedo (Tokyo) in 1857 where, according to Pat Barr in her appropriately titled book *The Coming of the Barbarians*, the Shogun announced to Harris:

'Intercourse shall be continued for ever! '

By the end of 1859, only two years later, Yokohama had been established as the most important port for foreign trade and by that time the Gankiro Teahouse had been built and began to flourish. It stood on the site where the new baseball stadium now stands in Yokohama Park near Kannai railway station and where an original Gankiro stone lantern and brass plaque now commemorate its brief existence from 1859 to 1866. The area is called Minatozaki. At that time the whole area was swamp-land and after the section of land for the 'Entertainment Quarters' had been drained, a long wooden bridge was built across the swamp between it and the busy seafront. Cherry trees were planted around the 'Pleasure Houses' to put visitors in a good mood.

The construction of the Gankiro Teahouse was undertaken by Sakichi Company of Shinagawa who already owned another 'Entertainment Quarters' at Shin-Yoshiwara in Tokyo. It was built under the auspices of the Bakufu government in order to attract Japanese merchants to Yokohama and to provide for the needs of the newly arriving foreigners, who were usually bachelors at this time.

59

With careful forethought, the Bakufu had earlier, in July 1859, prohibited any inns in the Kanagawa area to have any courtesans under their roofs and so such persons were forced to operate in this new establishment. One such young lady called Kiyu, who is depicted for eternity on a famous Ukiyoe print, refused to associate with *gaigin* (foreigners) and chose suicide instead.

The Gankiro Teahouse was opened in grand style and the whole of the foreign population attended the ceremony except for the missionaries and priests. The reason why it was located some way from the main town was that it was convenient for government supervision. The courtesans who worked there had to obtain a licence from the government which kept firm control on the activities of the establishment. Arrangements were made for newly-arrived men by the officials at the Customs House. The records show that almost every single foreign man in Yokohama at this time had an employee called a *'musume'* ('daughter' but really mistress) living at his house, and where two bachelors lived in the same house there were two of them.

By 1862 there were 15 such teahouses in the area but Gankiro was still the most famous and its interior and exterior were recorded on many woodblock prints which are rare and expensive collectors' items today.

During the day visitors paid just to have a look at the teahouse rooms and have a glance at the courtesans. In the evening foreign males from many different countries arrived. They held lavish banquets there and watched the courtesans perform intricate and delicate dances, or play and sing with their *samisen,* and often full-scale theatrical performances were put on. All the sensual pleasures were catered for in style: the palate tasted extraordinary food, the ear was soothed with oriental music, the eye feasted on the beautiful colours of the silk kimonos that moved to some haunting dance, the nose, no doubt, was caressed by a mixture of incense and perfumes, the brain all this while was being lulled and calmed by innumerable cups of sake, and so on.

But the rule that the courtesans had to be licensed in order to associate with foreign men was strictly adhered to. The Japanese term for such women was *'rashamen.'* The origin is not certain but *'rasha'* meant 'woolen' and *'men'* meant 'sheep.'

The foreign merchants were obviously well off in these pre-inflation times for the cost of a 'musume' was high. According to a recent book, well illustrated in colour with the prints from this time, written by Konishi Shiro called *Nishiki-E Bakumatsu no Rekiishi — Meji* (Kodansha), there were three ranks of mistresses depending on their calibre: 20, 15 or 10 ryo per month. At present-day values 1 ryo = 50,000 yen, and so the top rank were paid 1 million yen per month (about £4300/$7000). They had to pay a certain proportion of this to the management of the Gankiro Teahouse and thus the government had devised a clever means of keeping the foreigners' money within Japan and strengthening their own economy.

From the balconies of the Gankiro hung two or three pennants of cloth proclaiming in Japanese that: 'This place is designed for the amusement of foreigners.' It was a great tourist attraction for the Japanese who came to gaze into the windows and look at the foreigners in their strange Victorian garb. The foreigners' contribution to the amusements of Yokohama was the construction of a race-course nearby after a little more of the swamp had been drained and filled in.

Visitors to Yokohama in those days wrote down very little about the racecourse but were more fascinated by the Gankiro. The Bishop of Hong Kong went there in 1860 and commented:
'The Japanese officials...have also endeavoured to render Yokohama an attractive locality to young unmarried foreigners by establishing at the edge of the settlement and on a site approached by a narrow drawbridge over the canal, one of those infamous public institutions which have been already adverted to, containing its two hundred female inmates dispersed over a spacious series of apartments and all under government regulation and control. Not content with these flagitious methods of corrupting the foreign residents, the native officials contributed every facility for the perpetuation of domestic vice and impurity. Young men were encouraged to negotiate through the customs-house the terms of payment and selection of a partner in their dissolute mode of living. It is feared that the snare has not been set in vain...it is a deplorable scene of demoralisation and profligate life.'

The Bishop went on to pronounce that: 'The population of Yokohama is made up of the disorderly elements of Californian adventurers, Portuguese desperadoes and the moral refuse of European nations.'

Another visitor in 1862 described the Gankiro as follows:
'I visited the Gankeroo (sic) taking the precaution to go there in broad daylight, and, for my character's sake, in good company, and was a little startled at the systematic way in which the authorities conduct this establishment. Two officers showed us over the building, and pointed out its beauties with as much pride as if they were exhibiting an ancient temple sacred to their dearest gods. This was the courtyard; that was to be a fishpond with fountains; in this room refreshments might be procured; that was the theatre; those little nooks into which you entered by a sliding panel in the wall were dormitories, encumbered with no unnecessary furniture; there affixed to the wall was the tariff of charges, which I leave to the imagination; and in that house across the court, seated in rows on the verandah, were the 'moosemes' themselves. Would we step over, for it was only under male escort that we might enter the main building? My curiosity had, however, been sufficiently gratified, and I departed...'

Another memorable description of the Gankiro is given by the first British consul in Hakodate, C.P. Hodgson, who records the story of his visit in a book published in 1860:
'At Yukohama (sic)...I was perfectly astonished. I went with two of the principal European personages in Japan, and found a magnificent

palace; but before entering it, it was necessary to select, or, at any rate, make the appearance of selecting, one or more companions.

'To do this, a Yakunin (a government guard provided to protect westerners and report their activities) escorted us through all the courts of the seraglio, where ices, cakes, sweetmeats, and other Japanese delicacies were temptingly exposed, until at last we reached the "stables," for so they had been named.

'There were three rows of wooden boxes, some hundred mats long (1 mat = 1.8m), with a passage of half a mat between them; each row was subdivided into narrow "horse-stalls," little rooms with a small window or aperture towards the passage; and in each of these "stalls" was a female. At a given signal, either a clap of the hands or a cry, all the inhabitants rose from their cages, like dogs from their kennels, and put out their well-dressed heads. The visitor had to pass through a hedge, not of hawthorn or tea-trees, but of females, and if not full of pity, disgust and compassion, he must have become lost to feeling and any sense of shame or modesty. When an "object" has been selected, and its value estimated, the temporary proprietor retires, and may either have a room worthy of Sardanapalus or a garret fit for such monstrosities.

'The grand saloons (for I visited all) are really splendid — a fine room with fountains, fish, trees and flowers, marble and old lacquered ornaments, and a pretty view with Gayashaas (Geisha) or singing girls who are good and virtuous. The staircase was large and broad, and of marble; and the Yakunins were everywhere at the call of visitors; a clap of the hands brought together a bevy of men and maidservants.'

William Elliot Griffis, A.M., in his classic work *The Mikado's Empire* of 1883 was more understanding and realistic when discussing the 'moral status of Yokohama.' He explains that:

'Where heathen women are cheap, and wives from home are costly, chastity is not a characteristic trait of the single man.'

In 1866 a fire swept through the Yokohama settlement killing many people and destroying almost all the buildings. One of these buildings was the Gankiro Teahouse.

As T. Fugimoto explains in his book (1927) *The Story of the Geisha Girl:*

'Afterwards, the quarter was removed to Sugatami Street, next to Takashima Street, and at last to Eiraku and Magane Streets, as it is at present. The geisha girls are divided into two great circles, the Kan-hai and the Kan-gai; the former is in the central part, and the latter in the outer side of the city, the greater part of the girls living in the central part and amounting to over three thousands in their number.

'In the east suburb called Kanagawa there lives a great body of girls, independent of the two circles of the city. In the pleasure quarter of the district there was a grand famous brothel called Jimpuro, well known amongst foreigners as the No. 9 shop, but it closed business in AD 1903.'

Chapter 7

Number 9

'Away by the lands of the Japanese
Where the paper lanterns glow
And the crews of all the shipping drink
In the house of Blood Street Joe,
At twilight, when the landward breeze
Brings up the harbour noise,
And ebb of Yokohama Bay
Swigs chattering through the buoys.

THOSE LINES were written by Rudyard Kipling when he stayed in Yokohama in 1892 while he and his new wife were on their Cook's around-the-world tour. Unfortunately, they had to cut short their tour, obtain a refund on their tickets and retreat quickly back to England via Canada because of some mysterious trouble at the bank in Yokohama. Nevertheless, Kipling found out a good deal about Yokohama and also about the seamen who operated the steamships of that time, for the next year he wrote *McAndrew's Hymn* which is a humorous and powerful prayer offered by a tough Scottish ship's engineer. McAndrew had been at sea for 44 years and was regretting things that he had done when he was young, including:

'Years when I raked the Ports wi' pride to fill my cup o' wrong — Judge not, O Lord, my steps aside at Gay Street in Hong Kong! Blot out the wastrel hours of mine in sin when I abode — Jane Harrigan's an' Number Nine, the Reddick an' Grant Road!'

The 'Number Nine' referred to, amongst the other infamous red-light districts around the world at that time and familiar to all seamen, was a house in Yokohama. It stood just outside the city itself — in Kanagawa to the north-east — and the Japanese name for it was Jimpuro. It is curious that it came to be known by foreigners and Japanese alike as 'Number 9' — this seems such a mundane name with absolutely no exotic overtones.

Jimpuro was built specifically as a 'house of pleasure' under government control; it was located in an area where the less well-off patrons ventured. The high-class geisha girls were established nearer the centre of Yokohama but these establishments denied entrance to ordinary people like seamen, journalists and teachers, they restricted their clientèle to richer individuals like doctors, businessmen and politicians. These latter do not seem to have recorded any of their experiences in such places for posterity. This is a shame because so much of the past has disappeared and thus so little knowledge can be passed on to subsequent generations. But shame in such matters was a prominent feature of the majority of 'respectable' western men of that era. However, one journalist of that time did put pen to paper and described, through the medium of a short story, some experiences at Number 9.

He must have been very courageous for it was during the age when a bitter old woman was the most powerful figure in the world. Queen Victoria was not amused by many things and respectable ladies would swoon in a clammy faint if they heard or read anything referring specifically to any form of sexual activity. Victoria's subjects from the wealthier classes, throughout an Empire on which the sun never set, were even known to hang lace mini-curtains around the legs of their dining-room tables lest they excite a sexual response from any male observers!

This journalist, however, did take the precaution to write his story 'A Yoshiwara Episode' under the pseudonym 'A.M.' The book of stories is called *From Australia and Japan,* and was published by Walter Scott Ltd. in 1892. This was seven years before J.E. de Becker published *The Nightless City or the History of the Yoshiwara Yukawa* under the pseudonym of 'An English Student of Sociology.' This latter is a profusely illustrated account of every detail of the life, the laws and the events, as well as the history, of the Tokyo Yoshiwara. It is still being printed (by Tuttle) in paperback.

Perhaps at this point an explanation of some terms would be appropriate. 'Yoshiwara' was the Japanese name for the area in Tokyo developed in 1617 by the government to concentrate all the pleasure houses in one place. The name simply means 'reedy swamp' for such was the nature of the area before civilisation took it over. According to such Japanese people who knew about this area, the name referred to this particular part of Tokyo. But when foreigners began to arrive, they used the name to refer to any area in Japan that provided similar facilities; thus we find reference to 'Yokohama Yoshiwara', 'Kobe Yoshiwara' and so on. This is confusing to some Japanese people even today.

The story entitled 'A Yoshiwara Episode' is referred to in the Oxford English Dictionary (the complete version) as being one of the first published works to use the word 'rickshaw.' This is one of the first Japanese words to find its way into the English language and is derived from the three kanji characters 'jin-riki-sha' — meaning 'man-strengh-vehicle.' This is interesting, but even more interesting is the expression 'hunky dory' that appears in the same dictionary followed by the admission '19th.c; orig. unkn.' According to a prominent foreign citizen of Yokohama, the origin of this term is not unknown. When a foreign seaman jumped into a rickshaw at Yokohama dockside during the latter half of the nineteenth century and shouted 'Hunky Dory,' the man knew exactly where to run with his passenger. He had heard the sound 'Honcho dori' which is the name of the street, that still exists, that runs from the docks to the railway station and towards Kanagawa and Number 9. For that passenger in the rickshaw, everything was indeed hunky dory —

especially if he had been at sea for several months!

Be that as it may, this writer was told by the chief compiler of that renowned dictionary that such an idea was 'an afterthought' and there this semantic theory rests at present.

But enough of words! What happens in A.M.'s Yoshiwara episode? The hero, called Whitmore, ventures out to Hakone about a year after arriving in Japan. He had signed a contract to work as a sub-editor on the *Yokohama Chronicle* that is run by a terrible Irish character called Maloney — Patrick Maloney. At Hakone, Whitmore meets a Japanese mother and her daughter who are bound for Yokohama. The beautiful daughter, he learns, is about to be sold to Number 9. When he returns to Yokohama, he finds that he has won a fantastic sum of money in the Manila lottery, and after a period of lonely but thoughtful wandering in the back-streets he decides to take a ride in a rickshaw.

'Number 9!' he shouts and off he goes. The narrative continues:

'That was all he said. But the man seemed to understand, and darted off at a racing pace towards the patch of sky glowing with the reflection of the lights that had caught Whitmore's attention.

'Whitmore was whirled on (after going along Honcho dori) past the railway station and along the shore, his face and ears smarting and tingling with the stinging surface wind from the north. He drove by the kobansho, or policeman's box, receiving an elaborate salute from its occupant, and was whisked in through the gate of the Yoshiwara right into the full blaze of the garish lights streaming from the parti-coloured lanterns swinging at the doorways and from the cages. He dismounted, and strolled past the *saké* shops and tea-houses and the gaily-bedizened bevies of frailty on exhibition, squatting, pipe in hand, in long rows behind their lacquer brazier — each house with its distinctive crest — with the whole entourage repeated in duplicate in the huge glass-plate mirrors that in most cases formed the panelling of the walls of the showroom. Through streets on streets of this description he fared, with their motley crowds of all nationalities and tongues and colours.

'Past all the smaller houses Whitmore fared and made direct for a great and stately pile of buildings, with massive doors and latticed balconies, and a flood of light pouring from its front that made the garish splendour of the other establishments look pale and wan and mean.

'The journalist entered the doorway and sprang up the steps and passed under the gilded sign of "Nectarine." He was evidently well known there.'

This superb description is followed by a narrative that relates how he was greeted with words and bows that were a little too excessive and smarmy for him, and he knew that some of the honourable greetings and remarks of praise directed to him were just not true. He remarks:

'But in a country where politeness counts for so much, and veracity for so little, strict adherence to the letter of the truth is not to be expected generally, and certainly not in the Yoshiwara at all.'

After this Whitmore explains that the reason why he had become *persona grata* in such an establishment was because he felt that, as a professional journalist, he should know and experience everything. Also he was collecting material to write the history of the private lives of an Oriental Treaty Port — but he was determined not to publish it until he was 'safely out of reach of the shot-guns and riding-whips of the Yokohama community.'

Soon he meets the new, young courtesan whom he had first seen in Hakone, and he describes her as she is dressed for her new role:

'The girl sat on the sofa arrayed in all the gorgousness of Oriental magnificence; only she was minus that fearful and wonderful false hair-piece of tinsel hairpins, and free from that repulsive scent of oil that Japanese women affect so much. Her hair was twisted and piled upon her head, and kept in position by a silver arrow thrust through it like a skewer. She was utterly woe-begone, although she did make a brave effort to rouse herself and to receive her guest with the politeness and cheerfulness her miserable trade demanded. But when Whitmore took her hand — in spite of himself he marvelled at its symmetry, its pink nails, its long tapering fingers glittering with flashing rings — she shivered and shrank from his touch as if he had been a leper.'

Whitmore asks if she wants to return to her family in the country, and she indicates that she does, whereupon he agrees to pay ¥700 for her release. However, a sympathetic old waitress in the establishment hits on a better plan. The outcome is that Whitmore undertakes a *saké*-drinking contest with an old soak called Tajima — and he wins the bet; then, acting rather drunk, he is challenged to a game of 'go' by an expert on the staff — and again he wins; and finally, still appearing intoxicated, he is challenged to a 'kendo' match by an aging master called Sugihara — which he also wins! With this he has gained the freedom of the sweet damsel in distress and all the new clothes and jewellery that she has been given by the proprietors of Number 9.

At the end of this charming tale it is revealed that the kindly old waitress has been pouring green tea into his *saké* glass all through the drinking bout and his drunkenness was merely affected.

*   *   *

The Australian author, the late Harold S. Williams, who lived for over 60 years in Kobe and who studied the history of Japan in great detail, has written that:

'Number 9 was presided over by a madam known throughout that China coast and much of the Far East as 'Mother Jesus.' It was said that she was a kin of a certain well-known Japanese hotel family which, upon the opening of Yokohama to international trade in 1859, saw the opportunity of conducting there a business in a line more profitable than hotel-keeping!' Williams continues:

'Mother Jesus conducted the house in proper style. She could jolly along the rowdy ones, be stern with the obstreperous, and elegant with the mild and meek. In those days neither she, nor the old family of which she was a member, suffered socially by being associated with such an enterprise. However, in later years the family found the connection a bit of a cross, and liked to forget it.

'Mother Jesus had a fair knowledge of English, with which she greeted each visitor. Then she clapped her hands, and the girls, fully dressed in kimono, entered demurely from an adjoining room and lined up for presentation.'

Williams then recounts a certain misunderstanding that used to occur in Yokohama at this time:

'As there was another Number 9 address in Yokohama, namely a most ornate foreign residence known as Temple Court, owned by an American and located at No. 9 on the Bluff, which was the best foreign residential quarter in Yokohama, the rickshaw men were faced with a problem, when, at the shipside on the wharf, a new arrival gave the order 'You go chop-chop Number 9.' They had to decide whether he intended Mother Jesus' establishment, or that of the distinguished foreign resident on the Bluff.

'Generally the rickshaw men guessed correctly, but occasionally there were mistakes. And so, on being hauled up the steep hill to the Bluff, and on being deposited at the front gate of Temple Court, the passenger would be puzzled that the front door should be opened by a butler in a white coat.

'"Where are the girls?" the passenger would pantingly enquire. The error was apparent, and soon he was being hauled off to the correct destination at, of course, another fee for the rickshaw man.

'Sometimes the error was in the reverse order. The foreigner was decanted at Mother Jesus' establishment, instead of at Temple Court. He was greeted by Mother Jesus in English, and amazed when she clapped her hands and the girls lined up.'

Williams also informs us that in a museum in America — the Peabody Museum at Salem, Massachusetts — there is a small exhibit displaying a pair of Japanese slippers simply marked 'Number 9.' They were, he says, taken as souvenirs from Number 9 by a French resident of Yokohama many years ago, and when he died they remained in a trunk until about 1970. After they were discovered, they were presented to the Peabody Museum where they remain today.

Little else seems to have been published about Number 9 except for a number of postcards that presumably could be purchased at the place; but unlike the postcards of other scenes in Japan that visitors could buy at that time, hardly any of these were mailed back to friends at home.

Number 9 closed down in 1903 and all that remains is a lovely short-story, a few postcards, a reference by Kipling, a pair of slippers and, perhaps, the fading memories of a few centenarians.

It is now known that the author who used the pseudonym 'A.M.' was in fact Professor James Murdoch, a Scotsman. He was a wild-looking red-haired man, and a brilliant linguist and Oriental scholar who had been educated at Aberdeen University and at Göttingen

Few British readers would now feel the disgust of the Bishop of Hong Kong towards the brothels of the Treaty Ports which were sanctioned by the Japanese Government as economically and socially desirable: however, it is worth noting that in Britain during this period the 'flesh trade' flourished in every major city. Details of this aspect of British culture may be gleaned from the book *The Worm in the Bud, The World of Victorian Sexuality* by Ronald Pearsall (Penguin 1972) where an equally, if not more, disturbing system of prostitution operated.

From this book, we are told that in Victorian London 'Competition to be in the top flight of prostitutes (and there were an estimated 80,000 of them out of a population of 2,362,000) was fierce, though few of the aspirants had the qualities to make it. The successful not only had to perform well, but had to look well, talk intelligently, and if possible possess additional talents; a good singing voice was highly prized.' Here it would seem that the Japanese definition of a 'geisha girl' would have applied with equal meaning to this class of British girl. Or as Rudyard Kipling chorused: 'For the Colonel's lady an' Judy O'Grady are sisters under their skin'! Furthermore, much of Pearsall's 650-page book is devoted to homosexuality and perversion, and practices 'against the norm,' which may reflect the British public-school-military system of the times.

But for the international historian, the situation is now that in this sphere much is known about the Japanese system because it was officially recognised and records were kept, whereas in Britain one has to rely upon the private papers of doctors and self-acclaimed social commentators, as well as exaggerated folk-culture, for information which may be prejudiced and unreliable.

However, some speculation may be justified concerning the relationship between the central control of prostitution and street crime. Japan never had a 'Jack-the-Ripper' throughout the Meiji era, and still today as the old, controlled tradition proceeds and develops violence against the person on the streets of Japan is virtually unknown. Compare this to the present- day cities of Britain where young women feel afraid to leave their homes after dark, and even female pensioners are advised to chain their doors against rampaging intruders.

University in Germany where he studied Sanskrit. At the age of 25, he went to Australia where he was appointed headmaster of the prestigious Maryborough Grammar School in Queensland (1881-1885) after which he transferred to Brisbane Grammar School for three years before coming to Japan. In Japan he worked as a teacher and as a journalist, as well as writing short stories. He spoke and read Japanese very well, and wrote a scholarly three-volume *History of Japan*. In 1917 he left Japan with his second wife, a Japanese lady, and went to Sydney where he had been appointed Lecturer in Japanese Language and Literature, a newly created post. He had been a resident of Japan for 25 years, and the Sydney Chamber of Commerce had put pressure on the university to teach Japanese in order to have men who could help improve trade relationships between Australia and Japan. Murdoch died in 1921.

Chapter 8

Social Diseases and Smallpox

SHORTLY AFTER British troops had been stationed in Yokohama and other Treaty Ports of Japan in the 1860s following troubles (which included the murder of some Britons) between the newly-arrived foreign residents and some discontented Japanese who objected to their presence, another kind of trouble arose. This was due to the intimate fraternisation between the troops and Japanese prostitutes, in houses established in the so-called 'pleasure quarters',and, of course, took the form of venereal diseases. British sailors who indulged suffered similarly.

The first British consul in Hakodate, C.P. Hodgson, documented some of the temptations:

'In every open port of Japan there are certain houses, built and furnished at government expense, for foreigners. They are not the tea-houses we read of, where all the "moosmes," or maids, are either the daughters of the proprietor or their respectable servants,but houses of ill-fame.

'At Hakodate there was one of these houses, which I had occasion to enter with police officers more than once, to seize runaway sailors.'

Happily married Hodgson gave no more details of the Hakodate establishment, but did for the one at Yokohama, the famous pleasure-house called the Gankiro which has already been referred to. (See Ch. 6) Such places, however, increasingly worried the British authorities. Concern in London about the many members of Her Majesty's armed forces contacting so-called 'social diseases' through the services of such establishments (there were hundreds catering for all classes) led to secret orders for military and naval officers to meet to discuss the most effective means of controlling the multiplying bacteria and spirochetes in the infected humans and of preventing their spread to others. Before penicillin there was no complete cure, and the most effective strategy was to identify and isolate, often by force, all known carriers of the diseases.

The services of Dr George Newton were offered to the Shogun's government, the *bakufu,* in 1867 by Admiral Sir Henry Keppel, commander of the British China Station, free of charge, provided the authorities would build a special hospital and make regular medical examinations of all prostitutes compulsory. This was agreed upon and the *bakufu* provided some money, but civil strife in Japan the next year that led to a new government under the Emperor Meiji delayed completion of the hospital, and Japan's first Lock Hospital opened late in 1868. Meantime, Dr Newton realised the gravity and urgency of the situation and had been running a temporary clinic for venereal diseases in Yokohama, examining licensed prostitutes regularly for the first time in Japan.

At first, there was great opposition to this move by the owners and operators of the numerous brothels, and because corruption was rife cooperation from the police was not forthcoming. Also, there was a shortage of competent medical practitioners to carry out the regular inspections of the thousands of women in Yokohama, and the training of sufficient local men in the diagnosis techniques needed time. However, Dr Newton persisted and was rewarded by 1869 with complete cooperation from the authorities, including the police, and eventually by the brothel-keepers. He was consulted about introducing his system in other Treaty Ports, and in May 1871 a Lock Hospital began operating in Nagasaki where it was reported that over 56% of the women examined carried a contagious venereal disease.

Dr Newton's success in Yokohama was demonstrated when he recorded in The Lock Hospital Report that in the first quarter of 1871 a total of 14,450 examinations of prostitutes from 102 brothels, on weekly inspections, had been carried out and only 2% found to be diseased and forced to remain in the hospital. Also, out of 411 infected men who visited the hospital, 269 had been cured. So the value of the system was clear. Dr Newton died in 1871 and his place was taken by Dr George B. Hill who was also provided at the expense of the British government. In 1875 he reported that lock hospitals in Nagasaki, Hyogo (Kobe) and Osaka, the latter operated entirely by Japanese staff, were successfully controlling the dreaded diseases. Before the system was introduced at Kobe, twelve British seamen from HMS Sylvia, a survey ship, had been rendered useless by advancing syphilis, and so the British authorities realised that the benefits of the lock hospital system far outweighed the expense of providing a doctor to supervise it. Also, British naval medical inspectors made sudden, unannounced visits to various brothels. Not for pleasure, but to check that each keeper and inmate were cooperating with the hospital, to fight against corruption, and to make sure Japanese doctors were performing their duties adequately.

By 1879 Dr Hill was ready to move elsewhere and his successor, Dr Richard Charles Pasley Lawrenson, was accepted only after the British Consul General, Sir Harry Parkes, had interceded, for the Japanese foreign ministry wanted to dispense with this service provided by Britain and operate the system entirely with Japanese staff. So when Dr Lawrenson resigned in 1881 the authorities insisted that local staff take over all lock hospitals completely. The British finally agreed that they were competent, and that foreign doctors and inspectors were no longer essential, especially when the Minister of Home Affairs promised that Imperial officers would be strictly and carefully supervised.

*　　*　　*

After this there were conflicting views regarding the effectiveness of the system. Dr J.E. de Becker, the English lawyer, researched in detail the legal, social and medical aspects of prostitution in Japan during the 1890s and described how the spread of venereal diseases was accelerated by a practice called *'mawashi.'* In this a prostitute accepted several male guests and circulated between them all through the night. It was claimed that the woman engaged in *'mawashi'* washed herself after every connection but refused to use an antiseptic like iodoform because the smell offended some guests. Modern medical science now knows that this would not prevent the spread of some diseases anyway.

But control was effective to about the same degree as that maintained by the British doctors even though de Becker did point out cases of misleading statistics in official reports. He did record, however, that before 1868 it was a common sight to see noses eaten away by syphilis whereas in 1898 it was comparatively rare. In an earlier age such a disfiguration in a prostitute was continually repaired with coloured candle drippings as a primitive form of wax-surgery, a precursor of more sophisticated plastic-surgery, so she could continue in her trade in dim lighting conditions.

As a heated correspondence raged in the letters column of *The Japan Times* in early 1899 concerning the moral and pragmatic aspects of licensed prostitution in Japan, the systems of control became more formal in the Yoshiwara (redlight districts). 'Regulations for the Control of Prostitutes' issued by the Home Office in October 1900 required that they all register with the police in a 'Register of Prostitutes' and a personal file on each one was completed giving details of her life, reason and necessity for entering the business and place and term of engagement. Then each woman was notified that regular medical inspections were obligatory under the law and failure to comply attracted a fine of ¥1.95. A timetable of inspection days for each district (there were six in Tokyo) made clear what was required. However, if a woman was found to be infected she was confined in the hospital for treatment, and a further set of hospital regulations had to be complied with. In this case, with no source of income, her debts accumulated daily while what savings she had often dwindled away. Such a system led to suicide in many cases even though it was efficient in protecting society against the ravages of degenerate and disfiguring diseases in the pre-penicillin age.

*   *   *

Details concerning the relationship between poverty and prostitution in Meiji Japan can be found in Professor Mikiso Hane's excellent study *Peasants, Rebels and Outcasts: The Underside of Modern Japan* (Pantheon Books 1982) but the moral and medical issues were then not as distinct as they are today.

Few of the early travellers and residents from the West who recorded their experiences of Japan were concerned with prostitution and venereal diseases. This underworld was outside their experience, and taboos that had evolved in their Christian heritage made them tend to ignore it. Mr Hodgson was an exception in that his duties sometimes brought him in contact with it, but in writing he made it immediately clear that he visited Yokohama's Gankiro and the Hakodate pleasure-house in the presence of respectable collegues. Yet many did have a profound fear of smallpox which was a disease that was unambiguously and starkly visible all over Japan before 1890 and which was often remarked upon. Smallpox was responsible for the deaths of some foreigners and thousands of Japanese. Adventurers who went out into the countryside to explore the 'real Japan' were constantly at risk if not protected by vaccine; however, the diffusion of scientific knowledge and methods of treatment eventually eradicated the disease.

Vaccination against smallpox was first introduced into Japan about 1812 by Nakagawa Gorosi following his captivity in Russia, even though the same principles were discovered in China centuries previously. The Dutch doctor, Monike, in Nagasaki had also showed in 1848 how effective the method was, but medical care for the general populace was not, probably through economic reasons, felt important enough to pursue in a society rigidly divided by class. Possibly the class system divided both economically and physically by distance, with the *samurai* high on his horse and the lesser person kneeling on the ground, and this provided slight protection in a feudal society. But bacteria do not recognise class divisions, and to destroy them everybody has to be vaccinated. With the increased mobility of people as the industrial age dawned this became a matter of great urgency.

In 1858 a team of Japanese doctors founded a vaccination institute in Tokyo but there was much local opposition towards it because of the strange and unknown methods. But during a major outbreak of the disease in 1870-1, the new and insecure Meiji government foresaw that severe economic repercussions could follow if there were many deaths among the farming community, and it considered the proposals of Drs Newton and Siddall, following negotiations by Parkes, to undertake a programme of universal compulsory vaccination.

Dr Joseph Bower Siddall was the assistant of Dr William Willis who served the British Legation in Tokyo as a surgeon and interpreter. Both doctors had attended the wounded of both sides in the 1868 struggle between the Shogunate and Imperial forces — the first time that surgery was provided on battlefields in Japan. Willis managed the smallpox hospital on the Bluff in Yokohama that was established there in 1864, and he later married a Japanese lady and had one son.

Dr Siddall was a graduate of Aberdeen University and had been house-surgeon at St Thomas' Hospital, London, before being appointed surgeon to the British Legation in Tokyo in 1868. He took charge of a large temporary hospital for wounded soldiers of the Imperial forces at the request of the government as they were brought in from the battlegrounds, and initially had great difficulty in organising the hospital along western lines. Patients refused to remain in their beds, assistants would not keep the beds clean, nurses lacked authority because all the patients were men used to unquestioning obedience from women;

hygiene was also at risk because filthy bandages and poultices were buried outside and not burned. However, after refusing to continue an operation unless this situation changed, Siddall introduced strict hygienic methods into the hospital. Also he found Japanese students rapidly learned to use splints and bandages, and he taught some of them amputation techniques. Both Willis and Siddall later helped establish the Dai Biyoin (Great Hospital) in Tokyo.

Compulsory vaccination against smallpox was discussed at a meeting that Parkes arranged in January 1871 between a governor of Kanagawa and all the British and American military, naval and civilian medical officers. It was agreed, with complete support from the Japanese authorities, that vaccination stations with supervising hospitals should be established all over Japan.

The first stations were opened in Yokohama and nine towns nearby, with British doctors offering their services free. The authorities publicised the new service on noticeboards in every neighbourhood and most people cooperated well. In this new era, the simple country folk no longer believed that placing a sign outside their home stating that their children were not at home protected them from the scourge.

In 1874 the Emperor decreed that the entire population be vaccinated, all cooperated and visited nearby stations which had now spread to all parts of Japan, and within 15 years the disease virtually disappeared. It was obviously a team effort that brought this success, but the authorities chose Dr Siddall to be awarded the Order of the Rising Sun by the Emperor for it — the first time that this honour had been bestowed upon a foreigner.

* * *

The introduction of Aids into Japan recently, where a few have died from it, has been blamed squarely on foreigners. (*Daily Telegraph,* 26 November 1986.) This xenophobic response will no doubt increase as the media is given free rein to advise all Japanese to avoid having relationships with any foreigner, implying that all foreigners are Aids carriers. This attitude of the media, with its emphasis on sensationalism to cause intense panic, is no doubt encouraged by some new ultra-conservatives in the Ministry of Education who wish all young Japanese to avoid integration with the rest of the world. (*Times Education Supplement,* 8 August 1986). Using an historical event, like the spread of Aids in the 1980s or life-terminating military manoeuvres in the 1930s, to encourage nationalism and patriotism seems a retrogressive step. The British were adept at these tactics centuries ago when 'the French Disease' described syphillis and was used to create hatred between nations in Europe, now 'the White Man's Curse,' as Aids is described in Japan, promotes a similar ancient attitude. No mention, of course, is made of the Japanese travel business where 'Sex Tours' of several countries worldwide are arranged and have been enjoyed by thousands of Japanese businessmen over the last decade. The objective observer wonders what analysis of these sex tours for Japanese men has been made to determine whether any of them were responsible for bringing the Aids virus to Japan.

Chapter 9

Jonathan Goble — Bible-Basher and Inventor

WHAT OLD-TIME MYSTERY STORY of the Orient would have been complete without the statutory appearance of at least one rickshaw driver? A century ago 30,000 of these man-powered vehicles sped through Japanese city streets, carrying geisha girls to romantic assignments, potentates on their travels, priests on errands of mercy and rich businessmen to their warehouses to inspect the latest spices or silks from other parts of the East.

Today, there are less than 40 rickshaws in all Japan, and these are mere nostalgic novelties. Few people have a chance to see them except in the back-streets of some of Tokyo's entertainment districts where one may occasionally carry a heavily made-up geisha to her evening's work. As she sits under the hood of the neat, two-wheeled vehicle, does she ever think of its importance in the history of Japan and other parts of the oriental world?

The story begins in the mid-nineteenth century when Japan's rulers still maintained a policy of isolation. No foreigner was allowed to land in Japan, not even if he was shipwrecked. The authorities also wanted no Japanese to have any contact with the outside world. Laws were passed restricting the size of boats that could be built, so that these small craft had to hug the coast to avoid disaster in a storm. Many such boats were blown out into the Pacific and were never heard of again. One, however, was fortunate enough to be spotted by an American brig and the crew was taken to safety in San Francisco. They were fortunate in that they were alive, but fearful because they had broken the law of their own land. Only one from the crew of seventeen decided to return to Japan. His name was Sentaro-san, but his American seamen friends gave him the name of 'Sam Patch' and he has gone down in history as a kind of folk-hero who managed to escape from the rigid laws in Japan, travel abroad and eventually return to his own country where he is buried.

*　　*　　*

The first time that Sam sailed back to Japan was with the famous Commodore Perry squadron in 1854. He was in one of the American 'Black Ships' that sailed into Tokyo Bay to demand that Japan open her doors to foreigners and their traders. He could speak English fairly well by this time and had taught some of his American friends the rudiments of Japanese. One of the marines on board his ship was called Jonathan Goble whom Perry described as being 'a religious man who had taken a special interest in Sam; finding in his docility and intelligence promise of good fruit from a properly directed religious training. Goble had begun with him a system of instruction which he hoped would not only make the Japanese a fair English scholar, but a faithful Christian.'

Sam wrote a letter to his relatives, who must have taken him for dead, but the Japanese authorities stepped in and demanded an explanation for his presence on the dreaded Black Ships. Sam became afraid that he would be beheaded if he landed, so he went back to America to live with the Goble family for a few years.

By 1860 Japan was already trading with other nations and foreigners were setting up businesses in a few places on the coast — in the Treaty Ports such as Yokohama. Through Sam Patch, Goble was one of the few Americans who knew a good deal about Japan and its language and he decided that it was God's Will that he should return as a missionary of the Baptist 'Free Will' Missionary Society.

*   *   *

Apparently, this particular missionary society did not look after their emissaries very well. The Gobles were delayed for two months in San Francisco waiting for a ship and they had to support themselves by finding temporary manual labour. They eventually did arrive in Yokohama on 1 April 1860, and found a small Japanese-style house to live in. Again, it seems, his sponsors let him down and Goble was reduced to mending shoes in order to feed himself and his wife, who had become sick. He was an excellent cobbler and taught the Japanese shoe-makers how to repair and make western-style shoes.

The long sea voyage from America and the strange food in Japan combined with having to live in a small, draughty house affected Mrs Goble's health, and soon they returned to America to get away from the cholera-infested streets of Yokohama. It must have been a very despondent man who landed in America after spending so many months in Japan and achieving nothing in the way of Christian converts. The fascination of Japan must have remained with the Gobles, however, for after Mrs Goble had recovered her health, they returned once more. This time they were sponsored by the Baptist Missionary Union.

The devotion of these two people is not easily understood today: he to his faith and she to her husband. One has to reflect on how Eliza Goble must have feared that second sea voyage to Japan and dreaded the prospect of surviving on Japanese food again.

Eliza Goble lies in peace in the foreigners' cemetery in Yokohama but even in death she has not been always allowed to rest. The 1923 earthquake caused her grave to fall down the side of the Bluff towards Motomachi, and today her granite gravestone is located in the Jewish section of the cemetery. All those foreign women since her time who have followed their husbands to Japan should shed a tear for her. What a momentous 'culture shock' she must have endured in the Japan of the 1860s!

*   *   *

Eliza Goble knew that her husband was no saint. His bad temper was infamous and he often beat her. In 1873 he was forced to resign from fellowship with the other Baptists because he had battered his servant. One Sunday while he was preaching at the roadside — having studied the Japanese '*yoso*' (story-tellers) and adopted their style of '*robodendo*' (street-preaching) — about the evils of working on the sabbath, some carpenters nearby continued to hammer away. He grabbed a long bamboo pole and 'smote them about the legs and thighs until some of them lay senseless.'

Schoolboys delighted in running past the bamboo palings at the front of his house on the Bluff and making a noise with a stick on them. Goble would rush out of the house and clout any boy he could catch — one day it was the British Admiral's orderly doing it, and he was also dealt with in the same way.

In the late 1860s Eliza Goble fell sick again. Her husband was busy translating the Gospel according to St Matthew into Japanese — the first time that any part of the Bible had been translated using *hiragana* — the Japanese phonetic system of writing — throughout. He had also arranged for it to be printed by the traditional woodblock method. He probably did not feel confident to handle the subtleties of kanji characters (ideograms) for there were so many thousands more in use in those times than today. Despite this urgent work, and his apparent male chauvinism, he was concerned about his wife's health and well-being, especially since she had not been well enough to leave their house for some time. It would not have been wise for her to venture out on foot because the streets were muddy (there was only a very primitive drainage system) and the rain came down in sheets at that time of the year. Some kind of covered carriage would have been ideal for Mrs Goble, but the fact was that horses were too expensive for a missionary on a modest income. Goble did possess an old horse at one time to haul himself and his Biblical literature around the streets, but his temper had got the better of him one day and he had flogged it to death.

*   *   *

One evening Goble was reading a series of articles in his wife's monthly magazine *Godey's Lady's Book and Magazine* — America's first regular publication specifically for women. The series was entitled 'Some Account of Modern Coaches' and was illustrated by line drawings. The August 1860 edition described and illustrated a two-wheeled vehicle that was first used in Paris in 1669 and was called a 'Brouette.' The anonymous writer of these articles records that 'the body of this (vehicle) was like a sedan chair placed upon two wheels, and was dragged by men. The man in front supports the poles by a leather strap, and the machine is steadied and propelled by a man behind.'

Slowly it dawned on Goble that such a vehicle would be ideal for his wife. Horse-power in Japan was expensive, but human muscle power was cheap at that time. He made a sketch of what he wanted and went off to discuss the construction of the vehicle with a Japanese carpenter. Soon the first, rather primitive, 'jin riki sha' (man-powered vehicle) was born ... or rather such a vehicle had been revived in Japan after it had ceased to exist in Europe for over 100 years.

There is further circumstantial evidence to support Goble's later claim that he had built the first rickshaw in Japan in 1868. M. Aime Humbert, a Swiss minister who travelled extensively in Japan in 1864, recorded all he saw in his classic book *Manners and Customs of the Japanese* which was originally published in French. He gives details of the '*kago*' and '*norimon*' under the heading 'Modes of Conveyance,' but there is no mention at all of the rickshaw. But by 1871, the year that the German Baron de Hubner visited Japan, rickshaws had arrived. In his book, *A Ramble Round the World 1871*, he wrote: 'The "jinrikisha" only came into existence a year or two ago; but there are already more than 20,000 in Yedo (Tokyo).' So the date of their appearance seems to be confirmed.

By studying the 'Brouette' as illustrated in *Godey's Lady's Book and Magazine*, it will be noticed that on the shafts are two legs to allow the lifting-man at the front to lower the vehicle into a horizontal position when it is stationary, also the general box shape of it is apparent. A study of vehicles in Japanese prints from this period shows how the early rickshaws were box-shaped and had legs on the shafts. Could this really have been a coincidence? Or does it prove a connection between the 'brouette' as illustrated in the magazine and the early rickshaws? Yoshitora's ukiyoe print '*Tokyo orai kuruma-zukushi*' (Many different vehicles in Tokyo's busy streets) of April 1870 shows two such heavy rickshaws, as does Kunimasa IV's print of three months later.

As the years pass, so the legs and heavy box-like structure disappears, and the rickshaw takes on its light-weight aspect with the pram hood. Japanese ingenuity soon took over, and the wheels moved below the centre of gravity of the passenger and vehicle making it easier to pull and manoeuver. So what had in Europe been a clumsy, inefficient device requiring energy from the straining muscles of two men even on level ground, now became an efficient means of transport that was to gain importance in many countries and generate a large industry. But Goble gained no financial benefit from his 'invention,' and he had to be content in the knowledge that his idea had helped Japan in no small way in her struggle to become industrialised.

A graphic description of a rickshaw ride is found in J. Johnston Abraham's *The Surgeon's Log*. The ship's doctor and the chief engineer had visited Honmoku in Yokohama in 1904, and walking back to the docks in the early evening darkness they came across two rickshaws that they hired to carry them over Yamate-cho to their ship:

'The tinkle of a rickshaw bell came to us in the night. Then one kurumaya appeared from round the corner, with the lantern of his rickshaw lit; and he was quickly followed by another. We each got into one, and called out '*hatoba*' (pier). Then the men started.

'Going down from the Bluffs to the Bund there is a very long steep hill.

'"Hold tight," shouted the chief from the rickshaw in front. Our men had started slowly; but gradually they gained momentum; and soon we were flying down the incline at breakneck pace. Their feet seemed barely to touch the ground. I felt as though my last hour had come. Suddenly we came to a sharp turn; and the men swerved quickly, leaping sideways in the air, swinging the light cars round by their weight. Down they came on their feet again, and continued their breakneck run. It was like bob-sleighing without the snow. A feeling of exhilaration came over us; unconsciously I found myself shouting encouragement. Down we swept past rickshaws painfully crawling up the hill, past brightly lighted shops, past hurrying pedestrians, till at last, panting and exhausted, the men slowed up on the crowded level highway of the Bund.'

*   *   *

The rickshaw slowly put most of the '*kago*' (palanquin) men out of business. A journey in a swinging, bumping kago was more tortuous than walking over short distances — especially for large-sized foreigners — and in the newly-developing cities businessmen required a rapid means of travelling short distances. The rickshaw was ideal for this and saved a lot of time for many people, so it was here to stay until the railway and automobile eased it out of existence. In the meantime, the rickshaw had spread across to China, into India and all the way down to South Africa where muscular boys in leopard skins, lion's manes and animal bones hauled their rickshaws from place to place.

Over the next few years, the globe-trotters who came to Japan — and then published the inevitable book about the country — were intrigued by the *jinrikisha* and described them in delightful detail. But according to Miss Isabella L. Bird in her 1878 book *Unbeaten Tracks in Japan*, the term '*kuruma*' was more popular both with Japanese and foreigners. She hired several kurumas to carry her and her baggage the hundreds of miles north to Hokkaido, the first time that a western woman had been there. In 1889, Rudyard Kipling wrote a story set in

India called 'The Phantom Rickshaw,' so the shortened, Anglicised version of the Japanese word must have been well established by then. The next year the word was used as a verb, for in the *Pall Mall Gazette* of February 1890 there is an article with the unlikely title of: 'Chumming with Chinamen, jinrickshawing with Japanese, palavering with Peruvians.'

The Japanese government, like any other government would do, noted the commercial success of the rickshaw and thought it appropriate to impose a tax on these vehicles. Goble at this time had plans for the building of a school for the blind and applied to the government in Tokyo that he should receive a portion of this tax because he was the inventor of the vehicle which had provided so much employment in the country. He was unsuccessful — he never did make one yen from the rickshaw.

Somehow, Izumi Yasuke has become associated with the jinrikisha and his name appears in all Japanese dictionaries as being the inventor of the vehicle in 1869. It is also recorded that Yasuke received ¥200 for his invention. Can anyone be sure what exactly happened back in those days? The geisha girl probably does not really care either.

(Acknowledgement is due to Susan Manakul, researcher in the Library of Congress, for her help with this topic. NP.)

Chapter 10

Laurence Oliphant — Adventurous British Diplomat

IT ALL HAPPENED so quickly. It was a dark and quiet night in Edo (Tokyo) on 5 July 1861 when the 'ronin' (masterless samurai) decided to attack. They easily overpowered the only guard who was awake just after he had sounded the alarm with his bamboo rattle. Laurence Oliphant's dog was then aroused and began to bark loudly, awakening all the members of the British Legation. But already the ronin, their razor-sharp swords drawn aloft, had entered the building intent on killing every foreigner there.

Oliphant fumbled in the dark for his revolver, only to find that it had been locked in its box by his servant, Bligh. His hand came across his riding crop and he gripped it firmly as he strode towards the front of the converted temple to investigate. Before he got there, he was faced with a dark figure who immediately swung his sword down towards his head. The riding crop snaked out but did not trap the sword. Again the practised swordsman aimed a blow which did not find its mark, and again and again the riding crop flailed the air as Oliphant screamed for help. An overhead wooden beam prevented the sword from falling with all its force the first few times, but finally Oliphant felt the blade tear into the flesh of his shoulder and as the ronin prepared to make the final, fatal thrust, a shot rang out. The ronin ran off with a bullet in his arm.

The Consul of Nagasaki, Mr Morrison, had discharged his pistol over Oliphant's shoulder and saved his life. But then a second warrior appeared with drawn sword and Morrison pulled the trigger on the second barrel. The bullet ricocheted off the blade of the sword, however, and struck Morrison on the head. Still, it was enough to frighten off the swordsman and the two bleeding Englishmen staggered into the small office of Rutherford Alcock, the Chargé d'Affaires. Seconds before, Bligh had leapt in terror through the shoji-paper screen scattering broken scraps of wood and paper all over the office. Two ronin were climbing in the open window of his room and he had fled in panic, not bothering to slide back the screen. Luckily, as the bare-legged ronin slid over the table just inside the window, they felt the pins from an entomological collection enter their flesh and this slowed their progress.

Alcock tried to patch up Oliphant's deep wound. The rapid loss of blood was making him dizzy. Bligh gave him a cup of water and asked: 'Do you think they will torture us, sir, before they kill us?'

Outside the sound of violent sword-play was getting closer, and the four men silently fought off terror. Finally, a crash of shattering glass in the next room made them give up hope of ever leaving Japan alive. The seconds passed slowly and silently, for the shouting and slashing had ceased. Japanese government officers entered the room to greet the huddled Englishmen with smiles. They had won! And the diplomats under their care were all alive. Then the 'yakunin' guards rushed in, covered in the blood of the ronin. The last man to arrive was Charles Wirgman, the reporter-artist representing the *Illustrated London News* in Japan. He was covered in mud, for he had been hiding under the floor of the temple since he had heard the first sounds of violence. Immediately he asked Oliphant how his wound was inflicted, and after being told, he found his sketch-book and began drawing the scene of the fight. In his report, as published on 12 October 1861, he claimed that he actually saw Oliphant and Morrison fighting off their attackers!

The temple was in a shambles, and sighing with relief they all viewed the damage. Blood was splattered over furniture, and under a sideboard was the gory head from a body in the middle of the room. Oliphant, supported by Bligh, stepped on something soft. It was a human eye.

*   *   *

Alcock was furious at the regrettable incident. He had returned to Edo only the previous day after a long tour around Japan including visits to

Nagasaki, Osaka and Hyogo (Kobe). The restrictions that he had met
— his party could not enter Kyoto due to the power of the authorities
there — made him realise how limited was the authority of the Shogun
with whom the treaties had been signed, and how difficult it was going
to be for England and the other western nations to have good
relationships with Japan. Japan was in no way united, and the attack
emphasised this. The Emperor had not ratified the new treaties, and
the 'daimyo' (rulers of fiefs) who were not aligned with him could not
be forced to recognise them. In fact, a law passed at the time of Tokugawa
Ieyasu was still in force which legally allowed the killing of foreigners
by any Japanese. The Shogun, it seemed, was playing for time so that
his government, the Bakufu, could make military preparations. This
was confirmed to Alcock the previous day when he was handed two
letters. One was from the Shogun to Queen Victoria, the other to himself
from the Japanese foreign affairs ministers and both requested that the
opening of the treaty ports of Nigata and Hyogo and the commercial
cities of Osaka and Tokyo be postponed for a further seven years.

Of the 14 ronin that had attacked the legation, three were killed,
one was arrested and three committed 'harakiri' (ritual suicide). The
others escaped. Alcock demanded retribution and blamed the lack of
security on the lazy guards. The next day he sent an urgent message to
HMS *Ringdove* lying off Yokohama, and by noon 20 armed marines
arrived.

Oliphant had been in Japan only 10 days. He had been appointed
First Secretary under Alcock, but now he was being carried on board
the *Ringdove* to begin a voyage back to England. He had lost the use
of both his arms, and lying in a berth out on Tokyo Bay in the July
heat, he was far from comfortable. He suffered a sudden attack of boils,
prickly heat covered his face and ophthalmia affected both his eyes. In
this condition the news from Bligh, who had burst into his darkened
cabin, that a Japanese war junk was bearing down on them and that all
the armed men were now defending the legation on shore, did nothing
to inspire his faith in diplomacy. Luckily, the war junk was content with
merely ramming the *Ringdove* and making off. But Oliphant did leave
Japan alive never to return. His experiences had been traumatic, and
may have led to his loss of self-confidence in later years.

*   *   *

In fact, this had been Oliphant's second visit to Japan. The first had
delighted him in that he wrote to his mother: 'We were enchanted by
Japan' and that 'I would willingly go to Japan were I to get the
appointment of Consul-General there, you and papa would like it.' The
second part of his book *The Narrative of the Earl of Elgin's Mission to
China and Japan* is full of enthusiastic praise for the newly-opened
country. In 1857, he had been appointed personal secretary to Lord
Elgin on his first China mission. China had not impressed him at all,
but on landing in Nagasaki: 'Each day gave us fresh proofs of the amiable

and generous character of the people... The beauty and elegance of all we saw delighted and astonished us.'

Elgin's mission was to sign treaties between Japan and Britain. Britain's Foreign Secretary, Lord Clarendon, had instructed that it was to be a peaceful mission and forbade Elgin to use force to achieve his objectives. Unlike Perry's mission a few years' earlier when a whole squadron of large American warships, bristling with guns, appeared in Tokyo Bay, the British mission consisted only of *HMS Furious* escorted by a steam frigate, the *Retribution,* a gun-boat, the *Lee,* and an elegant, well-fitted 318-ton steam yacht, the *Emperor.* This latter vessel was a gift from Queen Victoria to the Emperor of Japan, and was to play a significant part in the negotiations.

In Nagasaki harbour, the Vice-Governor of the city came on board for lunch. Oliphant observed: 'He is a plebian-looking man with an extremely smiling countenance and very short legs. They are encased in loose trousers, not unlike knickerbockers, of damask embroidery, of a pattern that would be considered rather too gaudy for curtains. He bows repeatedly and rapidly and his two swords, like a double tail, cock up responsively.' During lunch it was noted, however, that he could handle a knife and fork like any gentleman, and it was after lunch that he asked for the yacht to be delivered into his care at Nagasaki and that the British refrain from proceeding to Edo. Elgin politely refused, and his little flotilla steamed on to Shimoda. Again the town governor took lunch on board and made a similar request. When Elgin insisted that his mission was to personally deliver the yacht to the Emperor, the governor laughed and amid his laughter told the officers on board that refusal would probably mean his death — and the death of all on the mission. Oliphant observed that a great joke was made of it, and as the governor was about to leave the lunch table, he began to wrap up samples of the remaining food, explaining that 'his children enjoyed foreign delicacies.' Members of his party then followed suit.

At Shimoda, the Dutchman, Heusken, was loaned as an interpreter by the American consul there. The diplomatic language in Japan was then Dutch, the procedure being to go from Japanese to Dutch with Japanese interpreters and from Dutch to English with Heusken. Dutch had been learned by many Japanese in previous years when Holland was the only country allowed to trade with Japan via the tiny island of Deshima in Nagasaki harbour.

Once inside Tokyo Bay, officials by the boatload came out to attempt to stop the British ships from getting close to Edo, but Elgin ignored them all and steamed on to drop anchor near the forbidden city. More officials came on board and ordered them to go back along the coast to Kanagawa, but Elgin instead composed a letter to the head of the government requesting a residence on shore for his use during the treaty negotiations. Next day, they moved further inshore, anchoring amongst the Japanese fleet, and a group of daimyo came on board for lunch. Many scribes in the group noted down all they saw and all that was said. Others in the group watched over the scribes and the daimyo — these were the *'ometsuke'* or censors, for the inefficient administration of Japan at this time depended heavily on a complex system of spying and counter-spying amongst various groups. All this was quite unknown to Elgin, and indeed to any other foreigners who came to Japan before the Restoration of the Emperor in 1868.

On 17 August, in the height of the summer heat, Elgin was informed that his party could go ashore. Each officer put on his full dress uniform and the naval vessels, flags flying, slowly threaded their way through the junks and barges to get in as close as possible to the shore. The ships' guns roared out as they dropped anchor and then the band played *Rule Britannia*.

*   *   *

When the party stepped on land a colourful procession was formed as the officers and members of the mission entered 'norimon' (Japanese palanquins — which were quite tiny) and were carried to their temple residence. Huge crowds lined the route, and the visitors were impressed by the orderly way the crowds were controlled by the police. Once inside the large temple they were surprised to find western furniture, but annoyed at the curiosity of the families that shared the building with them. Oliphant, while dressing one morning, found that two holes in the shoji-paper contained a pair of female eyes observing him: 'A toilet, as performed by an English gentleman, was a spectacle which afforded intense amusement to the young ladies of the family next door,' he recorded in his diary.

After a series of meetings with the Shogun's representatives, carried out in a spirit of good humour bordering on hilarity, the treaty was finally signed on 28 August 1858, and the yacht officially handed over amid celebrations. The treaty opened Nagasaki, Kanagawa and Hakodate to British residents and trade, providing extra-territorial rights for all British subjects who were also granted freedom of worship. The importation of opium was forbidden, but the Japanese government was responsible for controlling smuggling. Altogether 24 Articles were agreed to, and Elgin was satisfied with the result of his mission which allowed Britons to come to Japan for the first time since 1623.

Oliphant, however, had some misgivings about the whole affair. He felt he could sympathise to some extent with those Japanese nationalists who were prepared to guard Japan from contact with the West by even laying down their lives for the cause. In his diary he imagined a nationalistic Samurai arguing:

'We desire nothing which we have not got. It has not been proved to us that railroads and electric telegraphs make people happier. We tried the Christian religion, and it led to the destruction of thousands of our countrymen. We do not think that our civilisation would be increased by a knowledge of the latest improvements in gunnery, or the latest invention for the destruction of our fellow creatures. We are contented with *saké,* and desire neither brandy, rum, gin, whisky, nor any other spirituous production of progressive countries. We can bear to be deprived of opium...There are also a few diseases which do not exist amongst us, and the importation of which we do not think would increase our general happiness. At present our subjects are peaceable and well-conducted, of an honest and simple nature, not given to brawling and quarrelling; but from what we have seen of the Europeans who man the ships coming to our country, we do not think this simplicity and tranquility in our seaports would be likely to continue.'

This idealistic and Utopian notion of Japan was far from the reality. The complexities of Japanese feudalism with its associated injustices and brutalities were unknown to the early western observers.

Some years after his traumatic and contradictory experiences in Japan, Oliphant joined a strange 'religious' community in America. He gave up all his considerable wealth to the persuasive leader, and entered the sect concerned with mysticism, telepathy and, as Philip Henderson points out in his biography of Oliphant, sex. For Victorian times in Britain were also traumatic and contradictory — Christianity grappled with concepts of science, church-going soldiers were called upon to shoot unarmed 'natives' to expand the Empire while prostitution thrived amongst the masses in the industrial cities. Oliphant was aware of these contraries of his time, but was part of them. He later wrote that the Far East was 'abominable, not so much in itself, as because it is strewed all over with the records of our violence and fraud, and disregard of right.'

Still, in London many years after the attack on the legation, Oliphant was entertaining some Japanese and one of them is reported to have said: 'How glad I am you escaped safely, for I, to whom you have shown so much kindness, planned the whole affair!'

Chapter 11

Yokohama's Christ Church and the Great Earthquake

DURING the sixteenth and seventeenth centuries when Spanish and Portuguese Jesuits had first attempted to introduce Christian ideas and Catholic principles into Japan, the net result had been the untimely and brutal death of thousands of those who proclaimed themselves to be Christians. What would be the result when nineteenth century westerners came with their religion to Japan to live amongst and work with the Japanese? Naturally, the authorities on both sides were anxious.

The early treaties of the 1850s allowed foreigners to practise whatever religion they chose. But Christianity continued to be proscribed as far as the Japanese themselves were concerned. 'That evil sect' was how Christianity was described on edict boards erected in every village in Japan. Numerous edicts proclaimed that it was the duty of every Japanese to inform the authorities if anyone was associated with Christianity. Rewards were offered and many suffered. Spies monitored the movements of every foreigner and continually reported on their activities to the authorities. So any over-evangelical foreign Christian attempting to make a convert, could be certain that his protege would be led to prison, or worse.

*   *   *

In 1862, the British authorities sent to Yokohama a consul, a vice-consul, a policeman, a gaoler, a guard and a chaplain. A complete do-it-yourself set of characters that could administer to all the needs of a community within a community in a Treaty Port.

The first chaplain was the Reverend Buckworth Bailey whose 'parish' covered the whole Protestant community in Yokohama as well as the garrison of British soldiers stationed there. Looking after the moral welfare of the latter must have been a difficult task, for the opportunities for all kinds of 'sin' — as classified by Victorian Christians — were available in the city. The Rev. Bailey, however, was not deterred and threw his boundless energy into numerous projects. The first of these was the assisting in the building of a permanent church and parsonage on 105 and 101 Yamashita. This land was leased in perpetuity from the Japanese government and the project was financed half by the Protestant community and half by the British authorities. While this first church was being built, Church services were held each Sunday in the residence of the British Consul, Captain Vyse. But according to the

Japan Herald of August 1863 there were problems. Due to faults in the design of the roof of the new church the whole edifice was dangerously unstable, and not until iron rods had been inserted to truss it up could the building be used. The building finally was ready for 'business' in 1864 and the foreign community of some 3000 souls had at last the facility of the 180-seat Anglican church. Then plans were made to place a memorial window in the church dedicated to the memory of the ill-fated C.L. Richardson who had been slain by samurai the previous year.

Those who attended Sunday services could enjoy the spectacle of the band of the 9th Regiment marching down Camp Hill followed by others in their finest clothes in this regular 'church parade.' Inside the church the organ was played by John Griffins, as the congregation took their places in their own reserved positions in the pews. Some of the pews and furniture had been constructed by the Rev. Bailey's own hands. However, the Rev. Bailey's talents did not stop there. It was he who introduced the cultivation of European vegetables into Japan, and he also taught western cooking to some Japanese. In 1867 he founded the *Bankoku Shimbun Shi,* one of the first Japanese language newspapers, but it was not a financial success and soon disappeared. As the years passed, the popularity of the Rev. Bailey declined amongst the upper echelons of the community. Despite his many skills, his book-keeping was found to be wanting. Also, he caused something of a stir because he recorded an inaccurate date on the death certificate of a seaman who had died in the hospital.

'It was a case of Mr Bailey present and bad finances, or Mr Bailey absent and good finances!' shouted one of the church trustees at a meeting. The pressure increased and in 1872, after 10 years' service, the Rev. Bailey was forced from his £68 per annum post as first vicar of Christ Church.

*   *   *

In 1874 the British soldiers left Yokohama and the British government withdrew all financial support for Christ Church. Changes had taken place in Japan making their presence unnecessary. The Emperor had been restored as a political figure and stability was assured, the edict boards had been removed partly due to pressure put on the Imperial Japanese delegation, (headed by Prince Iwakura, whose mission took them to Europe and America in 1872) and now any Japanese was permitted to become a Christian.

A 'pew rent' was introduced to finance the Church, and increasingly the church became missionary orientated within the outer Japanese community, working with members of the Society for the Propagation of the Gospel. The Reverend E. Champneys Irwine was appointed in 1880 and the church flourished; this was the same year that the Mission to Seamen was established in Yokohama. But towards the end of the century it was found that the original wooden church building had become so unsafe, possibly due to the work of termites, that the Rev. Irwine had to hold his Sunday services in the Gaiety Theatre on the Bluff (Yamate).

A new building was planned and arrangements were made for it to stand on the site of the old army camp on top of the Bluff, for as business and industry expanded in Japan the land down in the original 'settlement' in Yamashita grew in commercial value. The new building was huge and was constructed of red bricks from Glasgow. The bricks arrived in Yokohama as ballast on British sailing ships. On 2 June 1901 the new building was consecrated by William Awdry, the Bishop of South Tokyo, and the tall Victorian lines of the building, typical of many built about the same time in the industrial towns of Britain, were admired by all. All, that is, except the members of the Rationalist Society who were then active in Yokohama and causing discomfort to the Rev. H.B. Walton who directed sermons against them.

*   *   *

But in 1908 an English divorce suit of Marshall vs. Marshall, brought some distressing facts to light concerning about 30 marriages conducted by the vicar of Christ Church. Because there had only been a ceremony in a church without being properly legally documented the judge found that he could not grant a divorce! This meant that all the 30-couples who had 'married' in Christ Church between 1899 and 1908 had been 'living in sin' (in the eyes of the law), and that all their children were illegitimate. Under English law at that time, the children would remain illegitimate — a serious disability within British society under the law — even if the parents consequently married properly — according to the civil code.

Up to 17 July 1899, extra-territoriality operated in Japan whereby a church marriage was perfectly legal in the Anglican churches just as it was in England. But after that date all foreigners came under Japanese law. Marriages had to be solemnised within the embassy or consulates to be legally valid and such was not the case with the Marshalls et al.

The news caused an uproar in the foreign community. The Bishop of Tokyo travelled to Christ Church to explain the situation and blamed himself for it. It was not until the matter had been discussed in Westminster, and a special Act of Parliament passed to make the 30 marriages legal and their children legitimate, that the whole unfortunate affair was forgotten.

World War I disrupted the foreign community in Yokohama as men left to join their own military forces. However, in the years that followed the new vicar, the Rev. E.M. Strong, assisted with the establishment of the first Girl Guides company in Japan. His duties included meeting new arrivals off the steam ships that docked at Osanbashi (South Pier) and during the royal tour of 1922 he welcomed the Prince of Wales who attended a service in Christ Church on St George's Day.

Friday, 31 August 1923 had been particularly hot and oppressive. Christ Church's organist, Mr Catto, was tired and uncomfortable after his practice session. As he washed his hands in the rectory before taking a cup of tea with the Rev. Strong, he glanced out of the bathroom window and looked into a window of the church. Inside he saw in the aisle a coffin on a bier that was covered with a Union Jack. He had heard of no death in the community and, according to the Rev. Casson's book *The Church on Colonel's Corner* published in 1962, he asked the Rev. Strong to explain. The latter was equally as surprised, and both hurried into the church to investigate. They found nothing — no coffin, no bier and no Union Jack. But the following day, 1 September 1923 the deaths in the community — both Christian and pagan — were considerable.

*   *   *

The earthquake struck at noon. The epicentre was only a few kilometres from Yokohama. The great red-brick building of Christ Church was smashed to pieces as the ground moved vertically up and down with immense violence. Almost all the records were destroyed. Fires spread and swept across the city. The dead and dying were everywhere on the Kanto Plains. The Rev. Strong survived and spent the next few days, despite a head injury, helping the survivors of the holocaust onto the ships in the bay. O.M. Poole in *The Death of Old Yokohama* records that the Rev. Strong 'proved tireless.' For his work he was later awarded the Order of the British Empire.

Some days later in Kobe he met Mr Catto the organist. 'Next time I see a coffin in a Church with a Union Jack on it, I shall put my toothbrush in my pocket,' Mr Catto is reputed to have said.

Within three months of the disaster two temporary wooden huts had arrived from America to be used as church and chaplaincy, and the Rev. C. Hodges became the new vicar. He began to organise the financing of a new church to be built on the same site as the one destroyed. Unfortunately, the Rev. Hodges died of pneumonia in Korea three years later, and he was replaced by the Rev. E.G. Bucknill who continued the work.

The British Ambassador, Sir John Tilley, laid the foundation stone with due ceremony in October 1930, and an English country church in the old Norman style arose from the soil of Japan. Seven months afterwards all was completed and the church consecrated. Regular services followed, but the end of the decade brought further problems.

*   *   *

When war broke out in the Pacific in December 1941, the Rev. T.P. Symonds was chaplain at Christ Church. He had only 20 people on the church roll for most had been evacuated from Japan and it was not long before he and the remaining foreigners were interned in prison camps.

A few days later he was transferred to the compound of the British Embassy in Tokyo, leaving many of his congregation and his organist, Mr I. Sykes who had been head of the Chartered Bank, confined in either the Yacht Club or the Grandstand race course. At Easter 1942, the Japanese authorities allowed a service to be held in Christ Church but two days after this Mr Sykes suffered a violent death and was buried in the foreign cemetery. In the meantime arrangements were made to transfer the church building and other property to the 'Nippon Sei Kokai' (Anglican Church in Japan), but after the agreement was signed the Japanese government disapproved of the Nippon Sei Kokai and it ceased to exist as an organised body. The military authorities of Japan took possession of the church building and used it as a Naval hospital store, and then as an officers' club and theatre.

On 29 May 1945 a direct hit from an incendiary bomb dropped from one of the US Air Force's 500 'Flying Fortresses' almost completely gutted the building. The square tower still remained intact as did most of the hall at the side of the small side-chapel. These provided some kind of shelter to families who had lost their homes in the air raids.

Following the surrender of Japan, the American occupation troops came across the building soon after they landed and a plan to restore it was put in hand. Work began almost immediately and a service was held there at Easter 1947 under dark iron girders and a sunny sky. By 1954 the building had been repaired and the Rev. G. Helft arrived to carry on as others had before him. One highlight of the post-war era was a visit in April 1959 of the Archbishop of Canterbury, the head of the Anglican church. The centenary was celebrated in 1962.

Chapter 12

Yokohama International School

PAUL NIPKOW, the moving force behind the foundation of Yokohama International School, could never have foreseen the unique nature of the educational institution that he was about to create. A school that was to flutter like a butterfly on the edge of financial disaster so many times, yet an establishment that, like the 'mizu shobai,' kept bobbing up like a cork because there was a real necessity for it in Japan.

Its story began in the early 1920s just after the Great Kanto Earthquake of 1 September 1923. The decade of flappers and jazz — 'moga' (a contraction of 'modern girl') and 'jazu' in Japanese — that followed the Great War in Europe which had completely changed the old social order soon filtered through to Japan. Cinemas and dance-halls began appearing, cabarets became popular and bars where wind-up gramophones filled the smoke-filled atmosphere with popular western music could be found in many neighbourhoods. These developments helped to create a feeling of newness about the world, and many began to question the old values that had been accepted for so long.

In England, A.S. Neill was organising a school based on positive liberation and freedom — much in the tradition suggested by Rousseau — and his ideas seem to have permeated to Mr Nipkow in Japan. There was no direct communication between them, but as has often been the case in the past, one man has made the same discovery as another quite independently and almost at the same time. Mr Nipkow's concept of education seemed to coincide with that of A.S. Neill. However, although they were both formulated in the early 1920s, Summerhill was an experiment from the outset, whereas Yokohama International School (YIS) was the result of the ideas of a Swiss businessman with a child in a privileged ghetto within an alien culture, and who had some ideas about internationalism as his guideline. He accepted the English language as being the most appropriate for the age, and put his own child into his dream. His dream came true, except for a few complications involving the weaknesses and gullibility of a few individual men. It is surprising how close the two institutions became in some ways, for the actual education in both was entrusted to educators from many different countries. The importance of a sense of 'community spirit' — so strong in Japan itself — has been a major influence on the students at YIS, a spirit that Neill deliberately generated at Summerhill.

                          *   *   *

The Yokohama United Club — the traditional exclusive men's club (on the seafront) which admitted western members only if they had a certain social and financial status — was one of the few buildings left standing after the Great Kanto Earthquake of September 1923. The following September, plans were being laid to build a new school for the foreign children which would be non-sectarian and admit any child regardless of his nationality or religion. Although there had already been established two fine Catholic schools — one for boys and the other for girls — as well as a host of small private schools for younger children which had come and gone on the Bluff — it was straight away agreed by the six men at the meeting held in the YUC that a new type of co-educational school was needed. Immediately, they formed a committee with Paul Nipkow as president, Horace Carew as treasurer and H.N. Morin as secretary. The new school was to be called 'Yokohama International School' while the responsibility for finding a qualified teacher was given to Paul Nipkow, with Horace Carew responsible for finding a site.

By the end of October a room had been rented at the YMCA and Mrs F.J. Gressit, a local lady, began to teach her class of six — all except one being children of the three committee members. At the end of November, Dr J. Henry Wild arrived from Switzerland whom Nipkow had appointed as the headmaster at ¥500 per month plus travelling expenses. But as the fees were only ¥100 per term per child, something obviously had to be done about raising money and obtaining new pupils. The services of Mr E. Hamilton Holmes, the British Consul-General in Yokohama, were sought and he was elected Honorary President. Most future meetings were then held at his residence on the Bluff. Holmes hinted that about ¥5000 could be obtained from the *Fai Way Fong* which was about to leave. This was a ship chartered by foreign firms in Yokohama just after the earthquake to be used as floating residences and offices for employees and representatives of those companies that had decided to return to Yokohama and carry on business. Holmes also stated that some £3000 remained unused in the 'Lord Mayor of London's Fund' for earthquake relief. Then there was talk of taking over the site of the old Yokohama Foreign School, of which no records remain, at Bluff 72 on which there was a mortgage of ¥8000.

Dr Wild was instructed by the committee to visit the American School in Tokyo, enquire about their system, and report back. Meanwhile, arrangements had been made to use the vacant chaplaincy at Christ Church for lessons, and on 6 January 1925 19 pupils arrived at their new, temporary classroom. This situation continued until September, by which time a site at Bluff 153 had been developed using a building donated by the Butterfield and Swire Company and lumber donated by the Union Church. Money donations had poured in from 43 sources including ¥1000 from Dr J.E. de Becker and ¥460 from the 'Hard Times Dance'! Yokohama Municipality contributed ¥2000.

Miss Johanna Carst, born in Yokohama in 1875, daughter of a Dutch captain who had arrived in 1865 and who had recently died in Kobe aged 88, was appointed kindergarten teacher. The Rev. Hodges of Christ Church was entrusted to teach English, and the new premises opened with good facilities, plenty of money and much optimism. Paul Nipkow had seen his hopes materialise in just one year.

* * *

From the start YIS was a community undertaking, to be owned and run by the foreign community and not by any individuals. It had to depend on donations as well as school fees, and on the freely given expertise of members of the community. Mr Sykes of the Royal Chartered Bank offered his expertise in arranging all financial matters.

Enrolment increased steadily in the first years, but donations were not so numerous even though some firms gave regularly every year. Dr Wild was replaced by fellow-countryman, Dr Peter, who was appointed by Nipkow while on a business-trip to Europe. He was replaced at the termination of his contract by a Canadian, Miss Shard, and after that the English lady, Miss Macfarlane, became headmistress in September 1933.

From 1929, some parents had begun to complain about the academic standards of the school, and Miss Carst's teaching methods were said to be old-fashioned. Rather than try and explain that 50% of all children in the world are below average in intelligence and ability, and that the offspring of Yokohama parents were no exception despite their superior affluence, it was decided to appoint a new kindergarten teacher so that Miss Carst taught only in the mornings. However, the pressure mounted and Miss Carst resigned at the end of the year. She continued to live in Yokohama until her death in 1964 at the age of 89.

Other complaints centred on the American structure of the school syllabus, which made it difficult for European students to be integrated on returning to their own country's educational system. In July 1929, it was decided to join the Parents National Educational Union (PNEU), a guiding body for England's private schools. British students were then encouraged to take the Common Entrance Examinations, and standards seemed to improve.

To further improve standards, in 1936 the Rev. R.P. Pott of Christ Church offered his services as a part-time teacher, four days a week, and agreed to 'undertake this arduous work in the interests of the community' in order to 'attain a higher standard of efficiency, especially in arithmetic' for ¥240 per month. Within a year the school population topped 100 and the Rev. Pott had become headmaster. A nursery class had been added to increase numbers, or as the school prospectus stated: 'In Japan, where children are left too much in the charge of amahs, progress is greatly retarded, and harmful habits are formed. It is for this reason we feel a definite need for a nursery class in the community.' A school uniform was now required, much to the delight of some mothers and to the disgust of others, the sales of which enabled the Rev. Pott to supplement his income. He also supplied milk to the students. As for the school sportswear it is unlikely he was responsible for supplying this since at one of the committee meetings he 'objected to the girls wearing shorts.'

Still, during the warm spring months of the late 1930s life went on in the Yokohama community as the rumbles of fascism increased around it. The PTA ladies raised ¥342 for the school during a Bridge Tea and one parent presented cricket bats and balls. Unfortunately, the school lacked sports facilities,but this need was supplied by others in the community. The YC and AC (Yokohama Country and Athletics Club) gave the use of its playing field on Wednesdays and the Ladies Lawn Tennis and Croquet Club nearby provided two courts on Mondays, while the vacant plot next to the school was loaned by the owner. For the most part, the community spirit worked well.

The tranquillity at YIS was suddenly shattered in July 1937 when, according to the minutes, the Rev. Pott suddenly resigned after an argument with a committee member. In order to continue as headmaster he insisted that a new constitution be implemented whereby the school would be run by the headmaster and 'four trustees' only. As no other person was qualified to be headmaster in Yokohama, and obtaining a new one from Europe or America would be expensive and a lengthy business before the days of air travel to Japan, the new constitution was adopted. Nipkow was rejected as a trustee.

By this time Nipkow's son had left the school, but he was still concerned for the progress of YIS. He was now Chairman of the Bluff Hospital committee, and the following November the hospital was approached to see if it would sell the school the lease of a 1863 *tsubo* (6036 square metres) site at 41 Karasawa, about two kilometres from the school, which had been used previously as an 'Infectious Diseases Ward.' The two buildings alone were worth more than ¥125,000, but as it was for YIS the hospital agreed to sell for a nominal ¥1000. However, it is suggested by later minutes that it was Rev. Pott himself who had bought the site for such a low figure! Of course, his four 'trustees' must have known this.

For over two years the Rev. Pott ran a boarding house on this site for YIS students as another side-business, although he insisted that he made a loss due to non-payment of fees, and because many families were leaving Japan as war became more obvious.

At YIS the German students were faced with a particularly difficult situation: in 1938 four German refugee boys arrived from Shanghai who were from Jewish families; they were taught with German students from pro-Nazi families including the son of the Ambassador, while others came from German anti-Nazi families. The Rev. Pott recalled that in school they all accepted one another without hesitation, yet outside school they were not expected to recognise one another!

At the end of 1939 there were only 65 students remaining, 32 being boarders; the boarding house and the lease of the land of the old hospital site were subsequently sold to an unknown buyer. Today, that extensive site is occupied by Sancta Maria School — a girls' Catholic School founded in 1961. The Rev. Pott then decided to volunteer for war service and resigned in June 1940. After his departure the minutes record the fact that some school fees had been paid into the Rev. Pott's private account with the Hong Kong and Shanghai Bank!

On 18 December 1940, an Extraordinary General Meeting was held at the school to close it down because of the war situation. The new headmaster, Mr Dixon, must have been very disappointed as he had only arrived from England in August. It was then that Paul Nipkow heard about the fate of the old hospital site, and he was furious. 'These buildings were only sold at a nominal fee of ¥1000 as a good gesture towards the school!' he shouted. 'The Trustees have lost everything including the lease of the land?' To which the chairman replied: 'Yes. All gone.' As he calmed down, Nipkow proposed that the remaining land be retained by the school for he knew that, just like earthquakes, wars also come and go. He was anticipating the school opening again after the war, and his proposal was accepted.

Meanwhile, on returning to England, the Rev. Pott was to spend three years as a curate, first in Paddington then in Brentwood, as well as two years as a chaplain in the Royal Naval Volunteer Reserve, before moving to the idyllic countryside of Norfolk where he became Vicar of Heacham in 1945 — a position he held for many years. In 1946 he was to start his own private school, St Michael's, in Ingoldisthorpe, where he was headmaster until 1970. During his retirement he was to have the privilege, on 11 January 1981, of preaching to the entire Royal Family at Sandringham and of then lunching while sitting between the Queen and the Queen Mother.

When asked about the old hospital site, the Rev. Pott strongly denied disposing of it before he left Japan and expressed an interest in how the present owners obtained it. 'It was left to a Mr Kumegai, who died in about 1947, to act on my behalf.' he said, 'Since I heard nothing I assumed that the property had fallen into Japanese government hands as "alien" property, and so was not surprised to receive anything. To avoid suggestion that I was party to some underhand deal, I can assure those interested that the land was unsold when I left the country.' The school minutes show that Mr Kumegai was at the final meeting when Mr Nipkow became so angry, but said nothing. So the mystery remains.

Explaining the reorganisation and row of 1937, the Rev. Pott insists that it was not he who resigned, as the minutes book records, but the entire committee resigned which left him and a small number of his supporters to take over. The issue, he stated, concerned the admission of Eurasian children to the school and he 'was not prepared to exclude any boys or girls on racial grounds.'

*   *   *

In 1941, the school buildings were rented to the 'German Refugees' organisation and so remained until May 1945 when a bomb from a B-29 destroyed everything.

It took until August 1953 before any compensation was received from the Japanese government after a detailed War Claim had been filed with the help of the British Consul. By this time the foreign community was increasing again, many having arrived from Shanghai after the communist revolution in China. And again there were children who needed schooling.

The Bluff School was started in 1954 for kindergarten children by 10 women and one man, but this was taken over by YIS when it started again in September 1955. One Swiss teaching headmaster and nine students showed that the pattern of 30 years before was repeating itself. The confidence of the community was demonstrated by a rapid growth in enrolment and in large and small donations. New grades and teachers were added as needed, and in 1958 a new building was added, then a third in 1962. By 1968 development had gone so well that an adjacent site, formerly an Occupation Forces fire station, was purchased and, despite rumours of graft, a large three-storied building was erected complete with laboratories, art and music facilities and extensive administration offices. 1973 saw the first senior class graduate. By this time graduation rings, yearbooks, school balls and fairs as well as annual field-trips to various parts of rural Japan and 'Awareness Days,' on which outside speakers from all walks of life communicate with high school students, had become firmly established. The British Council designated it as the GCE centre for Japan, affiliation was accepted by the Geneva-based International Schools Association and the East Asia Regional Council of Overseas Schools. Many students proceeded to universities and colleges in America, including Stanford and Reed, and in Europe, Australia and Asia. The Japanese authorities registered it as '*gakkonojin*' giving it the same status as a flower-arranging school!

Chapter 13

The Cornish Connection — Birth of Japan's Railways

JAPAN'S railway system, with its fast Shinkansen expresses that depart and arrive exactly on time, where tunnels have been blasted through mountains and under the sea to connect the main islands, is the envy of many nations. But as the present-day passenger sits on his comfortable seat behind the sealed, insulated windows and absorbs the glorious views of Mount Fuji that drift quietly by (glancing now and then at the large speedometer on the carriage wall that shows a steady 200 km. per hour) does he realise what struggles and problems the first railway engineers had in Japan? The mountainous terrain that covers most of Japan, the frequency of earthquakes and landslides, and the fact that all rails and rolling stock had to be imported by sea from England were challenges that had to be met before the wheels could roll across the land.

The first engineers all came from Britain, in the early years of the Meiji Restoration, although it was the US naval chief, Commodore Perry, who brought the first locomotive to Japan together with tracks and some rolling stock. That was in 1854, and within a few days this present to the Shogun was belching steam as it rolled along. However, it was only a miniature train, not much bigger than a child's toy, but it did create amusement, wonder and interest. Many of Perry's Japanese 'hosts' had heard about railway and steam engines before and seen pictures and diagrams of them in foreign books, but this was the first time that they had seen a real one. Even at this early date, they realised how important it could be to a country — especially in terms of military power.

Soon afterwards a Russian mission led by E.V. Putyatin brought another scale-model locomotive that burned alcohol, and T.B. Glover, a British merchant in Nagasaki, demonstrated a 762 mm. gauge steam locomotive called 'The Iron Duke' to an interested Japanese audience.

All these 'model' demonstrations were premature in terms of building an actual railway system, for under the Shogunate the country was divided and unstable, and no outside nation was prepared to lend Japan the capital needed to finance such a project. But in 1869, the year after the Meiji Restoration, when the country was united under the Emperor, the government made plans to introduce a national railway system. A British adviser, Henry Brunton, suggested building a line first from Tokyo to Yokohama because it was a relatively short distance and the terrain was not too difficult to build on; also the number of people in the area would ensure that it made a fair profit. He also suggested that the railway service be placed under the direct management of the government.

That same year, another Englishman, Horatio Nelson Lay, tried to persuade the Japanese government that he had access to a large loan from the British government to build such a railway line. But it turned out that Lay's credit rating was lower than he claimed; a discrepancy of a few per cent in the interest rates made the Japanese suspicious of him, and he soon disappeared from the scene.

A loan of 1 million pounds at an annual interest rate of 9 per cent was raised in London in 1870 and the first full-sized railway in Japan began to take shape. Earlier that year, 19 English engineers had arrived in Japan under contract to the government to plan and supervise the building programme. The most famous of these was Edmund Morel who was 29 years old when he arrived on a five-year contract; unfortunately, he completed only one year before he died of tuberculosis. Even so, Morel was very much involved in the line running from Shimbashi in Tokyo to Sakuragicho in Yokohama; furthermore, he pressed the Japanese government to establish a ministry in charge of engineering so that the country could eventually become independent of foreigners. Whenever work on the line was impossible because of inclement weather, he took the Japanese employees into his own house and lectured to them on surveying and engineering. Some of the English surveyors became irritated with the Japanese workforce because most of them were from samurai families and still wore their traditional Japanese clothes, together with their two swords — the steel in these swords apparently affecting the magnetic surveying compasses!

Morel died in September 1871. He is buried along with his Japanese 'wife,' who killed herself the same day he died, in Yokohama's foreigners' cemetery where a granite stone which was erected by Japan National Railways in 1962, proclaims his tomb to be a railway monument; there is another stone emblem in the shape of a punched passenger ticket which also celebrates his achievements. A white-blossom plum tree was planted over their final resting place, and it is reported in a Japanese history book that when it first flowered there were both red and white blossoms growing entwined together on the tree. A plaque in the entrance hall of Sakuragicho Station shows the figure of the young Morel in relief and records his contribution to Japan's first major step towards industrialisation.

Three of the other English engineers also died in Japan and three more were forced to return home because of ill-health. Sanitary conditions in Japan at this time were primitive, as they were in much of Europe.

The opening of the line was delayed again and again. People began to get impatient and sneer at the project, and in order to alleviate the criticisms a number of VIPs were taken for trial runs from Yokohama on the section of track that had been finished. As part of this public-relations exercise, these so-called 'first passengers' had to buy tickets and have them punched, although on this occasion the journey was for only five miles (as far as the track had been laid at the time).

Just over a year after Morel's death, on 14 October 1872, the first railway in Japan was opened by Emperor Meiji. It was a sunny day, Mount Fuji was visible from Tokyo, as a long procession of all the important people in the country walked under special celebration arches covered with many types of flowers to the Shimbashi railway station. Twenty thousand people watched, not one of them had a camera, and the only visual record of the occasion are some woodblock prints made by a few artists. None of these is sufficiently accurate to identify the actual steam locomotive that was used.

The next day a regular passenger service began. Two trains were used, both imported from England, which did four hourly runs in the morning and five in the afternoon. The carriages were not particuloarly comfortable — 'matchboxes on wheels' was how one passenger described them. The fares were high and only the well-off could afford to travel the full 18 miles by train; however, a daily average of 2800 did use the service for the first six months. The first-class fare was 1 yen 75 sen, second-class was 75 sen and third-class 37 sen. For 37 sen, the passenger could have bought over 2 kg. of first-grade rice, whereas the fare today for the same journey would buy only 100 gm. of rice, which shows how expensive it was in real terms.

Five minutes before departure time the barriers — manned by an Englishman — were closed so that right from the first day punctuality was the hall-mark of the Japanese railway service. During the first few years, all engine-drivers and guards were English but these were gradually replaced as Japanese personnel learned the required skills. Isabella Bird, a Scottish lady who travelled alone through much of the countryside of Japan in 1878, used the new railway to visit Tokyo: 'The Yokohama station is a handsome and suitable stone building,' she wrote, 'with a spacious approach, ticket offices on our British plan, roomy waiting rooms for different classes — uncarpeted, however, in consideration of Japanese clogs — and supplied with the daily papers. There is a department for the weighing and labelling of luggage, and on the broad, covered, stone platform at both termini, a barrier with turnstiles, through which, except by special favour, no ticketless person can pass.'

By force of habit, some of the Japanese passengers slipped off their footwear before they stepped into the carriages. They were obviously less than pleased not to find their shoes waiting for them at the end of their journey as they stepped out of their carriage. Signs were soon erected to warn people of this practice, and there were also signs prohibiting urinating out of the carriage windows — the fine was 5 yen.

The next line to be opened ran from Osaka to Kobe and was completed in May 1874. It did not follow the route that was first planned by the engineers and surveyors because of some sharp practice by several foreign land speculators from the business section of Kobe — hoping to cash in on the leasing value of land the railway company would be obliged to use. However, at the last moment the railway authorities decided to alter the route and the speculators lost out.

In 1874 there were 104 foreign railway engineers, 94 of them English. One of these was Richard Francis Trevithick (1845-1913) and he organised the building of the first steam locomotive to be made in Japan. He instructed his Japanese colleagues in various skills and techniques so that they were later able to set up bigger factories to make more locomotives and other rolling stock.

Trevithick was the grandson of the great Cornish engineer and inventor, Richard Trevithick (1771 - 1833) — the one who actually invented the very first steam locomotive that ran on rails in 1801. The great Trevithick is still remembered today in his native Cornwall. His cottage has been preserved, roads and houses are named after him, and the Trevithick Society is devoted to studying his family and achievements as well as other aspects of industrial archeology. At the age of 19, Richard Trevithick was the engineer in charge of several tin mines where he devised a new high-pressure steam pump to keep water out of the mines. This caused the pumps and engines of James Watt, the Scot after whom the 'wattage' of every electrical appliance is named, to become obsolete. Trevithick was responsible for a great many inventions, but the steam locomotive was undoubtedly his most important achievement even though George Stephenson was to take the glory, fame and money 20 years later. Richard Trevithick died penniless, and was buried in a pauper's grave with no marker or stone.

Another of his grandsons came to Kobe in 1877. This was Francis Henry Trevithick(1850 — 1931) who stayed in Japan for 20 years before returning to England because of ill-health. In 1894 the government railway authorities put him in charge of the construction of a line through the mountains in Karuizawa in central Japan. Although he loved Japan and was dedicated to his work, he did not relish his tour of duty in

Karuizawa, mainly because of the food — or the lack of it. When he arrived in Kobe, there was no meat, cheese or butter available because cattle were not kept in that part of Japan, and in the days before refrigeration these dairy products could not be imported. He quickly accustomed himself, therefore, to Kobe's diet of fish and fowl. But up in the mountains of Karuizawa there was not even fish and a government regulation forbade the carrying of firearms, so no birds or animals could be shot for food. He had to survive several months on rice and vegetables.

However, the money was good for both the Trevithick brothers — Francis Henry received 450 yen per month, and Richard Francis an affluent 675 yen. At that time one yen was worth one silver American dollar. The Japanese government also paid a generous pension to all their foreign engineers from when they retired until they died.

Both the Trevithick brothers married Japanese women. The only daughter of Richard Francis died young, but Francis Henry produced two sons and two daughters. The eldest son, Richard Yoshitaro, studied navigation and seamanship in London and later returned to Japan to join the NYK (Nippon Yusen Kaisha) steamship company. In 1916 he was made a captain and commanded the *Hakusan Maru* that ran between Yokohama and London. On these trips he would take sembei (rice crackers), *saké* and other Japanese food back to his retired father in England. He was obliged to assume Japanese nationality in order to command a Japanese ship, and so Mr Trevithick became Captain Okuno — taking his mother's family name. One of Captain Okuno's sons resided on the Bluff in Yokohama for many years, working for Lloyd's Company, until his untimely death in 1978. His teenage son, Yoshiharu Henry, continues the family line.

A great many of the foreign engineers and other foreign experts who went to Japan in the early Meiji era married Japanese girls and began families there. In the early 1970s, during the Japan National Railways' (JNR) jubilee celebrations, a search was initiated to trace the descendants in order that a gold plaque could be presented to them. Mr Yamanaka of the JNR and Mr Okuno took part in an NHK (Japan Broadcasting Corporation) programme, but no others were found. Perhaps the records of each family tree, the 'koseki,' were not kept as strictly then as nowadays, or perhaps attitudes towards foreign blood caused the records to be changed or deleted.

The progress of the railway system was rapid after the first wave of foreign engineers showed the way. Morel's suggestion that an engineering college be set up in Japan came to fruition in 1873 when Henry Dyer arrived from Glasgow to establish such an institution and became its first principal. Several other British teachers followed him out as it developed into the Imperial College of Engineering in Tokyo. The Japanese were quick to learn, and by 1888 there were only 14 foreign railwaymen employed by the government. These later engineers were mostly American and German.

Chapter 14

Henry Dyer — First Principal of Tokyo's Imperial College of Engineering

AS the steamship's engines thundered away, the young 24-year-old engineer who had just graduated from Glasgow University watched Southampton port disappear into the spring mists. It was April 1873, and Professor Henry Dyer, whose status had changed from undergraduate to professor in a few weeks, must have given considerable thought to his first task of how he would organise the new Imperial College of Engineering (Kobu Daigakko) in Tokyo. He had actually been appointed principal of the college before he had taken his final degree examinations.

Everything had happened so quickly that he was glad to have time on the voyage to think and plan. His fiancée, Marie Urquart, had remained in Glasgow, but he was accompanied by Tadasu Hayashi. Hayashi, later to receive the title of Baron and then Viscount and become the Japanese Ambassador to the Court of St James', was then private secretary to Hirobumi Ito, the Vice-Minister of Public Works and a member of the Japanese Embassy in England. It was the Ministry of Public Works that had seen the need for an engineering college in Tokyo to train Japanese students so that they would be able to take over from the foreign experts then working in their country, and develop for themselves all aspects of industrialisation in Japan.

In the five years since the Meiji Restoration, many Japanese students had attended colleges abroad in response to the Imperial Oath of April 1868: 'Knowledge shall be sought for throughout the world, so that the welfare of the Empire may be promoted!' Students were selected according to their abilities, and the countries they went to were carefully chosen according to which one was most advanced in a particular field of study. Thus, England was chosen by naval and marine students. France by those studying law and local government, Germany by military and medical students and America by those interested in business methods. For young, progressive Japanese, the world was just one huge classroom! But this method had its drawbacks. First, it was slow and uncoordinated, and also students had often to be re-educated in Japanese on their return from abroad. Many students made little progress abroad because of language difficulties; and so a new strategy was developed whereby high salaries would be offered to foreign educators to tempt them to come and teach in Japan.

100

Dyer was one of the first, and as his ship steamed into Yokohama port he carefully collected the papers he had been working on during the two-month voyage. He had drafted out rules, regulations, timetables and curricula for the proposed new engineering college and these he presented to the Acting Vice-Minister of Public Works, Yoso Yamao. His draft was accepted in its entirety with no changes thought necessary. By coincidence, Yamao was already known to Dyer for they had been in the same class during an evening course at Anderson's College in Glasgow back in the 1860s. The two men cooperated well, Dyer, as principal, was responsible for all educational arrangements, and Hayashi and Yamao, representing the Department of Public Works, managed the finances and administrative staff. Other young professors arrived from England and America, and the college opened its doors to the first batch of eager students. With no ancient traditions to uphold, and with almost fanatical support for westernisation, the whole team progressed at a rate unheard of before within any educational establishment. Soon, unfettered by any precedents, and believing whole-heartedly in their mission and their ability to create a system of learning embracing many innovations, the Imperial College of Engineering became the most advanced institution of its kind in the world. The distinguished British scientist, Lord Kelvin, who was also a personal friend of Dyer and under whom the latter had studied, mentioned this fact in a speech to inaugurate the James Watt engineering laboratory at Glasgow University.

*   *   *

The city of Tokyo itself was in a state of flux. The population of two million, which included nearly 400,000 samurai households, 280,000 from a segregated low-class caste and 23,000 beggars, witnessed daily the growing influence of the West in the physical changes to the city. The poorer people found that the process could improve their lot, while the samurai were now determined to become part of it and help direct it. The Ginza for example, was widened from 20 to 30 metres, it was paved in brick and lined with two-storied Victorian brick buildings under the supervision of the British architect Thomas Waters. The first railway was under construction. The midday gun echoed across the city daily, and a new drink, beer, introduced a few years earlier by William Copeland when he built a brewery in Yokohama, was becoming popular. Rickshaws had appeared on the streets in thousands, providing work for many of the poor, while the samurai had been forbidden to carry swords and wear top-knots, and married women no longer blackened their teeth or shaved their eyebrows. Important-looking westerners were everywhere, most living in the walled compound around Tsukiji temple, but since the great fire of 1872 which razed the whole area, many had taken residence in other parts of the city. A city where less than a decade before, no foreigner could walk alone unarmed without risk of being cut down by a samurai sword.

Dyer and his team of teachers were undoubtedly caught in the spirit of excitement and progress during these early days of rapid change. The professor of physics and telegraphy, W.E.Ayrton, a graduate of London University who had also studied under Lord Kelvin at Glasgow, 'created a laboratory for teaching applied electricity.' It was 'the first of its kind and served as a model for those which Ayrton himself organised in England later, and through them, for numerous other laboratories elsewhere.' In cooperation with Professor John Perry, he researched a host of basic electrical phenomena including terrestrial magnetism, dielectric constants and electrolytic polarisation. In London, after his five years in Tokyo, Ayrton again worked with Perry to invent many portable electrical measuring instruments — the ammeter, power meter and various types of voltmeter — which were prototypes for those still used today.

John Milne, the professor of geology and mining, was to become world-renowned as the father of seismology. Together with his colleagues, J.A. Ewing, professor of mechanical engineering, and T. Lomar Gray, several new instruments were invented and many important discoveries made. In the Chemistry faculty, Professor Edward Divers and R.A. Atkinson pioneered western chemistry teaching. There was some knowledge of this subject in Japan dating back to 1837 when the 'rangaku' (Dutch learning) scholar, Yoan Udagawa, wrote *Seimi Kaiso,* a book based on a translation of the Dutch book *Chemie fur Dilettanten* by Adolphus Yprey (1803). But this was a translation from the German of a book by J.B. Trommsdorf, which in turn was a translation from English of *An Epitome of Chemistry* by William Henry (London, 1801). Updated versions of Udagawa's book later contained sections on the work of Humphrey Davy, the famous Cornish scientist, and even before the Meiji Restoration Japanese students appreciated the importance of chemistry in Medicine.

Teaching in the English faculty were W. Gray Dixon, a graduate of Glasgow University, W. Craigie, and several Americans including W.E. Griffis and E. Warren Clarke. Only 22 years old on his arrival in 1876, Dixon was later replaced by his younger brother, James.

Most of the engineers and scientists at Imperial College also taught and were consultants at various government factories, or were expected to carry out additional duties outside the college. Divers, who was to replace Dyer as principal in 1882, was a supervisor at the Shinagawa glass factory, while Dyer taught at an Akabane factory, and he and others were frequently consulted on railway construction. Dyer was also responsible for introducing the first telephone to Japan in 1877 when instruments he ordered from London connected his office with the Public Works Dept. However, telephones for general use came many years later.

Almost all the staff of Imperial College, later to become Tokyo University, were members of the Asiatic Society of Japan, a learned society that celebrated its centenary in 1972 and still is very active. Many served on the committee for several years, contributing dozens of papers between them on topics ranging from 'The Specific Inductive Capacity of Gases' (Ayrton, 1876) to 'The Habits of the Blind in Japan' (Dixon, 1890). Dyer, himself, however, gave no talk to the society although he did serve on the committee.

* * *

After just one year in Japan, Dyer returned briefly to Britain in 1874. He had been authorised to appoint more staff for the expanding college, and while on this mission he married his fiancée, Marie, the daughter of a doctor, whom he brought with him back to Japan. Five children were born to them in Japan, the first son unfortunately died a few months after his birth, but three more sons and a daughter survived and spent their early years in Tokyo. By 1882, having been in Japan for nine years and with his eldest son now five years old, Dyer decided to return to Glasgow. He had firmly established the college in new, larger premises since his arrival, so that it functioned smoothly and efficiently with the latest teaching aids in fine laboratories unequalled anywhere. In this decision, he was probably considering the education of his own children, coupled with a fear that being absent too long might affect his chances of becoming re-established in Glasgow.

Glasgow was home to Dyer. Born at Bothwell, just a few miles outside the city, he won all the first prizes when he left Wilson's School at Shotts Iron Works. In 1863 the family moved to Glasgow itself, and young Henry was apprenticed as an engineer in a foundry which manufactured marine and winding engines, and pumps of all kinds. Some evenings he attended classes at Anderson's College (now the University of Strathclyde), and by the age of 20 had a sound practical and theoretical knowledge of engineering. He successfully applied for admission to the University of Glasgow, winning a Whitworth Scholarship worth £100 a year in 1870, the first Scot to do so. He was also the first graduate of Glasgow University to be awarded a BSc, a degree that Sir William Thomson (Lord Kelvin) had been anxious to introduce, in 1873.

When fellow Scotsman H.M. Matheson, the managing-director of Jardine and Matheson Co. and the London agent of the Japanese government, whose world-wide company had an infamous base in drug trafficking at the time of the Opium Wars in China, approached the authorities of Glasgow University to fulfil a commission to provide staff members for the newly-conceived Imperial College of Engineering in Tokyo, Dyer seemed a natural choice. Alex Kirk, Dyer's supervisor at the foundry had written about him: 'Your skill as a workman was thorough, not only were you capable of doing good work, but of doing it quickly.' While Professor Rankine, who had introduced him to the university, considered him 'the fittest man for the post.' Through these and other words of recommendation, Dyer's early career was similar to the rapid rise of Japan from feudalism to world power.

Back again in Glasgow, the Dyer family settled down. A modest fortune had been made in Japan, for his monthly salary of 660 yen as principal was supplemented for six years by an additional 860 yen for additional duties, and so the family could live in relative comfort. But Dyer himself soon became very frustrated. At the age of 34, crowned with success in the establishment of the world's foremost engineering college, Dyer found that he was unwanted in his own country. He had high hopes of occupying the Chair of Naval Architecture at Glasgow University. He applied for the position in both 1883 and 1886, but without success. Then his application to become principal of the Heriot Watt College in Edinburgh was rejected. He was refused any position of influence and all further progress in his educational career was denied him. It was a devastating anti-climax after his brilliant and highly successful years in Tokyo.

One reason for this rejection by his fellow countrymen may have been his socialist and pacifist views. As an engineer with a positive belief in building and constructing, Dyer was disgusted by the meaningless destruction of wars that could so rapidly wipe out the amazing architectural and construction feats produced by man's intellectual and physical understanding of the world. The scientist's understanding was successfully and progressively overcoming natural hazards and discomforts, and extending man's perceptual facilities by building steel bridges that would take railway trains and their passengers through hostile landscapes in comfort, by allowing men to talk with colleagues through wires over any distance, by even making earthquakes less destructive. But nationalistic politicians could only see a use for science and engineering in providing larger and more destructive weapons. It was a sad fact that a large proportion of Britain's population could not read Dyer's words in 1902, when Japan signed a military alliance with Britain (the Anglo-Japanese Alliance), and he commented in one of the many books he published after his Japan tour:

'It is a sad commentary on western civilisation when we find that an eastern power could not qualify itself for entrance to the comity of nations without, in the first place, spending a large part of its revenue on the appliances of destruction, and which could have been used to far greater advantage in improving the general conditions of the people.'

'A lengthened absence from Britain,' he continued in the same book, 'enables one, on his return, to observe British social conditions from a detached and comparative point of view which was not before possible, and he finds much in these conditions to excite the most painful anxiety. The ever-widening extremes of poverty and wealth, the conditions of life of our poorest classes, the production on a large scale of degenerates who are physically, mentally, and morally unfit for a fair share of the duties of citizenship, the uncertainty of employment, the growth of monopoly which is placing the conditions of the people at the mercy of a comparatively small number of capitalists, and the immense armaments which are sucking the life-blood of the nations, are all factors which give rise to very serious thought.'

Disillusioned, Dyer devoted the rest of his life to popular education in Scotland, being active in much social work. He lived in a terraced house in Glasgow until he died at the age of 70 in 1918, the year that 'The Great War for Civilisation' ended.

More than half a century after Dyer's death, engineering education in Japan and Britain are remarkably different. According to an article in *The Times Higher Education Supplement* headed 'Lessons in learning from the Japanese' (30 October 1981), Japan in 1978 produced 71,167 graduate engineers compared with only 6,897 in Britain. And in 1977 there were 271,956 graduate engineers and scientists working in Japanese industry compared with a mere 78,800 in the UK. Trade Union leader Clive Jenkins, disgusted at the financial cut-backs in this field of education, complained that higher education in Britain was 'now under-planned or not planned at all.' The problems that Dyer faced on his return from Japan appear to be still present, and Jenkins stated that the ills of Britain result from the essentially conservative nature of British society.

'As currently constructed,' Jenkins is quoted as saying, 'the universities (in Britain) are the last great bastion of feudal privilege. The British are only now realising they are at the end of the Empire. I think our social and educational structure is still geared to producing administrators for the rest of the world.'

Chapter 15

'Earthquake Milne'

THE scientific instrument was ready to record. The dynamite charge was set, and the leader of the project gave the signal to detonate. Like the roar of an old cannon, the chemical reaction released its energy as earth, stones, plants and jagged rocks were blasted into the air in the countryside outside Tokyo. Within his tiny earthwork, protected from above only by an old door, the supine leader stared at the delicate instrument he had constructed to measure the shock waves. He was little more than twenty feet from the explosion, and before the needle of the instrument reached its final position, a ton of earth and rubble crashed down on the door, smashing the instrument and flattening the professor. Although this particular experiment had failed, Professor John Milne survived the ordeal and crawled out from his hazardous position — much to the relief and subsequent amusement of his Japanese associates. The newly-appointed professor of geology and mining at Imperial College of

Engineering, Tokyo, was lucky to be alive, but he had faced dangers many times in the past in his pursuit of knowledge and was never deterred by such events.

Thousands of his other experiments concerning shock waves travelling through the earth were successful, and these were to lead the way to a truer understanding of the structure of our earth. Many accurate measuring instruments — seismographs — were to be designed and constructed by him in Japan, and then used world-wide to discover that the interior of the earth was composed of a core concentric with mantle and crust. Eventually, the remarkable theory of plate techtonics was to evolve from Milne's early pioneering work. Milne, accepted by many as the 'father of seismology,' was primarily concerned with studying earthquakes, using explosives to test his instruments, measure the speed of the waves and determine the geological formations beneath the surface. His interest was awakened when he experienced a strong tremor the first day he arrived in Japan in 1876. His work was to lead him and his colleagues into studying all aspects of earthquakes, from their psychological effects to ways of building quake-proof houses.

*   *   *

Born on 30 December 1850 in Liverpool, Milne's parents soon moved to Rochdale where his father had a successful wool-stapling business. First attending a 'Dame School,' then being a private pupil of a rector, the 13-year-old lad entered the Liverpool Collegiate Institute. His studies progressed well, and in his holidays he went off on solo trips around England and Ireland, mostly walking but once canoeing around the rivers and canals of southern England with his dog.

At 17 he attended King's College, London, studying a variety of scientific and mathematical subjects, but by 1871 his interests lay mainly in geology and mineralogy. That summer he sailed with a friend to Iceland where they examined volcanoes, geysers and minerals. The following year Milne was awarded a Royal Exhibition Scholarship to study at the Royal School of Mines, and after a year of concentrated study with some practical experience down mines in Cornwall and Lancashire, he sought employment.

For two years employed by a millionaire entrepreneur, he searched for coal and other minerals in Newfoundland; he also undertook a short expedition in the winter of 1873 with a Biblical scholar, Dr Charles Beke, to 'locate the true position of Mount Sinai where the Law had been delivered to Moses.' After writing long reports on these places, there came the offer of a post as Professor of Geology and Mining at Imperial College of Engineering, Tokyo. Immediately he accepted, but was apprehensive about the long sea journey as he suffered badly from sea-sickness. Finally, he decided to travel alone overland.

This was decades before the completion of the Trans-Siberian Railway, and rumours about packs of hungry wolves, gangs of wild exiles and miles of frozen plains did not deter him. He set off full of confidence to observe and record all the interesting facets of his long journey. By ship, rail, seatless carriage, riverboat and sledge, he moved across Europe and Russia, sharing hot tea with Cossacks in the Siberian winter, until a camel train brought him into China where he took a ship from Shanghai for Japan. Eleven months had elapsed since leaving England.

* * *

The first principal of the new Imperial College of Engineering, 28 year-old Henry Dyer from Glasgow, welcomed Milne on to his staff, and he settled into a routine of teaching. The timetable was full, and students were instructed to begin their studies at 6 am and finish at 10 pm with eight hours spent in class every day, for Japan urgently needed to educate men to implement the policy of industrialisation the Meiji government had decided to pursue. Each student followed an intense programme of English, the medium of instruction, and Milne was aware of the value of his notes handed out to them. Gathered together, his lecture notes on crystallography were later published as a standard textbook, which supplemented his ¥300 monthly salary.

Milne's contract also stated that he had to travel around Japan to determine the geology of the islands, and to then suggest likely locations for obtaining mineral resources. However, he was not allowed to become involved in any business ventures. 1878 saw him cruising around the Kurile Islands, observing seals and sea-otters (long since disappeared through hunting), measuring heights of mountains, and meeting the few inhabitants. Other college holidays took him to the edges of active volcanoes on Oshima and Asama, attempting to measure the depths of craters with wires and line.

Back in Tokyo, he devised experiments and models to demonstrate the formation of volcanoes, sprinkling heaps of sand and gravel with water to simulate the effects of rainfall. By 1879, his studies of Japan's pre-history had led him, accompanied by the American Professor Morse, to excavate several tumuli. He presented seven papers to the Asiatic Society of Japan for which he acted as a councillor for seven years. His examination of the language, customs and religious practices in Japan, suggested to him that the place of origin of the Japanese people was Polynesia, a theory since proved to be incorrect.

Two British lecturers at the college, John Perry and Professor William Edward Ayrton, had begun studies of earthquakes before Milne arrived. They found that records of over 2000 quakes existed in Japanese archives, and magnetic seismometers were in use that had been designed by a Tokyo spectacle maker who had noticed that a magnet on his wall had lost its power just before an earthquake. However, these instruments were neither accurate nor sensitive. They also knew that the first seismoscope was invented in 136 AD by the Chinese Chang Heng, but by the 1870s little scientific advance had been made. In Europe, where the scientific revolution had created instruments for measuring almost all natural phenomena, earthquakes were relatively few, so no need arose to study and measure them. More profitable lines of research continually presented themselves there. But if profitable and safe industries were to arise in Japan, earthquakes would require close attention. Milne, building on his knowledge of geology and experience in mining, saw their importance and determined to understand them and fight their destructive effects. Soon this study obsessed him and almost took over his life. He was to write over two million words on the subject of seismology.

His approach was firstly to design, test and develop instruments based on known scientific principles that could measure, record and time earth movements in all three dimensions. No easy task when everything tends to move, including the instrument, during a 'quake. But, using the principle of inertia and with invaluable cooperation from his new colleagues, James Alfred Ewing, Professor of Mechanical Engineering, and Thomas Gray, Professor of Telegraphic Engineering, he succeeded. The Gray-Milne seismograph soon became standard world-wide.

Next, he had these instruments distributed over a wide area of the country so that data of shocks of varying intensity arriving at different times at different stations could be collected. With such data Milne could build up seismic maps and isoseismal diagrams. The rapidly developing Japanese postal system cooperated fully in providing an efficient communications network. Much of the initial impetus for his scheme came from the moderate Kanto Plain quake of 22 February 1880. Milne was awakened at 12.50 am and immediately inspected the seismographs in his house. The next day he received further data from a colleague in Yokohama with a similar seismic station, and he sent out hundreds of questionnaires via the *Japan Gazette* to assess the damage over a large area.

The interest generated led to the formation of The Seismological Society of Japan, the very first body of its kind in the world. At its first meeting, at Imperial College on 26 April 1880, Milne presented the first paper. Within a short while 15 seismic stations were established in telegraph offices all around Tokyo where accurate clocks, regulated daily from the Tokyo headquarters, were available. By the end of his 20-year stay in Japan, Milne saw the number increase to nearly 1000. His energetic efforts in this work, where he continually sent out and received thousands of postcards bringing earthquake data from all points in Japan, and which he used to compile a huge catalogue of reports on 8331 quakes between 1885 and 1893, caused him to be nicknamed 'Earthquake Milne' by the other foreign residents.

*   *   *

But this was just the groundwork. The noble objective was to minimise or prevent the awful destruction of quakes, and to find ways to predict and control them, for the benefit of all human life. Cooperating with Professor F. Omori and Professor K. Tatsuno, who held the Chair in Architecture at Imperial College, buildings were designed with shock-proof characteristics, and which incorporated many traditional features of ancient Japanese building techniques. Test rigs were constructed to simulate earthquake action, and materials and structures shaken violently. Strict mathematical analysis, guided by Professor Omori, followed. Other countries in earthquake zones then showed interest in this work, as the reputation of the Tokyo team became widespread. The Minister of Education, Arinori Mori, in 1888, set up a committee of engineers and architects to advise on quake-proof construction of which Milne was a prominent member. Many recommendations of this original committee are still to be found in Japanese building regulations today.

That year the Emperor Meiji decorated Milne with the Order of Merit with the Cordon of the Sacred Treasure, and he was elevated to 'Chokunin' status, which meant he had many special privileges including a life-long pension of ¥1000 a year when he left Japan.

By 1893, seismographs had been designed sensitive enough to detect shock waves from quakes on the other side of the earth. Photographic techniques could record these as seismograms more conveniently and permanently than the old pen-on-smoked-glass method. By the time Milne left Japan, in 1895, an Earthquake Investigation Committee had been established by Imperial ordinance as well as a Chair of Seismology at Imperial College.

At the age of 45, he decided to return to England with his Japanese wife, Tone, whom he had met in Hakodate in 1877. She was the daughter of a Buddhist abbot, Jokyo Horikawa, who owned the Ganjo-ji (Temple). Educated in the Kaitakushi Girls' School in Tokyo, she resented having to serve *saké* to male teachers, and she objected even more to being educated to become 'a good housewife for a farmer in Hokkaido.' Their marriage in the Ranazu-ku temple in 1881 caused some malicious gossip amongst the class-conscious Victorians in the British foreign community, and comment by some Japanese concerned with preserving racial purity. By 1895 their relationship had matured and they sailed from Yokohama, after a brief second marriage ceremony at the British Consulate to legalise their union under British law, to take up residence at Shide, Isle of Wight.

Milne had chosen this particular location because the solid geological formations beneath the house were ideal for his seismographs. Here his sensitive instruments could detect small quakes epicentered in Japan or any part of the world. Soon, ably assisted by his closest friend Shinobu Hirota, two stations were made operational on the island. Many vibrations of local origin occurred on the seismograms that had to be eliminated, for trains and even nearby horses caused swings of the needle. At one station in the cellar of the Royal Victoria Yacht Club at Ryde, where the effects of tidal loading were being investigated, large regular swings on the trace appeared at the same time each week. No other station recorded them. After eliminating all possible local causes — gunnery practice, quarry blasting and trains passing — Milne found that they occurred when the butler and housekeeper at the club had their afternoons off together.

Initially, he had difficulties in obtaining accurate time checks. For many years previously the Japanese government and Post Office had cooperated closely with him, providing telegraphic time signals. But in Britain he was frustrated by the perversity of the red tape of officialdom in its feudal extreme. The British Postmaster-general, unmoved by requests from the British Association and the Astronomer-Royal supporting Milne, refused to provide daily time signals unless Milne personally agreed to pay £22 a year for the service plus total costs of installations — vast sums in those days. For a time he made use of a primitive, but accurate, sun-dial, then when the French began broadcasting radio time signals from the Eiffel Tower, a friend constructed a crystal receiver for Milne and the problem was solved. A neat solution before the time that the feudal elite of Britain imposed licensing on all radio receivers.

Shide was for a while the centre of a network of seismic stations all around the old British Empire. But a further stage of complete international cooperation from every point on the earth was sought, especially by Milne, so that scientific data could be gathered on an even wider scale. But national governments found it hard to agree on finances and locations. Milne received no financial aid from the British government, even though seismic studies initiated by him had saved hundreds of thousands of pounds by quickly locating quakes that had severed submarine telegraph cables essential to business. Still, eventually an international network was established that today has additional duties of detecting underground nuclear explosions.

Milne died in 1913 after the science he had created outstripped his comprehension, and Tone remained at Shide until 1919 and the end of the infamous Great War before returning to Hakodate where she died in 1925. A memorial in Hakodate was raised to the couple in 1926. But the story does not end there. Great interest in the life of Milne was revived in Britain in 1980 when L.K. Herbert-Gustar and P.A. Nott, two teachers in the Isle of Wight, produced the excellent book: *John Milne: Father of Modern Seismology* (Paul Norbury Publications). A Japanese translation followed shortly. And the director of the Meteorological Agency's seismological observatory at Matsushiro, the most advanced in the world, recently surveyed his equipment that can provide instant information, through computers, on earthquake activity and issue immediate tsunami warnings, and commented:

'How we wish John Milne could be with us today!'

Chapter 16

Japlish

PART OF THE TRADITIONAL CULTURE of western residents living in Japan is to smile with indulgent amusement at shop signs, advertisements and other written notices in Japlish. 'Japlish' is a word invented in the nineteenth century which describes attempts by Japanese to display a message using the English language in a way that would not be generally acceptable in English-speaking countries. It is one example of using English in a deviant way. Although some may describe it as 'bad English,' in fact it is merely a variation of English and some variations may eventually become permanently established in the standard dictionaries and grammars.

This tradition has existed since the 1850s when westerners were first allowed back into Japan and a few residents and visitors set about collecting and recording these ingenious variations to add spice to their globe-trotter travel books. Several academics attempted to investigate this phenomenon, especially with regard to the spoken pidgin languages that evolved in the context of the development of languages in general.

A sports-bag, bought in 1980, is inscribed with the legend 'Poor Look Boy with Rich,' and another proclaims 'The World's Most Beautifully.' So the tradition still endures and examples are legion, with every so-called rule of grammar broken several times over, and even spelling is deviant at times. Most of the variations can be explained in terms of hurried, literal translations being made with a dictionary, but some phrases seem to express a poetical nuance of novel ingenuity, while others are unconsciously outrageous. One baker, or his printer, inserted an 'm' instead of an 'n' to advertise his 'Delicious Hot Steaming Bums.' Variations in spellings in every alphabetical language do occur over time, just as variations of character formation take place in eastern languages, but foreign influence tends to introduce new words rather than change old ones!

The interaction and absorption of one language into another can perhaps be understood in terms of the history of man's technical and economic progress. Why did hundreds of different languages evolve? The answer must surely lie in the long-term isolation of tribes during the extended stable era following the Agricultural Revolution some 30,000 years ago. In our own age of the computer, the information explosion, exponential population growth and nuclear weapons, it is not easy to conceive of a slow, isolated existence that allowed completely independent and different languages to take shape among groups of people struggling to survive the perversities of nature in fertile or not-so-fertile valleys and plains all over the world. As the centuries passed,

111

greater success in cultivation techniques caused certain populations to increase, and tribes polarised together into national units. As means of transport improved, so did arms, and with the invention of money, mathematics, religion and taxation out of necessity, a more complex society arose that was designed to primarily defend its national identity. But such nationalism, once a useful survival device, has finally produced the present real danger of human extermination by man-made devices. There exist two opposing trends: science and technology and industry encouraging smooth international intercourse with a comfortable and controlled life for all, while political forces tend to distrust any crossing of national barriers, even proscribing rules for languages!

*   *   *

During the Meiji era (1868-1912) in Japan, the Japlish signboard over a shop attracted customers from foreign tourist ships. In other words, it worked. Customers came to the shop, business was done, and the amusement of the western visitor at the sign was an added bonus. In a foreign country, the average traveller tends to bring his or her feeling of national identity to the fore, so a sign using ABC, albeit in an unfamiliar way, attracted him or her. This strategy is still used in Spain and France for British tourists, and in the European capitals for Japanese tourists.

Hundreds of English words were absorbed into the Japanese language, after katakanisation, following the arrival of Commodore Matthew Perry in 1854, just as many Dutch and Portuguese words had already been introduced 220 years earlier. But also many Japanese loan words came into the English language (as well as other European languages) to take their place in the standard dictionaries, such as 'Tsunami' for a tidal wave that follows an earthquake, 'rickshaw,' 'judo,' 'kamikaze,' 'hibachi' and 'tycoon.'

This has always been a natural and logical process, for when one culture meets another, new concepts and phenomena are found by both sides. In Britain, with the collapse of the Roman Empire, the English language had become richer and thought clearer, especially in legal matters, through acquiring new lexis and constructions from Latin to express new ideas hitherto undefined. The Norman invasion of 1066 began a similar process although the effects were not as intellectually significant. A characteristic of these later invaders was their unwillingness or inability to do actual physical work, and so most words relating to work remained Anglo-Saxon. For example, live animals cared for and reared on land stolen by the new hierarchy, like 'pig,' 'sheep' and 'cattle,' are of Saxon origin. Whereas the dead meat as feasted upon by the new rulers, 'pork,' 'mutton' and 'beef,' are of Norman-French origin. The 'stalls,' 'styes' and 'byres' for housing food-producing animals were Saxon words, while the steel-clad knight kept his steed in a 'stable,' — an imported Norman word. 'Milk' is Saxon, 'cream' Norman!

Such aspects of etymology reflect the conditions of the time, much of which still exist. Further, the basic lexis of Saxon origin referring to the sexual parts and activities, the so-called four-lettered words, have withstood all attempts to eliminate them by the descendants of the Norman rulers. Their religious standards, social institutions and psychological inhibitions have for various strange reasons, attempted to deny the reality of the mechanics of human reproduction. This may have been due to their lack of work experience with animals, and the husbandry necessary to supply meat, coupled in a queer way with romantic notions of love. Also, the Normans established institutions for one sex only, which naturally encouraged homosexuality in all its extravagances, and the Saxon word objectively referring to a sodomist has continually been feared and hated by the British establishment for this reason. It would appear that the persistent and current use of that word very often used to describe tax collectors and other government officials in Britain is a 900-year tradition of defiance against the Norman invasion!

*   *   *

By the time that Japan was involved with the English language, the aggressive nature of the British rulers had extended round the world. The phenomenon known as 'The British Empire' had developed through more sophisticated weapons and warships that brought destruction, exploitation and misery to several continents. It also brought the English language. And this was responsible for making it the second most-spoken language, after Mandarin Chinese, in the world today. But certainly it is the most widely distributed language, in all its variations. George Orwell was one who rationally and bitterly criticised 'the equivocal moral position of Britain, with its democratic phrases and its coolie empire,' but the gun-boats fired their shells and the English language spread. The moral position was rarely discussed.

The merchants, traders and experts from the West who travelled to the Far East and Japan during the early Meiji era were primarily concerned with making money and doing a job of construction to build the 'new' Japan. To buy, sell, obtain credit, give credit, exchange and haggle. To organise a team of inexperienced labourers, to have a supply of materials provided. Not for these tough individuals the niceties of previously learning the language at a college, or studying it carefully with various learning aids on arrival. It was improvisation all the way, the thrashing out of some effective means of communication so that the business in hand could be done. The agents of the bigger trading houses did have close connections with their consuls who spoke the native languages, but the majority were left to sink or swim on their own.

In India and the China coast, they relied on members of the local population learning a deviant and simplified version of English that contained a sprinkling of local words and phrases. This became known as Pidgin-English, or business-English. 'Hey Johnny, you go chop-chop bund godown fetch number one bossman!' The present tense generally sufficed, and prepositions and articles were unnecessary. It was an inventive survival language, never written down except in part by a few academics.

                              *   *   *

In Japan the situation was reversed in that the common currency of communication was Pidgin-Japanese. This reversal is understandable in historical terms, for the advance eastward by the armed westerners through India and China was relatively slow and long, with few restrictions on men crossing national borders or entering different language zones. English was probably known in the Chinese ports, by a few who had travelled west and then returned, before the first merchants arrived. But the opening of Japan was a sudden quantum jump, for the national borders had been closed for 220 years to all outsiders. Dutch was already known by '*rangaku*' scholars, but by the nineteenth century Holland had become a minor power. English was unheard of, but spoken Japanese was not as difficult as Chinese for the western vocal and aural apparatus to utter and comprehend, and these factors contributed to the evolution of Pidgin-Japanese. But even here it was a two-way compromise as English and other foreign words became part of the matrix of communication that the tea-house girls, rickshaw-pullers and coolies soon learned as part of their trade. Economy of vocabulary and sense of humour were characteristics of this now obsolete patois.

Due to the advent of more profitable trade, bringing the luxury of professional interpreters, more intelligent merchants and more effective universal education, it has been almost irretrievably lost. Professor Basil-Hall Chamberlain writing in the 1890s implied that it was current then. A pamphlet called 'Exercises in the Yokohama Dialect' by a Mr Hoffman Atkinson, published first in 1874 or possibly earlier, was intended as a 'grammar' in Pidgin-Japanese for newcomers to the Treaty Ports. Tongue-in-cheek with humorous phonetic spellings — 'cheese eye' (small), 'mods cashey' (difficult), 'abooneye pon pon' (earthquake) — it went through several reprints until 1915 after the 'Bishop of Homoco' had requested a revised and corrected edition. It thus seemed that Pidgin-Japanese evolved and changed rapidly, but the fact that this unique pamphlet was not subsequently reprinted may indicate the beginning of the decline of the patois. Japan's improving economic situation and better communications in the post-World War I era may have caused this decline.

In the 1930s and '40s, there was a renewed academic interest in the topic with F. J. Daniels emphasising its importance in studying the development of mainstream Japanese (but not foreseeing what a flood, indeed a deluge, of foreign words and expressions would be absorbed into Japanese during the American Occupation and economic boom years of the post-World War II era).

Experts claim that Atkinson's pamphlet was accurate, despite the humour, and that a dentist was known as a 'ha-daikusan,' or a tooth-carpenter, and a lighthouse was referred to as a 'fune-haiken-saraban-nai-rosoku,' or a ship-watch-candle-light-inside. Chamberlain also comments that in Pidgin-Japanese the Lord's Prayer began: 'Ottosan nikai arimas,' or 'Grandfather is up on the second floor!'

*   *   *

The early traders, merchants and technical experts in the Treaty Ports were creative enough to produce a unique language of their own out of necessity in their quest for commercial and industrial intercourse, despite their lack of formal education in linguistics. But they were not bilingual. However, with the broadening of educational facilities, many of their children were naturally bilingual, especially the offspring of those who settled down with Japanese wives. Yet many of these children, with their special skill and experience, were discriminated against in their formal higher education. Nationalism reared its ugly head again. 'Mistakes' made by such children in one language or the other were regarded as indicating a lower intelligence level, but were in fact due merely to the influence or interference of one language, or thought process, on the other.

In the post-World War II era the status of teachers declined in the West with the implementation of universal education which had become necessary because of the economic need for an intelligent workforce, and teachers proliferated as soldiers serving the minds of youth. As an increasing number of international schools began to evolve into their present sophisticated form, so similar discrimination appeared against those teachers who had had experience in them. In their country of origin they became suspect by monocular education administrators at the lower echelons of political power. Like the pre-war bilingual students, they tended to be regarded as outcasts by each well-defined nation, perhaps as a strange and dangerous species whose wider experience had given them values and insights that were too comprehensive and permissive, and therefore irrelevant to the vegetative attitudes expected of those who should work for the glory of one nation. This tragic rejection of a uniquely valuable human resource, like the bilingual children before them, appears to be wasteful and detrimental to any kind of future evolution of the human species. But this attitude is slowly changing, which it must do if mankind is to have a future.

As the ongoing development of languages continues with the adaption and adoption of lexis from each other, like the introduction of 'pasokon' (personal computer) into Japanese, we can only wonder how much the spreading growth of the knowledge of a computer-language will give a more universal insight into the nature of language itself. Perhaps creating the base for an international unity that no empire builders could achieve.

PART III

Western Teachers and Technocrats

ESSENTIAL for the transmission of human culture from one generation to another, or from one location to another, are teachers. Traditionally, a teacher is envisaged as a knowledgeable person in a classroom in front of rows of younger students, but this limited and formal image is only part of the process of education. Much more effective teachers are those who work with their students and become an integrated part in the common aims of the group, a group that can see or foresee the fruit of their efforts. Such were the majority of 'experts' from the West who were invited to Japan after 1868 to graft the institutions and establishments that had resulted from the flowering of science and technology in Europe and America onto Japan. These men were at first supplemented by missionaries who did valuable work in studying the Japanese language, as well as teaching English and the basics of western science and technology.

As the majority of the teachers and technocrats were British, and were graduates from 'public schools,' they had an indoctrinated sense of their own inborn superiority, while many of the Baptist missionaries from America were similarly confident in their own sense of righteousness, so there were bound to be conflicts when they came into contact with Japanese society. Generally, these conflicts were resolved with a greater understanding on both sides ensuing, but sometimes a deadlock was reached and then contracts were not renewed.

Despite these difficulties, compounded frequently by a degree of arrogance on the part of some Japanese, the flow of western scientific culture into Japan was rapid, profitable and permanent. It was the first time that such a phenomenon — the transference and absorption of technology on such a massive scale from one culture to another — had ever taken place.

116

Chapter 17

W.E. Griffis — Early Commentator in Meiji Japan

SHE WAS A MERE 17-year-old, firm of limb and shapely in figure. As she cleaned the oil-lamp wearing the traditional garb of Japanese servant girls of that time, the 27-year-old American master of the house twisted his body in his chair, gritted his teeth and remembered a quotation from the Bible about 'lust.' He had arrived in the country town of Fukui in south-eastern Japan in March 1871, and now, five months later, he was gaining the reputation of being a first-class teacher in science. His professional life was a great success and he believed that he was influencing the history of Japan by being one of the first *yatoi* (government hired foreigners) to teach some of the future leaders of Japan. However he was not completely happy and satisfied with life.

One of the reasons he came to Japan was because he had been rejected by a certain Miss Ellen Johnson back in New Brunswick. Now, with Miss Johnson receding further into the back of his mind, this anonymous maid was tempting his natural instincts that his strong Lutheran Christian upbringing had taught him to reject with visions of eternal burning in Hell. He resolved his dilemma by writing a letter of confession to his sister, Maggie, and by having the maid removed from his service. He also confessed to his friend, Dr Verbeck, in Tokyo who wrote back to him: 'Do not think of temptations! If your religion does not hold you up, think of your parents and sisters, of your future wife! Name, influence, respect, future happiness, present peace, all would be irretrievably gone!'

William Elliot Griffis overcame temptation and went back to his writing, for even though his residence in Japan was to last only three-and-a-half years, the amount he wrote was phenomenal. Almost every aspect of life in Japan was touched on by Griffis and his works are a mine of information for the historian.

*   *   *

When he was only seven years old he had watched the launching of the frigate *Susquehanna* that was later to bring Matthew Perry to Japan; after that, when he was at school, his classmate was the son of the American Minister, Pruyn, who had visited Japan; and later still he was a teacher of the first group of Japanese students who had come to study in America at Rutgers Grammar School in 1869. These tenuous connections, along with his heart-rending experience with Miss Johnson,

117

convinced Griffis that he was God's chosen instrument to help in bringing
the benefits of western civilisation to feudal Japan. Afterwards when
he had worked in and finally left Japan, he believed his mission to be
teaching and explaining Japan and the Japanese to his fellow Americans.

Arriving by the steamship *Great Republic* on 29 December 1870 at
Yokohama Port, he was met by the Reverend J.C. Hepburn and his
wife who introduced him to the other Christian priests and missionaries
in the community. Two days later he was preaching a sermon — 'One
is your master, even Christ' — at the new Presbyterian Chapel. Soon
he was off to Tokyo by way of the old Tokaido where he met the
Reverend Guido Verbeck who assisted him in making arrangements for
his teaching post with Prince Echizen of Fukui, one of the last feudal
lords.

Griffis had to wait six weeks in Tokyo and he soon saw for himself
the conflicts and contradictions of that city. He was impressed by the
exquisite table manners of his Japanese hosts during European-style
banquets that included ale, sherry, claret and champagne, but, on the
other hand, he was aware that in other parts of the city vice was rampant
and two-sworded *ronin* (masterless samurai) roamed the streets and that
these men considered it to be an act of great patriotism to cut down any
western 'barbarian.' As a precaution Griffis always carried a loaded
Smith and Wesson revolver, while the Japanese authorities provided
bodyguards for their Tokyo yatoi. When two fellow teachers, Dallas
and Ring, who had posts at the Imperial College of Engineering decided
one night to dismiss their bodyguards and go off to search for women,
they were attacked from the rear by two ronin and suffered serious
wounds. Griffis and Verbeck helped nurse these two waywards, but
agreed with each other that: 'If they had lived a moral life, they would
have been safe enough that night.'

                              *   *   *

Griffis arrived in Fukui on 4 March and was received with great
hospitality. Prince Echizen, Matsudaira Shungaku, gave him a reception
in his castle and after brief formal introductions, the wine and beer
flowed so that within a short time a warm, informal atmosphere
prevailed. Three days later he taught his first lesson and to honour the
occasion the director of the school awarded him with a plump goose
and another official presented him with champagne and some carved
monkeys. He seemed well satisfied and wrote to his sister that his future
ambitions were 'to make Fukui College the best in Japan, to make a
national text-book on Chemistry, to advocate the education of women,
to abolish the drinking of *saké*, the wearing of swords and the
promiscuous bathing of the sexes!'

His teaching load was quite light — only four hours per day — and
he had fewer than 22 students per class. Each Sunday he was free and
after a few weeks he began to give Bible classes. He admitted to his

sister that he could only drive off homesickness and loneliness by keeping incessantly busy. Only two people were fluent in English at Fukui at this time: his interpreter, Iwabuchi, and another teacher from Britain called Alfred Lucy. 'Lucy,' wrote Griffis, 'is rather a pale, quiet young man of about my age, and is a smart fellow with a head packed full of information, and talks the Jap language fluently,' however Lucy 'like 99 of every hundred single men in Japan, had taken a temporary wife.' This moral gulf between these two foreign teachers affected their relationship although they did take many walks, rides and hunting expeditions together. Griffis' loneliness became more painful, almost impossible to bear, when Lucy departed for Tokyo in the summer.

Griffis taught science which required not only books but also apparatus. He managed to find a 'few glass tubes, some utensils and materials' in Yokohama before he went to Fukui; in addition to this he imported apparatus — using his sister as his agent — from America. Also he had a blacksmith, a tinsmith and a joiner to make apparatus for him under his instructions. Nonetheless, he was a little disturbed when he was asked 'to teach the men in the war departments of Echizen how to blow up a man-of-war with submarine mines!' It dawned on him that many of his students were interested in science only because of its military value.

*   *   *

It was perhaps a combination of this fact, together with his loneliness, that caused him to move to Tokyo after only nine months in Fukui and take up an appointment at the Daigaku Nanko in January 1872. But in Tokyo there were further problems on the education scene. He complained that many of his foreign colleagues had rather doubtful qualifications. They came 'from the bar-room, the brothel, the gambling saloon' and they 'brought the graces, the language and the manners of those places into the school room,' to quote the English writer F.V. Dickins, who went on to pronounce in his frank and witty style: 'The majority of the "Professors" in the schools of Tokyo were graduates of the dry-goods counter, the forecastle, the camp and the shambles, or belonged to that vast array of unclassified humanity that floats like waifs in every seaport.'

This exaggerated tirade was probably based on a modicum of truth for, as today, foreign teachers were well appreciated by the Japanese — especially in financial rewards. Ogata Hiroyasu, a modern historian, points out that some of the foreign teachers were paid ¥600 monthly whereas the Daigaku's president received only ¥400. About 14% of the total education budget went towards the salaries of foreigners! Who could blame a few charlatans from trying to muscle in on the scene?

Griffis soon chose a few friends in Tokyo and settled into his new life. His sister, Maggie, sailed to Japan and he found her a position at a girls' school. Her presence helped to overcome his loneliness, but he still continued to write for three hours every day and much of his work was published in magazines in America. He was slowly becoming quite famous through his reports on the mysterious country of Japan.

It may have been that some of his articles did not please the Japanese authorities, for from about this time his position as a yatoi began to become precarious. His clash with Japanese bureaucracy eventually led to his departure.

*   *   *

It all started with the Independence Day (4 July) festivities held by the American teachers of Tokyo in 1873. They were warned by the police that fireworks were a fire hazard in the foreigners' compound. The American ghetto, perhaps fired by patriotism and alcohol, chose to ignore the instructions — confident that their 'extra-territoriality' would prevent them from being prosecuted. The rockets soared upwards and the fire-crackers exploded. But the loss of face of the Japanese police would not allow the matter to rest there.

A few days later the school authorities punished its foreign teachers by increasing their holidays: they would be free on six days every month: the 1st., 6th., 11th., 16th., 21st., and 26th. — the same as for Japanese teachers. But the foreign teachers were not happy with this arrangement; they protested and threatened to resign because it was only occasionally and irregularly that these days fell on the Sabbath. Life for them would be impossible if they had to work on Sundays.

Griffis fought this decision. But his protests only brought him more trouble and he was told that his contract would not be renewed. He was shocked, and sought the help of all his influential friends both American and Japanese. Amongst his students at Tokyo and Fukui were two future prime ministers, several ambassadors, a few foreign ministers and many businessmen and scholars — but all his efforts were of no avail. At the end of the summer term 1874, his work as a yatoi was finished and he began to pack his bags and trunks.

*   *   *

On 18 July 1874, despite thoughts of travelling around the world with his sister and his old friend Ed Warren-Clarke, Griffis sailed straight back to America. He was now 31 years old and he knew that he could have obtained a good teaching post in any American school, but his baggage contained a pile of hand-written papers about Japan and he wanted to edit and publish these. He now saw himself as a 'bridge between East and West.' In 1876 his 700-page book *The Mikado's Empire* was first published, and by 1913 there had been twelve editions.

In 1879 he married a Miss Stanton and the remainder of his life was devoted almost exclusively to the publication of books and articles about Japan. After 1900 he became increasingly concerned about the lack of recognition in Japan of the work done by the yatoi. He placed advertisements in American magazines asking for information about the early yatoi and he wrote about some of them. Another yatoi, the railway engineer, Francis Trevithick, who put down much of the first iron tracks and bridges across Japan, complained about the lack of recognition of his brother, also a yatoi.

'Richard Trevithick of Kobe,' he wrote 'will never be known in Japan by the Japanese as the designer and builder of the first Japanese locomotive, the credit being already given to a Japanese who has very little mechanical knowledge.' Even today in various museums in Japan one finds that the multitude of schoolchildren that pass through are presented with large pictures of kimonoed persons who had something to do with the introduction of scientific knowledge into Japan, but who had nothing to do with initial discoveries and developments. The circle is complete when one realises that it is probably the educational system that is to blame. Recently, however, many fine illustrated books have been published in Japanese in which due credit is given to the yatoi and other foreigners.

*   *   *

In 1926, Griffis returned on a sentimental journey to Japan as a guest of the Japanese government. He had previously been awarded a medal by the Emperor (Order of the Rising Sun, fourth class) at which he had shown surprise for he admitted that he had never been without criticism of Japan.

On this final visit he noted the immense progress that had taken place since his first arrival almost 60 years before. He revisited Fukui and all of his past haunts, making speeches about the secure and long-term friendship that had been built up between Japan and America. The next year, aged 85, he died in America, 14 years before Pearl Harbor.

Chapter 18

E. Warren Clarke — Preacher and Science Teacher

'FIRE! FIRE!' the shouts went up at the Kaisei Gakko (Imperial College of Engineering), which subsequently became Tokyo University. People were running hither and thither with wooden poles and buckets of water, giving and taking orders, as the smoke billowed up from the tiled roof. Some of the students were in a panic, throwing beds, books and furniture out of the windows of the two-storied structure which was made mostly of wood. The Fire Brigade soon arrived with a clumsy hand-pump and a human chain was formed so that buckets of water could be passed up the stairs and then up a ladder into the loft — the site of the fire.

Mr Warren Clarke did not panic as he heard the commotion while he was half-way through a chemistry lesson in the laboratory. He dismissed his class and told them to walk out calmly. Then he heaved a large metallic device onto his back, instructed his two assistants to bring two more similar devices, and mounted the ladder which led to the burning loft. Struggling to get through the hole with the large device, he burned his arms. Once inside he began to operate his device — an object unknown in Japan at that time. It was a Babcock fire-extinguisher that he had filled with acid only the day before.

*   *   *

A jet of white liquid shot across the loft and the carbon dioxide gas that it produced soon reduced the flames. After emptying the first extinguisher he carefully picked his way back over the smouldering rafters to the entrance hole and asked a fireman to play some water on his face. As he lifted the second extinguisher into the loft, he knew he could put out the rest of the flames, but when that one was empty there were still flickerings here and there and the third one was passed up. He felt confident that he could very soon finish the job. But he did not reckon on the local fire-brigade!

Just at that moment some roof tiles began to fall from above, narrowly missing him, and he looked up to see the firemen breaking a large hole in the roof so that water could be thrown in, in the traditional way. He tried to tell them to desist as fresh air would make the flames burst forth again. They continued to remove tiles and received a blast from the extinguisher! At the same moment the floor began to give way under him as another team of the fire-brigade broke through the floor with poles — again he shouted at them but they insisted on doing their job.

He moved to a corner, reflecting that he might either be roasted alive, decapitated by a falling tile from above or skewered by a pole from below. He did survive and managed to extinguish the fire completely. However, this science teacher extraordinary spent the next two days recovering in bed and thinking about his near-cremation.

*   *   *

He had arrived in Japan on 25 October 1871 at the request of W.E. Griffis to take up a position teaching science to Japanese students in Shizuoka. Once in Yokohama, he was met by officials of the 'Daijokan' — Council of State — and asked to sign his contract. As he read through the English translation, he found a clause that forbade him from teaching Christianity or any religious subject during his three year stay. He was sorely tempted to sign it anyway, for the $300 per month salary was a great deal for a teacher in those days but he stuck to his principles and wrote to the government officials that 'it would be impossible for a Christian to dwell three years in the midst of a pagan people, and keep entire silence on the subjects nearest to his heart.' Surprisingly, it took only three days to have the clause deleted and a new contract drawn up.

During his stay in Japan, Clarke spent much of his time holding Bible classes and trying to convert the 'pagans' as well as, on one occasion, singing hymns and preaching from the Great Buddha (Daibutzu) at Kamakura — much to the annoyance and embarrassment of the ordinary foreign merchants present.

After an adventurous journey to Shizuoka by *kago* and rickshaw, he moved into a temple and began preparations for teaching science at the nearby school. He taught through an interpreter and found great delight and satisfaction in demonstrating experiments to his students who were very anxious to learn from him. He was impressed by their quickness of mind and the rapid progress they made.

His house-servant and cook was the renowned 'Sam Patch' who proved his worth in cooking bread, pies and puddings — delights to an American palate so far from any bakery. Sam seems to have been a lovable buffoon, but indispensable to all the foreign people he worked for.

*   *   *

One Saturday, Clarke returned to his temple-home to find that a robbery had taken place. Some of his money was missing, but worse than that, one of his personal body-guards had been murdered by the thief. His fingers had been sliced off by the razor-sharp sword showing that he had tried to resist the attack before the death blow fell. The robber was traced and brought back to Shizuoka to be tried and beheaded. Clarke remarked that 'if it were not too terrible, I could describe the way they sometimes "try" such criminals by torture.' However W.E. Griffis stated in his book written about this time (*The Mikado's Empire, 1876*) that torture was not used to extract evidence after the Meiji Restoration.

This event prompted the authorities to build Clarke a new house and proposed that he designed an American-style house to be built by local artisans. The site was to be in the grounds of the dilapidated Shizuoka Castle, and all went well apart from the construction of the brick chimney. The workmen had never heard of such a thing. It was finally put in last of all after the completed floors and roof had a hole broken through them. He was happy in his new residence apart from the bouts of intense loneliness that was so often experienced by foreigners in these early days.

Clarke's scientific talents and knowledge were used to the full by the people around him. Not only was this 'big, white chief' expected to design his house and explain the mysteries of science, but he was also asked to vaccinate children against smallpox and locate coal mines and gold veins by examining rocks brought to him.

On his frequent excursions into the countryside, he was annoyed by the fleas in *futons* (mattresses) at inns where he slept and by the embarrassment of having to bathe in public, but generally he enjoyed himself. The boar and deer hunts were exciting and provided a goodly supply of meat for his larder. One particular duck shoot, however, he remembered with distaste for some of the participants made him the target! Several times he was shot at but he lived to tell the tale. The only victim that day was a young Japanese boy who died from his wounds some days later.

*   *   *

Back in Shizuoka he continued to amaze audiences with the wonders of science — his electric motors, air-pumps, steam engines, Leyden jars and Whimhurst machines were famous in the area. On one occasion he connected several thousand volts of electricity to a row of armed samurai warriors using a huge Ruhmkorff coil and the shock they received spilt them onto the floor — swords and all! A rather foolhardy demonstration one would have thought, for the samurai blamed the foreigners for upsetting the traditional ways of Japan and causing many of them to be unemployed.

Clarke was the first man to measure the height of Mount Fuji. From the atmospheric pressure and temperature, he calculated the height to be 11,560 feet which is quite close to subsequent measurements made with more precision. Bad weather and frightened, run-away helpers who feared the gods of the mountain did not allow him to use his instruments to their full capacity.

*   *   *

After two long years of lonely isolation in Shizuoka, Clarke was ordered to come to work at the Imperial College in Tokyo. It was not without a little sadness and regret that he left exile and made the hundred-mile journey to the capital accompanied by men carrying his scientific apparatus on their backs. On arriving in Yokohama he experienced a mild 'culture shock' in reverse. He travelled to Shinegawa by the new railway service and was met by Mr Hatakeyama, the Director of Imperial College who had studied in America. He was introduced to some of the other teachers including Dr Veeder, professor of physics. Clarke was appointed professor of chemistry.

Once established in Tokyo, he began to explore the city. The canals fascinated him and he bought a small one-man canoe and paddled himself around observing all the sights from the water. Out on Tokyo Bay, he put up his umbrella and shot along with the wind at a great speed!

*   *   *

The climax of Clarke's stay in Japan, described in the book he published in 1878 called *Life and Adventure in Japan,* was the time he gave a slide show to the Emperor Meiji and his entourage using his 'stereopticon.' Two military bands, comprising a total of 60 musicians, provided the sound-track for the exhibition which mostly showed scenes of different countries.

Windsor Castle, Sandringham and the Houses of Parliament appeared on the screen as the band played 'God Save the Queen,' then scenes of Niagara Falls and New York were shown with the appropriate music, followed by views of France, Italy, Germany and Switzerland. By this time the music from the two massed bands had lost its volume, and Clarke noticed that many of the musicians — from the Naval College — had sneaked into the hall and were enjoying the show just behind the Emperor.

In 1875 Clarke sailed away from Japan never to return.

Chapter 19

Guido Verbeck

THE AMERICAN PROTESTANT missionaries who arrived in Japan immediately after the Treaty Ports were opened in the 1850s were anxious to influence affairs there. They tried to cultivate friends in high places in government, often successfully in the early days, and impart to them their version of Christian truth in the hope that this would influence later decisions of national and international importance. It is not easy to assess the overall, long-term effect of their activities, but it was undoubtedly considerable.

Many of these missionaries were fairly simple men, as their literary efforts reveal, with little formal education or depth of intellectual reasoning. Such people, with merely a childish trust in the words of the Bible, did not realise that it was an impossible aim to attempt to persuade an entire oriental nation to visualise God and Christ as they did. The attempt to impose the Christian religion on Japan, to make the populace slaves to ancient western dogma, was perhaps just as improper as the attempt by cotton farmers in the Deep South in the United States to control the lives of coloured families living there. Very few of the missionaries who arrived were aware of this basic fallacy, but one who did was Guido Fridolin Verbeck.

Verbeck was born in Holland in 1830 and had Dutch nationality, but lost it when, as a young man, he went to America. Refused American citizenship, he spent most of his life a stateless person until a request for Japanese nationality was finally granted in 1891. This may have

influenced his outlook, making it broader and more universal than that
of most other missionaries, and allowing him a more practical vision
which enabled his influence in Japan to be remarkable.

Trained as a civil engineer in Holland, and fluent in four languages,
Verbeck arrived in America in 1852 to operate a foundry owned by the
Reverent Otto Tank, a friend of the family. Isolated Tanktown, however,
did not please him, he wanted to see more of America. 'I am determined
to become a good Yankee,' he told his friends, and by 1855 they had
persuaded him to enter a Theological School associated with the
Reformed Dutch Church in Auburn, N.Y. Here he met Maria Manion,
whom he later married, and the Reverend S.R. Brown who had recently
returned from missionary work in China, and who was anxious to return
to the Far East. On completing his studies at Auburn, Verbeck was
recommended by Brown to Dr Isaac Ferris, in charge of the Reformed
Dutch Missionary Board, as a useful missionary for newly-opened Japan.
The long-standing Dutch-connection at Nagasaki was well known, and
the Board considered a Dutch-speaking missionary with a good education
could aid their purpose. Verbeck was quickly accepted, ordained,
married and sailed from New York for Shanghai in May 1859,
accompanied by his new wife and the Browns.

*   *   *

The voyage round the Cape of Good Hope, stopping at many places of
interest to consult with other missionaries, took nearly six months. The
ship was detained in Hong Kong for one month to repair storm damage.
Leaving his wife, who had conceived a child at the beginning of the long
voyage, in Shanghai, Verbeck reached Nagasaki on 7 November to make
arrangements for accommodation. In this he was assisted by two bachelor
missionaries already in residence, John Liggins and M.C. Williams. He
eventually found a large old house in the Japanese quarter that needed
repair. In the speech of the men he hired for this work, he noticed many
Dutch words had crept into the Japanese language during contact with
Dutch traders in Deshima Island. 'Briki' (blick = tin) and 'giyaman'
(diamond) were uttered by the men as they fitted window glass, as well
as other words of Spanish and Portuguese origin.

On 29 December his wife arrived from Shanghai, heavily pregnant.
Two servants were available to help her with housework and cooking,
and on 26 January 1860 she gave birth to a girl, Emma Japonica, who
was to live only two weeks. But this was to be only the first of nine
children that Maria was to produce over the next 21 years, the last being
born when Verbeck was 51 years old.

Supported by their mission boards, the missionaries began to learn
Japanese. A tedious and frustrating task in those days with no dictionaries
or grammars to aid them. The help offered by old Dr Siebold, who had
lived in Nagasaki from 1823 to 1829 was hardly useful, for he was now
senile and rather eccentric, and not tuned in to the thoughts and

ambitions of these men. However, unlike Yokohama and Tokyo where *ronin* were a constant threat to foreigners and where government spies checked their every move, Nagasaki was a peaceful city. Even so, thieves were a constant menace and Verbeck's house was sometimes robbed. The foreign merchants and seamen generally detested the pious missionary set, and the Catholic priests from France naturally showed little friendship towards them. Verbeck, however, through his strength of character and boundless energy in investigating Japanese society, made several friends and soon he was holding English classes in his own house.

So successful were these classes that Verbeck was invited to become principal of a school of foreign languages and science the government had established in Nagasaki, mainly for training interpreters. The authorities were obviously unaware that Verbeck was secretly teaching two students the words of the Bible, for Christianity was still a prohibited religion up to 1873. Every village and neighbourhood had its edict boards that proclaimed the law, and the anti-Christian edict read: 'The Christian religion has been prohibited for many years. If anyone is suspected, a report must be made at once.' It then listed the rewards, which ranged from 500 silver coins for informing on one's father, to 300 for informing on a family sheltering a Christian. This law, which originated in 1614, made any missionary work in conversion impossible, for the convert would be imprisoned for three years, or until he recanted, then executed at the end of his sentence. As late as 1871, Einsoke Ichikawa died in jail while awaiting trial accused of possession of a Japanese translation of the New Testament. The pleading of several missionaries and the American Ambassador had no effect, the reply being that Japan was not answerable to foreigners for her treatment of Japanese subjects. Previously, treaties in China had ensured special privileges for Chinese Christians, and this had caused much friction. Japan refused to make the same mistake.

*   *   *

Verbeck was always careful in all his activities; often secretive but totally sincere, he was superbly diplomatic, trying to please all and offend none. His letters back to his mission board reporting on his work and progress always made the right sounds, and his dealings with important Japanese officials and with his students, many of whom proceeded to positions of power, reflected his admirable and intuitive understanding of Japanese society. The expert British linguist Ernest Satow was later to recognise traces of American political theory in the Japanese constitution of 1889 written by, among others, Shigenobu Okuma and Taneomi Soejima, both former students with Verbeck in Nagasaki, who had learned their English by studying the American Constitution and the Bible.

At the other end of the social scale, Verbeck seemed concerned at times with the lack of human dignity of the lower classes. His growing

knowledge of the written language allowed him to realise that in carefully
graded public bath-houses, the last pool was for 'Beggars and Horses,'
and the numbering symbols for labourers was the same as for animals.
Reminiscent, perhaps, of the sign erected by the British in a Shanghai
park: 'No Dogs or Chinese.'

The reputation of Verbeck as a sensitive and popular teacher soon
spread through all the southern clans, who, in the civil war and revolution
that took place in 1868, were to support the Emperor and restore him
to a prominent position. When the troubles were over, and when the
Emperor and the new government, which contained a large faction from
the southern clans, were established in Tokyo, Verbeck was asked in
1869 to move to the capital. He was to be the principal of a similar
school for western languages and sciences (Kaisei Gakko), and be
responsible for much of the administration, including the appointment
of foreign teachers for his and other schools. Naturally, he preferred to
appoint like-minded men and obtained a number through the mission
boards in America, including W.E. Griffis, a puritanic and intolerant
character who was the first to publish a biography of Verbeck after his
hero's death. In the rush to open the school, Verbeck had to fill five
teaching positions 'with people I have found in Yokohama.' This
displeased the newcomer, Griffis, who on his arrival accused them of
being 'teachers who would smoke their pipes in the classroom, swear
at the students, absent themselves from their post because alcohol had
fuddled their brains,or would be found in disreputable places.' Verbeck's
hiring of poor-quality teachers (he had no professional qualifications in
education) was to affect his position later, and upset his relationship
with other foreign teachers.

*   *   *

By March 1871, there were 12 foreign teachers at the school where 994
students from the samurai class could learn English, French and German.
The teachers all lived within the compound of the school, and each was
obliged to take two armed guards with him for protection when he left
the compound. Verbeck, in addition to guards, always carried a loaded
gun in the right-hand pocket of his coat when he ventured out.

From his arrival in Tokyo, Verbeck, like all foreigners employed
by the government, was obliged to be an adviser to various government
departments. Two years before their departure,he had given advice to
the members of the Japanese mission who were to travel through the
United States and Europe on a fact-finding and diplomatic tour under
the leadership of his friend, Tomomi Iwakura. It is said that Verbeck
initiated the idea for such a mission, and nine members were former
students of his. The long-term purpose was to bring an end to the
privileges of extra-territoriality (whereby foreigners in Japan were
outside Japanese law, being governed only by their own consul) and to
alter the one-sided tariff controls agreed by Japan under force in the

1.

2.

1. Gankiro teahouse. 2. No.9 Yokohama. 3. Girls from No.9. 4. 1890s pin-up

3.

4.

5.

6.

ペリー艦隊
来航記念碑
The Monument
for the Arrival of
U. S. N. Commodore
Perry's Squadron

5. Matthew Perry. 6. Perry monument,
Shimoda. 7. William Adams memorial at Ito.
8. Rickshaw puller c.1900. 9. Christchurch,
Yokohama.

8.

7.

9.

10. Attack on British legation 1862

11. Laurence Oliphant

12. Henry Dyer

13. Jonathan Goble

14. The Bluff, Yokohama, 1861

15.

16.

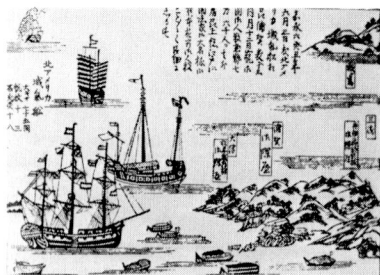

17.

15. 'Life in Japan' c.1900. **16.** Broadsheet announcing Perry's arrival 1853.
17. Monument to first 'daily' of 1871

19.

電信創業の地
明治2年 (1869) 12月25日 この場所にあった横浜電信局と
東京電信局の間にわが国ではじめて電報の取扱が
行なわれました。
昭和38年12月25日
日本電信電話公社

TELEGRAPH SERVICE LAUNCHED HERE

THIS IS THE ORIGINAL SITE IN JAPAN WHERE
TELEGRAPH SERVICE WAS LAUNCHED ON DECEMBER 25, 1869,
UTILIZING THE LINE BETWEEN BOTH YOKOHAMA AND TOKYO
TELEGRAPH OFFICES.
DECEMBER 25, 1963.
NIPPON TELEGRAPH & TELEPHONE PUBLIC CORPORATION

21.

18. Yokohama's fiftieth anniversary 1909. **19.** Osaka mint completed 1870. **20.** Plaque noting first telephone service 1869. **21.** Replica of Brunton's first iron bridge in Yokohama, 1874

22. Ernest Fenollosa

23. William Henry Brunton

24. T.B. Glover

25. W.H. Stone

26. William Eliot Griffis

27. John Milne

28.

29.

THE "FAR EAST"
Back from Europe.
The latest fashion in ORIENTAL mashers.

30.

LONG LIVE JAPAN!

Our Allies

Copyright

31.

32.

WOOD LANE ENTRANCE JAPAN-BRITISH EXHIBITION

28. Coaling at Nagasaki. **29.** Satirical British postcard c.1900. **30.** Postcard commemorating Anglo-Japanese Alliance of 1901. **31.** Postcard commemorating 1921 Crown Prince visit to Britain. **32.** Japan-British Exhibition 1910 (Wood Lane, London)

33. Clive Holland. 34. Japanese oil wells 1919. 35. Devastation of 1923 earthquake. 36. Ginza Beer Hall during US Occupation

NIPPON BEER   GINZA BEER HALL TOKYO JAPAN

treaties. On their return, Iwakura and other members were so impressed by the importance they had observed of Christianity in western life that they immediately recommended complete religious freedom in Japan, and the removal of the edict boards. For if this was not done, the Iwakura Mission agreed, Japan would never be regarded as an equal by other nations. Soon, all the anti-Christian edict boards had disappeared. This, together with the Gregorian calendar which had been adopted earlier in the year (1873) also to appease western nations, caused the missionaries to praise God and their own influence!

By the summer of 1873, the strain of work forced Verbeck to take a rest and he returned to Zeist, his birthplace. From there he visited Vienna and London, crossed the Atlantic to New York and sailed from San Francisco for Japan. All without a passport of any kind!

When he returned he found the school was being reorganised to become part of Imperial College, and he accepted a post as an attaché or adviser to the Genroin (senate) with special emphasis on education. He advised on curricula, on qualification regulations for foreign teachers, and he recommended that German, rather than Dutch or British, medical studies be introduced because of German superiority in medicine at the time. Most of his ideas were implemented, and were to affect future development. He held this position until 1877, and then the Emperor awarded him with the Imperial Order of the Rising Sun, Third Class. Verbeck was a man of broad learning and not a specialist, and progress in Japan now demanded specialists. He was no longer needed and his association with the Japanese government ended. Also a great anti-western movement had developed that blamed western influences, especially Christianity, for Japan's problems. Most Japanese intellectuals who were Confucian in their thinking preferred the more pragmatic and rationalistic philosophies from Europe, and books appeared that severely criticised Christian doctrine and practices. By 1883 there were only 4000 adult Japanese church members through the whole country.

*   *   *

Despite all this, Verbeck had always maintained his integrity and was still well appreciated in many circles. He was offered a teaching post in the exclusive 'Kuazuko Gakko' (Peers' School for young noblemen), but he refused it as he did not want to be reduced to 'the drudgery of teaching spelling and grammar.' 'Leave mere secular teaching to secular teachers,' he proclaimed, for it was as a revivalist preacher in Japan that he saw his next rôle.

But first there were family matters; his elder children were taken to a school in California, and he recovered his health again by resting there a few months. His return to Japan saw him undertaking a series of preaching tours, and becoming increasingly involved in the translation of Christian literature. This activity was to last almost two decades, interspersed with some teaching and lecturing at the Peers' School and some missionary schools in Tokyo. In March 1891, now 61 years old,

Verbeck applied to the Japanese Minister of Foreign Affairs, Viscount Awoki, to enquire if he and his family could acquire passports as they had lived in Japan for over 30 years. On 4 July the reply granting this request arrived and enclosed was a document entitled 'Special Passport' that bore the names of each member of the Verbeck family. After 40 years as a stateless person, he now assumed Japanese nationality as an unprecedented favour by the government.

In early 1898, Verbeck's health once more deteriorated, but he remained active almost to his last breath, preaching, writing and planning to present a Japanese translation of the Bible to the Emperor. Then on 10 March, he died, and was buried at Aoyama. The Emperor donated 500 yen for funeral expenses, and the funeral was attended by representatives of the Imperial Court and many other officials, as well as friends and ex-students. Tributes to his life and work in Japan followed in the press in America and Japan: a man whose influence was remarkable during the late Bakumatsu and early Meiji eras.

Chapter 20

Ernest Fenollosa

'YOU HAVE TAUGHT my people to know their own art; in going back to your great country, I charge you, teach them also!' was the order given by the Meiji Emperor to Ernest Fenollosa in 1886. This was seconded by Professor Yaichi Haga who stated: 'An American, Fenollosa, taught us how to admire the unique beauty of our art.' Such was the praise bestowed upon the 33-year-old Harvard graduate who had worked in Japan for just eight years and who was, through his translations of Noh plays and Japanese poetry, to influence the work of Ezra Pound and W.B. Yeats. Also European Impressionist painters like Monet, Cézanne and Van Gogh were to come under the spell of traditional Japanese art thanks to the efforts of Fenollosa and his associates.

Due to Japanese enthusiasm and wonder for all western achievements after the Meiji Restoration, and the disruptions in Japanese society that this caused, little time and money were found for traditional Japanese art. Most of the efforts of ambitious Japanese artists appeared to be directed towards the techniques of western artists — imitating them, emulating them and, like their military counterparts, endeavouring to surpass them. Fenollosa had had some training and practice as a painter and could appreciate the difficult techniques as represented by the works of sumi-e and ukiyo-e artists and by the sculpture as found in Japan's temples and castles.

Fenollosa was also not without an appreciation of the commercial value of such art, and accumulated a vast collection for himself. He was in a privileged position: he worked for the Japanese government and was thus free to travel anywhere in Japan, he was well paid and so had funds to pursue his interests. He learned the language and studied Japan's history and culture. In this way he became aware of the aesthetic and artistic qualities of Japanese art that is not always appreciated by those born into the society.

                         *   *   *

Born in 1853, the year that Commodore Perry first sailed into Tokyo Bay with his 'Black Ships', Fenollosa was the son of a Spanish concert musician who had earlier arrived from Malaga with a military band. Settling in Salem, Massachusetts, and setting himself up as a music teacher, the father had married one of his students whose family had a shipping business that traded in the Far East. From an early age, young Ernest became familiar with treasures from the East — porcelain, silks and lacquerware.

The family was Episcopalian, after the father had rejected his Roman Catholic upbringing, and at Harvard University Fenollosa helped to found the Herbert Spencer Club. Spencer's philosophy and his interpretation of evolution in terms of the unity of nature and the interrelationships of all phenomena appealed to Fenollosa, as it did to his friend Lafcadio Hearn, and was responsible for his intuitive understanding of the concepts of Shintoism and Buddhism during his studies in Japan.

Friends of the Fenollosa family in Salem included George Peabody and Edward S. Morse, and it was Morse, who had spent some time in Japan teaching and studying fossils, who used his influence to have Fenollosa appointed in 1878 as a lecturer in political economy and philosophy at the University of Tokyo. This university relied mostly on American and European lecturers to pave the way to industrialisation and 'modernisation,' and all the students had to learn English first in order to follow the lectures. Many of the students — Japan's future leaders - were confused by the variety of western ideas presented to them by young graduates of Harvard or Oxbridge with their diverse range of accents and idiomatic expressions.

A few days after his arrival in Tokyo, Fenollosa visited some curio shops and purchased a selection of traditional wall-hangings which appealed to him. His interest was aroused and he wanted to find out more about such art. But all he found was that very little had been written in English on Japanese art by that time, and in conversation with his friends Viscount Kaneko and Marquis Kuroda he found out that no art museums existed. Many private collections had been broken up as daimyo had lost their wealth and given their accumulation of art objects to their samurai and retainers. Some retainer families had been dismissed after serving their master's family for several centuries. Eventually these art treasures appeared in the general market.

Kuroda, however, had managed to keep his collection intact, but remarked: 'An American cannot judge; this art is beyond him.' Fenollosa, however, was amazed when he examined Kuroda's collection of art objects, and after a short study of recent history realised what was happening in Japan. Most Japanese now regarded their own traditional art as barbaric and obsolete, all eyes were towards the West. French and Italian professors were teaching Japanese students the techniques of European art, while Japanese masters from old families found no outlet for their superb work. No schools would employ them because of the westernisation policy. The soft sumi-e brush had been replaced by the hard pencil.

*   *   *

When the first western tourists arrived at the treaty ports in Japan they were often offered valueless bric-a-bac made by tenth-rate craftsmen who cheaply produced goods specifically for the foreign market. This mass of worthless trivia was sold either as genuine antiques or the work of masters of art. Only ukiyo-e woodblock prints, which had previously been regarded as low-class art by the Japanese, survived with any form of authenticity but here, too, much rubbish was produced for the new market. Many hereditary masters had given up practising their art altogether. Kano Hogai, the elderly head of the Kano school, supported himself by selling baskets and brooms and his wife did weaving to help their miserable income. Fenollosa searched him out and began taking lessons from him, paying him $12 per month from his $500 salary. Old Kano was a friend of Fenollosa until his death in 1888. 'The greatest Japanese painter of recent times...my most valued teacher,' remarked Fenollosa, who later wrote a poem about him.

It was only during his summer vacations that Fenollosa could study art and travel around Japan in search of art treasures from the past. Intercourse between the old *han* (fiefs) had been very limited, and so the new Meiji government had no idea what art treasures existed across their now united country. Fenollosa set about documenting all that he found. By 1882 he was appointed by the government to carry this out full-time, and two years later he was made Commissioner of Fine Arts for the Japanese Empire. The other Imperial Commissioner was Okakura Kakuzo, author of *The Book of Tea,* and together they helped organise the Imperial Art School in Tokyo which was designed to preserve and encourage the traditional arts of Japan.

Out amongst the ancient temples and castles, many of which were run-down, Fenollosa discovered treasure after treasure. Some he bought from impoverished priests and some he merely photographed or sketched. In the Yamanaka emporium in Osaka, for example, he bought a masterpiece by Monotonobu for 25 yen; two decades later it was worth thousands. In 1884, at the Horiuji temple in Nara, he and Okakura found one of the most beautiful statues of ancient Korean art. It stood in the Yumedono pavilion that had not been opened for 200 years. At first the priests were reluctant to reopen it and predicted earthquakes and destruction if anyone entered. But Fenollosa's insistence and his government papers made them relent. 'I shall never forget our feelings as the long-disused key rattled in the rusty lock,' he wrote. 'Within the shrine appeared a tall mass closely wrapped about in swathing bands of cotton cloth upon which the dust of ages had gathered.' After unwinding 500 metres of the cloth 'the final folds of the covering fell away, and this marvellous statue, unique in the world, came forth to human sight for the first time in centuries. It was a little taller than life, but hollow in the back, carved most carefully from some hard wood which had been covered with gilding, now stained to the yellow brown of bronze. The head was ornamented with a wonderful crown of Korean open-work gilt bronze, from which hung long streamers of the same material set with jewels. We saw at once that it was the supreme masterpiece of Korean creation.'

*   *   *

That year Fenollosa wrote to Morse: 'Of course it is natural that some of the old fogy Japanese are suspicious and unwilling to trust me. I am proving that some of their supposed treasures are relatively worthless and bringing forth the real gems from unknown holes. I have bought several pictures dating from 700 and 900 A.D. Already people here in Tokyo are saying that my collection must be kept here in Japan for the Japanese. I have bought a number of the very greatest treasures secretly. The Japanese as yet do not know I have them. I wish I could see them all safely housed forever in the Boston Art Museum; and yet, if the Emperor or the Mombusho (government education ministry) should wish to buy my collection, wouldn't it be my duty to humanity to let them have it?' Morse replied: 'Many fine things of Japanese art are now in the market, like those we are buying. It is like the life-blood of Japan seeping from a hidden wound. They do not know how sad it is to let their beautiful treasures leave the country.'

Shortly afterwards, Okakura explained the situation to government officials in Tokyo, emphasising the urgency, and the law of 'Koko Ho' (national treasures) was passed. This required that each piece of ancient art should be registered and it restricted their export. Soon national museums of art were opened in Tokyo, Nara and Kyoto.

Meanwhile, Fenollosa had sold his entire collection of over one thousand paintings to Dr Weld of Boston! These now make up the famous Weld-Fenollosa collection in the Boston Museum of Fine Art.

By 1885 there came a swing in Japan away from blind westernisation. All schools reintroduced the use of Japanese ink, paper and brushes for art classes. A new nobility was created from the heirs of the old court aristocracy, including samurai, and they had power in a House of Peers set up to balance the elected lower house. Fewer and fewer foreigners were employed by the Japanese government in this swing, the first of many, towards nationalism. In the field of traditional art there was a revival, and Fenollosa felt that his efforts had been all worthwhile.

*   *   *

Before the Meiji Restoration, every daimyo possessed his own Noh stage and collection of props. Performances were an essential part of official ceremonies. But after the restoration this type of theatrical art disappeared completely. Minoru Umewaka was a Noh actor in the Shogun's main troupe. When Perry's fleet arrived he was performing in the Shogun's garden and the news stopped the play for a time. In the years that followed fewer performances took place, the stages and props were destroyed and the actors sought other employment.

In 1871, Umewaka began to train his two sons in the ancient art; he bought a stage from an impecunious daimyo, and purchased masks, robes, etc. from other nobles. He gathered around him some of the old actors. His own texts and stage directions had been preserved and soon he was mounting private performances. A decade later Fenollosa met Umewaka and it was found that the American was quite proficient in performing some Noh songs and chants. For the next two years he studied the postures, dances and chants under Umewaka, and he made rough translations of about 50 of the texts. It was Ezra Pound, Fenollosa's literary executor, who later rewrote some of these as well as other translations of oriental poetry by Fenollosa. W.B. Yeates had access to all this material which inspired his first dance play 'At the Hawk's Well.'

*   *   *

In 1896, Fenollosa resigned his post as Commissioner of Fine Arts and returned to America to become the Curator of Oriental Art at the Boston Museum. Five years later he left his wife, divorced and married again — quite a scandal at that time in Boston and it forced his resignation. The next year he returned to Tokyo with his new wife, teaching English and continuing his studies of Japan's culture. This lasted until 1907 when he returned once again to America where he met with great success and popularity from his lecture tours specialising in oriental aesthetics. In 1908 he led a group of students on a tour of European art museums. In London in the September of that year he died suddenly. At first his ashes were interred at Highgate cemetry near the remains of Karl Marx, but a short time afterwards the bronze casket was transported to Japan. It was buried near the Miidera temple under some cryptomeria trees overlooking Lake Biwa. A large stone monument was erected to him at the Tokyo Art School, and under the chiselled bust the poet Yone Noguchi's words proclaimed that Fenollosa was 'the very discoverer of Japanese art for Japan.'

Chapter 21

John Black and Japan's
Early Newspapers

SOME HISTORIANS claim that newspapers existed in Japan long before the arrival of westerners in the mid-nineteenth century, citing, for example, the woodblock-printed daily bulletins that the Shogun, Iyeyasu, sent back to his ministers in Yedo in 1600 during the battle of Sekigahara. Similar sheets appeared when the Black ships arrived in 1853, but unlike the earlier example, these were sold to the general public on the street. By this time the authorities had allowed unofficial newsletters to circulate — these were called *Yomiuri* meaning 'read and sell' — which were hawked about the streets by vendors who read portions of them out loud. Their contents were very concise and factual and no attempt was made to comment or criticise. They were more like broadsheets that circulated in England during Shakespeare's time.

However it was only with the arrival of westerners in Japan that western-style newspapers began to appear. As G.B. Sansom says: 'The development of the press in Japan is a definite example of direct western influence, since newspapers published by foreign residents in Japan provided an example that the Japanese could study at first hand.' Quite soon after the opening of the Treaty ports the foreign residents started to publish their own newspapers. The first was the *Nagasaki Shipping List and Advertiser* (1861) which was concerned mostly with commerce; less than a year later it became the weekly Japan Herald under British management. The American-owned *Japan Express* followed in 1862 and a few years later the *Japan Gazette,* as well as the famous *Japan Punch,* produced by Charles Wirgman, came into existence.

The most prominent journalist in Japan at that time was the Scotsman J.R. Black. His stay in Japan was only by chance. He was in his thirties when he arrived in Yokohama in about 1864 (the exact date is unknown) on his way from Australia to Britain. Up to that time his life had been a failure for, even though he had received a good education and studied at Christ's Hospital, London, and then trained for a career in the Royal Navy as was the tradition in his family, he soon decided that the navy would not make him the type of man he wanted to be. He left the navy and went to southern Australia, attracted by the gold rush, to start a business along with his wife, Charlotte Elizabeth. Their first son, Henry James, was born there. Sadly things went wrong and they decided to return to England to try to make a new start. The ship stopped over in Yokohama for a few days and Black met Albert W.

Hansard, a businessman, who also published the *Japan Herald* — a weekly that came out every Saturday. Hansard and Black discussed the development of Japan, Black doing most of the listening. He became interested in staying but doubted his ability to succeed amongst the tough, hard-headed businessmen that inhabited the settlement in Yokohama at that time, especially after his previous failures. Hansard, recognising the quick mind and good educational background of Black, and being a hard businessman himself, offered Black the job of editor-in-chief of his *Japan Herald.* The *Herald* had become the official organ for the publications of the foreign legations in Japan and had no small influence on the Japanese government. Black liked the idea of this sort of power and believed that his English education and sense of fair play could be used to help in the development of Japan as an industrial power. He took up the post and worked on the *Herald* until Hansard sold it and returned to England in 1867.

Black was critical of the political manoeuvres taking place in Japan during his time with the *Herald.* He supported the last Shogun, Tokugawa Keiki, and was angry when Keiki was forced to resign his power and retire to Mito — he believed that this had sparked the bloody civil war and the Saga and Satsuma rebellions. However, Black was not aware of the dilemma of the Shogun's government. It had promised the supporters of the Emperor that they would expel all foreigners and revert to being an isolated country just as soon as Japan had learned enough to defend herself against foreign invasion, and also it had promised the foreign governments that Japan would enforce the treaties that had been agreed upon!

As well as matters of high political importance, Black was also concerned in his journalistic career with seemingly trivial affairs in the foreign community and the native community around it. He criticised the sanitary conditions in Yokohama, reported the arrival of Mr Risley and the first circus in Japan and expressed distaste of certain lewd shows taking place in certain quarters. His views were acknowledged, conditions improved and all the offensive shows in Tokyo were closed down.

Delighted with his success on the *Herald* and supported by others in the community, Black started publishing his own newspaper on 12 October 1867 — the *Japan Gazette,* Yokohama's first evening daily — which was an immediate success. After the Meiji Restoration in 1868, he continued to be constructively critical of events and occurrences in Japan but he was becoming more concerned with informing other countries about Japan. He resigned from the Gazette in 1870 and began to publish an illustrated journal that was more of a literary and cultural nature. It was a fortnightly publication called *The Far East* and he intended it to be a vehicle for 'cultivating good-will and brotherhood between the outer world and the subjects of the most ancient imperial dynasty in the world.' It contained travel articles about Japan and China, translations of Japanese literature and news about life in the treaty ports

— all illustrated by photographs taken by both foreign and Japanese cameramen. It soon became very popular and the number of pages increased to forty in 1873. The August edition of 1875 was the last one; Black had found another interest.

Many newspapers had appeared in Japanese by this time but Black was not happy with the situation. In fact he was disgusted. He deplored certain 'filthy paragraphs' that made them 'worse than contemptible in the eyes of foreigners. Also he deplored the censorship laws that had been passed in 1869. Two important vernacular newspapers, the *Mainichi Shimbun* in Yokohama and *The Nishi Shimbun* in Tokyo, were in daily circulation when Black started his *Nisshin Shinjishi* (The Reliable Daily News) but he complained they 'neither dared to write leading articles nor to comment seriously on the occurrences of the day' and that they were 'principally an advertising medium.' He made plans to publish and edit the *Nisshin Shinjishi* — 'the first Newspaper (worthy of the name) ever published in the native language in Japan' — as it says proudly on the title page of an important book that he wrote called *Young Japan*. Whether Black or his publisher made this claim is unknown, for the book was first published after his death.

It was his friend, Mr F. Da Roza, who did most of the preparations for the enterprise and da Roza also appointed the former Vice-Governor of Hakodate as the Japanese editor. These men could not obtain metal kanji type in Tokyo, so they improvised by having several artisans employed in their office cutting the characters in wood. They started with a mere 1200 characters, but almost every day new ones were required to report new stories or ideas and after some time they had accumulated over 12,000 of them — all hand-carved. The first copy came off the press on 23 April 1872 and was immediately popular. It appeared at first only three times a week and consisted of four pages, but within a month it had become a daily and grown to eight pages. Before the end of the year they had found a supply of metal type in Tokyo — at the cost of only one sen each.

The Meiji government saw the value of Black's kind of honest reporting and its thoughtful constructive criticism, and it allowed him to publish under his extra-territorial rights the proceedings of the Sain, one of the chambers of the Council of State. In fact, he was almost encouraged to criticise government policy. The authorities soon regretted granting this freedom to Black, for he revealed the secret facts behind a cabinet crisis and strongly criticised high-ranking officials who lacked proper education, he commented on the arbitary fashion in which the law operated together with the bribery that was so often involved. In an editorial he severely criticised the government's prohibition of publishing news about the 1874 Saga rebellion and later against the intended invasion of Formosa. Black's criticism may have been logical and legitimate, but his outspokenness had caused other vernacular newspapers to emulate his tactics. Dozens had been started.

It seemed, at first sight, impossible for the Japanese government to control Black for he was not subject to Japanese law under the extra-territoriality agreements. However the problem (for the Japanese government) was resolved when Black accepted a post as a foreign adviser to the Japanese government at ¥300 per month plus ¥50 rent allowance. The conditions of his contract swore him to secrecy in his work and he had to sever all connections with his newspaper. He happily signed it. Following Black's appointment, the British Minister was asked to issue an Order in Council forbidding all British subjects to engage in vernacular journalism and, when this was signed, Black was dismissed from his post in July 1875. Naturally he was furious.

In that same year new laws were passed in Japan sharply limiting the freedom of the press, and for two years there was a constant procession of editors and journalists to prison. Editorials became allegorical and ambiguous and many newspapers were published naming dummy editors, who were paid more than the real anonymous editor, but who were willing to spend time in prison. This system lasted well into the twentieth century. In due course, the authorities learned that one way to control a newspaper was to buy it and appoint its own editor.

Black attempted to defy all these new laws and in January 1876 he started yet another newspaper, the *Bankoku Shimbun*. Seven days later the government fined him and punished his workers. The British minister, Sir Harry Parkes, published a regulation that forebade any British subject from publishing a Japanese newspaper — the penalty was three months in prison or a $500 fine. Journalism in Japan ended for Black.

A short time after this Black moved to Shanghai where he started two publications, but in 1879 he returned to Japan in poor health and worked on his book *Young Japan: Yokohama and Yedo 1858 — 1879*. Death overtook him before he finished it and he was buried in Yokohama's foreign cemetery.

His wife died soon afterwards and was buried with him. His son took a Japanese wife and became a Japanese subject with the name Ishii-Buraku. He was an extraordinary character. He had spent most of his childhood in Japan and was fluent in the language. After spending three years at school in England, from his fifteenth to eighteenth year, he returned to Japan and remained there until his death in 1923. By profession he was a traditional Japanese story-teller who travelled over the whole of Japan performing in towns and villages.

Chapter 22

Josiah Conder — Tokyo's Pioneer Architect

A LIFE-SIZED STATUE of the English architect Josiah Conder, made by Japanese artist Taketaro Shinkai, was unveiled on the campus of Tokyo University in 1922. Conder had died two years previously, in June 1920. He had been buried at the Gotokuji Temple in Tokyo while many of the great buildings he had designed and constructed were still standing. But in the year following the dedication of his statue, 1923, the Great Kanto Earthquake caused some of them to collapse in ruins and others to be gutted. Nevertheless, many structures did survive as did his memorial statue which still stands in front of No. 1 Hall of the Engineering Department.

Josiah Conder was born in September 1852 in London and was educated at the Commercial School in Bedford. For four years from the age of 16 he became an articled pupil to Profesor T. Roger Smith during which time he attended courses on the principles of architectural drawing at the South Kensington Art School.

Following this apprenticeship in basic building design and techniques, he became assistant to William Burges in 1874 during which time he attended life-drawing classes at the Slade School of Art. He then transferred again to assist Mr Walter Lonsdale as a cartoon painter and was also concerned with stained glass work and other specialist techniques. In 1875 he made several trips to sketch buildings in England and France. And after he had won the prized Soane Medallion, awarded by the Royal Institute of British Architects (to which he was admitted as a Fellow in 1884) for his design of a country house, he travelled extensively in France and Italy.

But Conder's interest and experience was not limited only to buildings in Europe. His first employer and mentor, Professor Smith of University College, who was twice president of the RIBA, had worked abroad in India where architects had to adapt to a quite different environment. Specialising in public buildings, Smith had built a hospital in Bombay in 1865, and wrote a detailed paper 'On Buildings for European Occupation in Tropical Climates Especially in India.' Thus part of Conder's educational background was this experience of Smith working under difficult circumstances in other countries. So that when Conder was appointed Professor of Architecture at the new Imperial College of Engineering in Tokyo in 1877 at the age of 24, he was fully prepared for the challenge that building in Japan would provide.

The head of Tokyo's Imperial College of Engineering at the time was
Henry Dyer, a young graduate of Glasgow University who had studied
under William Thomson (later Lord Kelvin) and who had arrived as the
founding principal five years earlier. Dyer welcomed Conder and
introduced him to the other young, mostly in their mid-twenties, British
professors and lecturers. One of these was John Milne, later to be known
as the founder of seismology, whose pioneering research on earthquakes
must have considerably influenced Conder's design work.

Soon he was conducting courses for his keen Japanese students who
within a few years were to take part in a huge construction programme
of western-style buildings in every major centre in Japan. Conder was
also employed as an architect to the Ministry of Public Works, and thus
received two salaries like several other of the professors.

Western-style architecture by 1877, prior to Conder's arrival, was
not unknown in Japan. A few strange-looking and unstable houses had
been constructed in the Treaty Ports for the first westerners by eager
Japanese craftsmen determined to please. But such hybrid structures
were not based on any tried and tested building principles; in due course
these attempts to produce foreign-style buildings were described as
'foreign to every known style of architecture.'

However, Thomas James Waters, an Englishman trained as a civil
engineer, had designed and constructed several important buildings:
some barracks for the Imperial Guard in 1871, the government mint at
Osaka and the so-called 'brick-zone' of the fashionable Ginza quarter.
Another Briton, R.H. Brunton, also a civil engineer, had been
constructing lighthouses and other large buildings in Japan using western
techniques since his arrival in 1868. Brunton claimed to have completed
40 public buildings before he left in 1876, and to have trained a great
many Japanese artisans in western building skills, especially carpenters
and metal-workers.

A French architect, C. de Boinville, had arrived in 1872 as an
employee of the Ministry of Public Works. He completed the mint at
Osaka, after Waters' efforts had been set back by a fire, and went on
to build a wool factory at Senju and the auditorium of the Kobu Daigakko
(College of Engineering or 'Dyer's College') which could accommodate
4000 people. 'Two great galleries run round the hall, supported by fifty
or more gilded colonnades,' was how one observer described the interior.
The three-storeyed exterior was impressive with huge neo-Gothic
windows edged with classical columns and a large stone Imperial
chrysanthemum in each upper corner of every floor.

For a while western-style architecture was predominatly French
because of de Boinville. Then, in 1876, the Italian architect, G.V.
Cappelletti, came at the invitation of the Ministry of Public Works to
teach at the Arts School. He later worked for the Imperial Army, building
its General Staff headquarters and the Military Museum. However, it
was Conder who brought a definite general style to such work in Japan,
and although today his name is largely unknown he is acclaimed by

some historians as 'The Father of western architecture in Japan.'

*   *   *

Predictably, one of Conder's major concerns was the centuries-old hazard and dread of fire. Vast numbers of wooden buildings throughout Japan were consumed by fire at an alarming rate. Even 'large dwellings of the nobles,' wrote Conder in 1878 to the RIBA, 'have been burned to the ground through the introduction of European heating appliances into wooden walls without precautions and protection. The Tokyo Foreign Office, one of the purest old Japanese buildings in the capital, which was entirely destroyed this year by fire, is said to have been set on fire from a stove pipe running through a wooden wall without any protection whatever.' As a result of this catastrophe Conder persuaded the authorities that, as far as institutional requirements were concerned, brick buildings should be constructed whenever possible, and arranged for shiploads of bricks to be imported from Britain. Before 1870 brick buildings were unknown in Japan, and it is believed that Conder was responsible for bringing in experienced artisans to set up Japan's own brick-making industry.

Conder's first assignment was Tokyo's School for the Blind — a rather nondescript structure completed in 1878. Next came the museum of antiquities (Tokyo Imperial Museum) at Uyeno, then he designed and decorated reception rooms for the Ministry of Colonisation. This building was later to become the Bank of Japan, and was an exercise in pure western style with chimneys, fireplaces and truss-structure roofs secured with iron bolts. The foundations incorporated a new western technique to help render the building earthquake-proof: after excavating the site on marshy ground near the Sumida River, Conder drove in steel piling around the perimeter then poured in cement onto a timber raft held together in a strong lattice. Upon this base brick piles were placed to support the superstructure. The violent shaking of the 1923 earthquake resulted in the building being completely burned out but the brick structure held firm and remained vertical with no cracking of the walls.

Within four years of his arrival in Japan Conder's talents had been recognised; from 1881-3, for example, he was engaged on a small palace for HIH Prince Kitashirakawa, the Official Guest House known as the *Rokumeikan* ('Deer Cry Pavilion') used for grand balls where foreign and Japanese worthies mixed socially, and a large palace for Prince Arisugawa, the army commander who had suppressed the Satsuma Rebellion of 1877.

By now the first graduates in architecture, tutored and instructed by Conder, had left the Imperial College and were engaged in various building projects around Japan. Within ten years almost all government building work was done using only Japanese architects, but all of those had been Conder's students and his influence was to last well into the twentieth century and the age of reinforced concrete. Men like Tatsuno O. Kingo, Sone Tatsuya and Kawai Kozo continued the newly-introduced tradition of building with bricks and dressed stone in the unique western style that had evolved.

*   *   *

Conder had also become well established in his own private practice as an architect and consultant, supplementing his $400 monthly salary from the government. He built residences for nobles and Ministers of State, the Italian, German and Austrian embassies, along with the Tokyo Club, the Yokohama United Club, Yokohama Royal Hotel, Nagasaki Hotel and the Nicolai (Russian Orthodox) Cathedral. (The Cathedral project was not his own design as he worked from plans of a Russian architect.)

His best work, however, was in the development of the Marunouchi district in central Tokyo as a business centre where in 1890 the Mitsubishi Company had bought 65 acres of barren land from the government. Beginning with Mitsubishi No. 1 Building, completed in 1894, each building had substantial load-bearing brick walls rising through three, four or five storeys to steep tiled roofs with latticed ridge-tiles. The Renaissance windows with simply embellished lintels were large and many, yet in proportion within the total structure showing perfect horizontal punctuation, allowing for bright rooms. The main pedimented entrance was set in the centre of the facade in a protruding tower-porch structure dominated by a steeply-pitched dormer feature which was repeated again at each end as terminal features making for an aesthetic composition. The planning of the whole district with its wide tree-lined boulevards was equally pleasing to the senses. The interiors were in a grand style where classical columns with Corinthian capitals and high ceilings with decorated friezes gave a feeling of space and was also functional. These buildings not only survived the 1923 earthquake but the 1945 bombings as well.

Conder only left Japan for short periods between his arrival in 1877 and his death in 1920. In 1881 he married a Japanese girl, Kameko Mayeba, and they had one daughter, Helen Aiko, who married a retired Swedish naval officer, Commander L. Grut, in 1906. In later life Conder enjoyed being with his six grandchildren, even though the boys attended school in Sweden. Conder's death occurred just eleven days after that of Kameko.

Josiah Conder's work in Japan was well appreciated at the time and in 1884 he was decorated with the Order of the Rising Sun (Fourth Class.) Ten years later he was awarded the Order of the Sacred Treasure (Third Class) and the official rank of Chokunin. He was the first honorary president of the Society of Japanese Architects, and after he ceased lecturing at Tokyo Imperial University he held the title of Emeritus Professor of Architecture there.

As a member of the Asiatic Society of Japan he contributed papers on traditional Japanese costumes, armoury and gardening, but his longer works on domestic architecture, especially that of theatres, and landscape gardening brought detailed knowledge of Japan to the West and his books are still classics. For in Europe during this era, beginning in about 1870, there existed a passionate appreciation of Japanese art which had probably been introduced to Conder by his mentor, William Burges, during his earlier years in London. The Anglo-Japanese room designed by Whistler and Godwin in the 1878 International Exhibition in Paris helped to spread this enthusiasm, and in many of Conder's decorative designs and motifs on wallpaper particularly, the influence was naturally strong. So in some ways even Conder's western expertise and style was influenced by the ancient arts of Japan.

In 1962, Professor E. Thagaki of Tokyo University, the descendant of Conder's old college, wrote that Conder 'was regarded as the leading architect in Japan during his time. He made it his aim to develop a new style that would be suited to the Japanese climate and topography, and his efforts to achieve that goal can be seen in his buildings.' This is a fitting tribute to an architect who built bridges between East and West, even though now most of his original structures have disappeared because of Japan's accelerated economic development and the demands on space in over-crowded central Tokyo.

Chapter 23

Captain Frank Brinkley

THE SEVERED HEAD with congealed blood adhering to it, had been impaled on an iron spike and placed next to the entrance of Yoshida Bridge which led across to the Yokohama settlement. Guards watched over it for three days, and the inscription in Japanese characters below told how Shimizu Seiji had been executed by the sword for his part in the murder of two British soldiers.

Major Baldwin and Lieutenant Bird, of H.M. 20th Regiment, had been visiting the shrine at Enoshima Island and the Great Daibutsu at Kamakura on horseback in November 1864. They were riding along the coast when from behind two figures appeared wielding razor-sharp swords. With one swift upward stroke, Baldwin was cut from his hip to his shoulder, his spine sliced right through. Bird, riding just ahead, heard Baldwin's body fall dead to the ground, drew his revolver and fired one shot at his assailant before he, too, felt slash after slash of the sword's blade deep in his flesh.

These murders brought to 30 the total number of foreigners slaughtered since the opening of Japan in the late 1850s. The irony of it was that the 20th Regiment had been transported to the Japanese Treaty Ports to prevent such murders taking place. The theory was that a strong military presence would deter such attacks, for the political instability made the newcomers — diplomats and businessmen alike — afraid and nervous. Japan was still divided into 34 feudal territories, each under an independent daimyo, and there was intense conflict between those who welcomed foreign trade and those who supported the continuation of a policy of isolation. Rebellions, murders, sabotage and arson resulted from these conflicts in 'Old Japan,' and it was never clear to foreign diplomats where power lay and who to deal with. For the Shogun, the absolute military leader over all the daimyo, was unable to maintain his leadership with such chaos raging.

Sir Rutherford Alcock, the British consul-general, demanded immediate action by the Roju (Shogun's senior officials) to trackdown and punish the offenders. As the law stood in Japan, it was not a crime to kill foreigners, indeed it was encouraged in some quarters. But this time action was taken, the assassins were captured, tried and executed in the presence of British officials, and for the first time in Japan's history, the murder of foreigners was publicly declared to be a crime. Alcock was pleased with this sign of progress and showed his approval by granting the request of the Japanese Commissioners for Foreign Affairs for the appointment of British military instructors to train Japanese.

It was a strange and complex diplomatic relationship that existed. Western nations had imposed unequal treaties on Japan by a show of military force, insisting on extra-territoriality and special trading privileges. But when trouble arose, inspired by indignant samurai, Britain and France sent for their militia to protect the new settlers. The military was used to impose and influence the Japanese code of justice, making affairs even more unequal and tending dangerously towards colonialism. One of the 1200 British troops stationed in Yokohama and fully aware of this delicate balance of power was Lieutenant Francis Brinkley.

*   *   *

Born in Ireland of English parents in 1841, Brinkley had been educated for the British army, and after passing out of Woolwich, he entered the Royal Artillery as a gunner. His battery was stationed in Hong Kong for a short time, but was then ordered to Yokohama. In his early twenties, he was impressed by Japan and its people, and made efforts to learn the language and customs, and to appreciate the unique art found there. He was never to regret these early struggles, nor to lose his enthusiasm for the country, for he spent the rest of his life in Japan and made his own contributions to Japan's modernisation programme.

Brinkley became one of the first foreign instructors in the embryonic Japanese navy. It seems odd these days that a soldier trained in the British army could be employed by the navy of another country. No doubt his fluency in Japanese was an important factor, and his connections with the diplomatic corps also provided a lever. There was a great rivalry and intrigue at this level between western nations to aid

Japan's developing institutions. Japan chose, with some persuasion from Alcock and his successor Harry Parkes, that her navy was to follow British lines, whereas her army was to be influenced by German methods.

Historians disagree on the details of Brinkley's early career with the Japanese navy. One American professor reports that, at the age of 26 Brinkley worked for the Navy Ministry (Institute of Gunnery) under the Military Affairs Minister for the Fukui han (fief) from 1867 to 1871. On the other hand, a British expert reports that in 1870 Brinkley began to work with a new Meiji administration along with Lieutenant A.G.S. Hawes. His obituary in The Times seems to favour the latter thesis.

After the beginning of the Meiji era in 1868, records become clearer. Clearer, but no less odd. Brinkley did work for the Imperial Navy Ministry until 1873 as a gunnery instructor along with Hawes, and his salary was $500 per month. Then at $412 per month, he became Head of the Navy School, where he taught only English. And finally, at a salary of $350 per month, he worked for the Public Works Ministry from 1878 to 1880 as an English and mathematics teacher. This steady plunge in salary and change in duties reflects Japan's determination to form a navy independent of foreign support, as well as Brinkley's adaptability and his determination to remain in Japan.

Hawes and Brinkley were asked to teach the naval recruits in English, using an interpreter. But the inaccuracies that occurred when his instructions were translated led Brinkley to insist that he taught in Japanese; at the same time he wrote a textbook for the study of English. Hawes, who was a retired officer in the Royal Marine Light Infantry, had a more intimate knowledge of the workings of the British Navy, and his mission was to organise 'the system of instruction and discipline to be observed in the Japanese men-of-war ships.' In doing this, he had to break with many old traditions which angered his sword-bearing ex-samurai students. He pointed out the political dangers of having all the officers and men on one ship from the same *han,* and insisted they should be mixed. He introduced uniforms, and abolished the carrying of swords.

By 1872, a pattern of instruction had been established by Brinkley and Hawes which in turn formed part of the academic base for the Imperial Naval College which opened that year. More instructors were sought from England, and in July 1873 a mission of 33 men under Commander A.L. Douglas arrived to serve in Japan for three years. Douglas, sometimes referred to as 'the father of the Japanese Navy,' was a strict disciplinarian but was not allowed, under the terms of his contract, to inflict punishment on any Japanese subordinate or seaman for violation of regulations! But as most of the men were ex-samurai with a strict military code themselves, this caused no problems. Furthermore, Douglas and the other foreign instructors were forbidden to engage in any business beyond their work; but his generous monthly salary of $320 made that easy to bear. Even the ordinary seamen in the mission received $36.

The naval cadets, 129 in the first year, spent three years in the college and then a final year training on ships. One of these was the old *HMS Beagle,* associated with Charles Darwin and his historic voyage around the world gathering evidence for his theory of evolution, which had been bought from Britain and renamed the *Kenko*. The seamanship of these early cadets impressed the British commander of the China Station, who wrote that they were 'admirably smart, rapid and silent,' and 'their performance on deck could not have been surpassed on British ships.'

In 1871, 12 Japanese naval cadets went to England to study with the Royal Navy. Amongst them was Heihachiro Togo, the future admiral so skilful in the Russo-Japanese War of 1904/5 when his heroic efforts earned him the title of 'the Nelson of Japan.' After his four years' study on English training ships (he was refused entry into the English Naval College), Togo made a 30,000 mile voyage to Australia via Cape Horn on the sailing ship *HMS Hampshire*. On returning to England, he studied mathematics at Cambridge University before returning to Yokohama in May 1878 on the *Hiei,* which was a new corvette built at Kingston-upon-Hull in north-east England for the infant Japanese Navy. Britain supplied many naval vessels to Japan during this period, but ship-building facilities at Yokosuka, supervised by French engineers, were developing so that larger and stronger men-of-war could be built locally.

Japan's Imperial Navy steadily grew in size and potency until, under admiral Togo, within 30 years of the passing out of the first cadets, it totally destroyed the Russian Navy in the straits between Japan and Korea. By the 1920s it had become so large that America and Britain tried to find ways of restricting its size. The London Naval Conference of 1930 insisted that the ratio of British, American and Japanese warships should be 5-5-3. This arms limitation agreement was designed to ensure world peace and stability. However, the aggressive militarists were now grasping power in Japan, and the quality of naval personnel had changed. As Edwin Reischauer put it: 'The samurai colouring of the officers of early Meiji days had been largely lost. By the twenties, military officers, like most other Japanese leaders, were the products of an educational system, not of a social class. The army and navy were among Japan's most modern institutions, but in their ideas, many officers were closer to the peasants than were other leaders.' The educational system had dehumanised the military leaders who, in the face of an escalating population, food and energy problems, used simple, irrational slogans of propaganda to stir the majority into accepting the inevitability of war. Those intelligent enough to seek escape from such cancerous processes, found that the relatively empty lands of Australia, Canada and America had erected barriers against Japanese immigrants. Eventually, with World War II, the Imperial Japanese Navy was totally destroyed.

*   *   *

Perhaps Brinkley would have been saddened if he had lived to be a centenarian and saw the destruction of an institution he had helped to create. But he was a realist, and his vision changed with age, for his energies were later directed towards more constructive pursuits. Fighting his monocular military education, he became more of an individualist. His friendship with the volatile Charles Rickerby, who had been an English resident in Yokohama since 1862, changed his attitude to life. Rickerby had resigned as manager of the Central Bank of Western India, the first bank in Japan, to become the first editor and part-owner of the very first *Japan Times,* in 1865. In 1878, after several upsets with his colleagues for criticising injustices inflicted upon Japan by foreign officialdom, his *Japan Times, New Series* published Brinkley's work *Times of Taiko* in several instalments. Taiko was Hideyoshi, a folk hero who helped to unite Japan during the anarchic sixteenth century.

Three years later, Brinkley was appointed editor-in-chief of Rickerby's new paper, the *Japan Mail,* which incorporated the old *Japan Times.* The *Mail,* a fortnightly of 28 or 32 pages, contained all shipping movements, including complete passenger lists, as well as details of the Yokohama Race Meets and proceedings in the Consular Courts. The Asiatic and Seismological Societies reported their meetings in its pages, and numerous articles of literary, artistic and scientific interest appeared, including one headed 'Japanese Elephants' by Dr Naumann who had discovered some fossil remains at Yokosuka. New laws and regulations, rickshaw fares for example, that may concern foreigners were detailed, and one section printed letters to the editor. There was little advertising, mostly for fire insurance.

A plethora of foreign newspapers had by this time sprung up, each rivalling the other in their myopic criticism of the Japanese government But the *Mail* stood aloof, and was the only voice supporting the government for the revision of the unequal treaties, although Brinkley endorsed Rickerby's view that his newspaper had a right to criticise the government in a friendly way and offer advice. Through the long and intimate understanding of Japan by Brinkley and Rickerby, the *Mail* gained the reputation of being the only foreign newspaper that tried to interpret the Japanese position fairly. Strict censorship laws controlled Japanese newspapers but did not affect foreign ones, some of which delighted in libellous accusations against members of the government. The*Mail* opposed the blatant anti-Japanese ravings of the *Japan Herald* and *Gazette,* and accused them of abusing the 'freedom of the press.' For this, a caricature of Brinkley appeared in the *Japan Punch,* depicting him as a 'Japanese Flunky.' The *Hyogo News* of Kobe implied that the *Mail* was in the pay of the government, to which Brinkley replied: 'This paper is not an official organ in any sense of the word. It receives no subsidy whatsoever from the Japanese Government, and the opinions expressed in its columns are entirely the outcome of independent conviction.'

By this time Brinkley was involved in many activities in Japan. He was on the boards of many companies, including the NYK shipping company, and he did translation work for the authorities, including

material for the Columbian Exposition of 1893 in Chicago. He began
to write monumental history texts: *Japan and China* (1903) and *A History
of the Japanese People* (1912) with Baron Kikuchi who, in the foreword,
wrote: 'A history of Japan has indeed long been a desideratum. Now
just the right man has been found in the author who, an Englishman by
birth, is almost Japanese in his understanding of, and sympathy with,
the Japanese people.' He was also asked to write the section on 'Japan'
for the *Encyclopaedia Britannica,* and was chief correspondent for *The
Times* of London for 15 years. In 1885, Brinkley was proclaimed 'a
well-known connoisseur, and without doubt, our greatest authority upon
Oriental Keramics' when he held an exhibition and sale of 800 pieces
of his porcelain and pottery collection at the Edward Grey Gallery in
New York.

*   *   *

Captain Frank Brinkley received his rank from the Japanese Navy and
was decorated by the Emperor. He married 'an accomplished Japanese
lady' who, according to *The Times,* 'presided over his house with the
inborn tact and unassuming grace peculiar to the best type of Japanese
womanhood.' Their children, according to the male-orientated
nationality laws that still hold today, could only be British even though
they were born in Japan. His daughter, who chose to spend her life in
Yokohama, was required to register annually as an alien at the
Immigration Office! But as she grew older during the post-war era, she
kept forgetting to undertake this duty on time, much to the chagrin of
the authorities. Her devoted friends, in a similar position themselves,
had to conduct this dear lady to the office, help her fill in the appropriate
forms, and make peace and order between the authorities and one of
the offspring of one of Japan's true sons! For Brinkley, when he died
in Tokyo in October 1912, had spent his last 50 years working in Japan
and had seen at first hand the country change from a state of antiquated
feudalism and civil war to an industrial country allied to Britain on equal
terms, and capable of destroying a western nation with the latest
techniques of warfare.

Chapter 24

Edmund Holtham — Railway Engineer

THE FIRE THAT DESTROYED Edmund Holtham's Tokyo house in
February 1880 consumed the notes and materials he had been secretly
collecting for his 'great work.' But the book he did eventually publish

in London three years later, entitled *Eight Years in Japan, 1873-1881,* revealed better than any other the achievements and frustrations of British engineers who worked in Japan during early Meiji years.

Holtham arrived in Yokohama on a clear, calm day in November 1873 with a contract to the Ministry of Public Works; there was no one to welcome him so he spent a quiet weekend at the Grand Hotel enjoying oysters and wine. After making contact with the Chief Railway Engineer, R. Vicars Boyle, he spent three weeks inspecting the one existing Tokyo/Yokohama railway line that had opened the previous year, and which had so many engineering faults that it had to be completely remade, under Holtham's supervision, in 1878. He then sailed for Kobe to begin his work in earnest. Registering at the British consulate, requiring a fee of $5, he and some other newly-arrived fellow engineers entered the Kobe Club with its billiard tables, bowling alley and library where they became acquainted with 'fifty wild young merchant princes, all very affable and condescending.'

The following day confirmed his observations on the Tokyo/Yokohama line, that 'railway engineering in Japan was not as railway engineering elsewhere,' for there were several obvious errors in the iron construction work of the Kobe station and its workshops, while the walls for a 45 cm. water channel under the track 'would have served for the abutments of a 50-foot bridge'! Along the track under preparation he found three tunnels, two for a single line and the other for a double line. The explanation lay with a communication error, according to Chief Vicars Boyle, who had taken over railway supervision after the untimely death of Edmund Morel.

*   *   *

The next day was spent inspecting the whole of the incomplete line by walking most of the way to Osaka, and returning by steam-launch. The launch skipper was sceptical and angry about the future railway because of the effect it would have on his business, and it was later discovered that he actually tried to bribe officials to delay the opening of the Kobe/Osaka line. Ten more days passed quietly as stores were obtained for Holtham's journey to the interior on a surveying mission. He never did quite approve of Treaty Port life, being born himself in a village by the sea in England, and he was content to leave Kobe just before Christmas Day and depart from its childish sailors, policemen and Chinese merchants and its smells of tea-firing godowns that wafted through the settlement. The colourful flags of each nation flying above important-looking consulates did not impress him, nor the 'missionaries who swarm and multiply in godly contentment' and who 'enjoyed a good time with the help of children's pocket-money and the contributions of the ignorant.'

In the hills beyond Kyoto and along the wooded valleys beside Lake Biwa, with a surveying compass in his hand and a well-defined job to

do, Holtham was at his happiest. Out in the wild countryside, he felt a
certain empathy for village people, and made attempts to learn their
language, for they, after all, had learned enough about 'the ways of
English visitors' to be able to produce for him western steaks and
omelettes. And with his 'travelling stock of beer and whiskey,' he felt
quite at home.

The residence of the three British surveyors at Nagahama, the village
on the shores of Lake Biwa, was part of a Buddhist priest's house. From
this centre they scientifically planned a proposed railway route through
the mountains to Tsuruga on the Japan Sea coast. The frequent falls of
heavy snow, the amount of tree-felling necessary and the steep, rough
terrain made it tough and tedious work. This discomfort was added to
when a bundle of new regulations arrived in January 1874 that stated
that the department would cease to supply goods for private use to field
officers. So all the luxuries they had previously ordered in Kobe to make
their stay in the winter mountains more comfortable did not arrive. The
fragile Japanese-made chairs broke into pieces under their heavy weights
(Holtham weighed nearly 200 pounds) as they furiously discussed this
blow, and it seemed that their improvised table would have to be used
for the whole duration. But when Billy, another British engineer, arrived
with his portable harmonium and replenishments of Bass beer in the
early summer of 1874, the frustrations had been largely forgotten as
they all spent the long evenings in the local tea-house singing 'Oh!
Kafoozleum!' and other ribald ditties.

Meat was obtained by shooting birds and other game, despite a
government regulation forbidding foreigners to fire guns outside the
Treaty Port limits. The local authorities, however, promised to turn a
blind eye provided no person or property was injured. But the next
year, a stray pellet unfortunately hit a boy who was bending down out
of sight working in a millet field. The hunter, unaware of the accident,
was just about to eat his bag of pigeons at home when an interpreter
arrived to tell what had occurred. Rumours about a mad foreigner
murdering a child with a deadly revolver quickly circulated in the
community, while the bruised victim was carried to the nearest hospital
in great ceremony. But as no official action was taken following a detailed
report by Holtham to several government departments, the boy walked
back to his home and later demanded money from his 'assassin.'

*   *   *

The fervent energy of the spies planted by the Japanese government
among the adventure-seeking foreign technologists during this period
created much resentment. It did not take Holtham and his compatriots
long to realise that among the Japanese staff assigned to them, some
were hardfaced spies who continuously made detailed reports on the
'private conduct and personal failings of the foreign staff,' and that
'every action was noted.' The reports contained 'ingenious surmise,

ludicrous misapprehensions and contemptible slander' which once resulted in the ridiculous accusation that one British engineer was illegally selling braces as a side business. Private trading of any sort was forbidden by all foreign government employees, and it took the intervention of Inouye Masaru, the Head of the Railway Bureau, to quash the charge and demote the over-zealous spy.

Far more important considerations concerned the well-paid engineers who wanted to build substantial and secure lines across the shifting and unstable landscape. The political implications of their work slowly became apparent to Holtham, but he was far more concerned with overcoming practical difficulties. These pioneers of 1875, despite the constant threat of having their contracts terminated at the end of the year due to alleged lack of funds, wanted to see the completion of a basic railway system in Japan for the benefit of all. The next year they worked with fervour on the Osaka/Kyoto line, excavating and dredging the loose stones of the wide river bottoms that punctuate Japan's mountainous terrain, sending down the British diver or one of the Japanese he had trained, into the murk of the wells to ensure the correct placement of the foundations of railway bridges. The primitive diving gear used at the time meant that death was a constant companion, yet political pressure made sure that the lines became operational as close to the planned schedule as possible.

The accidental drowning of Mr Smith, the foreman of the masons, while swimming for pleasure in an excavated pool, upset Holtham for a time, but he was impressed by the efforts made by the Japanese divers to rescue him.

The death of their colleague, Charles Sheppard, in 1875 had caused much sadness among the railway fraternity. Then when John England, the Chief Assistant in Tokyo, died of cancer in 1877, Holtham was instructed to sail to the capital to take over his work. While he was waiting for a ship at Kobe during the September storms of 1877, the new single track from Kobe to Osaka was constantly used for shuttling Imperial troops between the cities because of the Satsuma Rebellion. A mistake by a driver in an empty down-train caused Japan's first serious railway accident. The train pulled out from a station siding and gathered speed to continue its journey to Kobe after an up-train had passed. However, that train was a special troop carrier, and the regular scheduled train was following a few minutes behind. The head-on collision resulted in the loss of three lives and considerable injury. The two engines were completely wrecked; Holtham arrived on the scene to assist in clearing the wreckage the day before he sailed.

*   *   *

A cholera epidemic was raging in Tokyo and Yokohama when he arrived, but Holtham was kept too busy to worry about it. The only other British railway engineer in Tokyo was Theodore Shann who was supervising the construction of a new bridge across the Tama River at Haneda. This, the largest bridge in Japan so far, was opened by Minister Ito in November. All the other 40 bridges on the 29 km. Shimbashi/Yokohama line needed to be renewed after only five years' service, for Japan's first railway line was, according to Holtham, 'a model of what things should not be.' His first task, however, was to introduce a system of piece-work payments for labourers and craftsmen, and to try to rid his more senior assistants of their 'dreamy temperament.'

After his New Year Imperial reception, where all second-rank foreign employees paid their annual respects to the Emperor and Empress by humbly filing up to them and silently bowing, Holtham settled into supervising the running of the trains, and the 'rebuilding of nearly every work throughout the line' which entailed converting 'a very rickety single line into a double line, worthy of the road between the chief city of the empire and its port.' However, the reduction in the number of British engineers, who generally had more practical experience than recent graduates of Imperial College, made progress slow at times. But as the months of his fifth year in Japan passed, he became more satisfied with the work of his Japanese staff, and the next year, 1879, several Japanese train drivers began operating on certain services, replacing British drivers. They proved to be excellent operators, economising on coal, and drawing only one-sixth of the British driver's salary.

Floods and obstructions were a constant threat on the Tokyo/ Yokohama line, the former an unavoidable factor of climate and the latter from a deliberate destructive human impulse. Drivers, in the early years, were continually afraid of pieces of stone, iron and wood placed on the track, and not always by children. Once a piece of rail was positioned across the track which almost resulted in a terrible smash. But worse destruction came from the floods at the end of 1878 when fast-moving water covered the tracks around Kawasaki and undermined the sleepers.

Holtham was out in the rain early to inspect the damage. The banks of the Tama River had broken, and the platform of Kawasaki station was under a metre of water, but the solid masonry and iron bridges that had so recently replaced the old wooden trestle-work bridges stood firm in the torrents. The railway service was closed for two days while trucks of ballast arrived for repairs. Holtham, with coat off and shirt sleeves rolled up to his armpits, shovelled ballast under the sleepers with the coolies, and when the bubbling water prevented them seeing where the gaps were, he was on his knees in the mud feeling under the water for spaces that needed filling. Afterwards, he realised that, in Japanese eyes, he had debased himself by doing such manual labour, for the Japanese supervisors and officials always wore clean white gloves to indicate they were above such menial tasks.

Two men were drowned while repairing a railway bridge, but in Haneda village nearer the sea, many more were lost. No scientific records

on the flood levels had been kept in Japan, and this made the planning
of railway routes difficult. Holtham's strategy was to ask the oldest
inhabitant of a village to indicate where the water of the highest flood
he could remember had come to, thus obtaining data for his planning.

*   *   *

Living in Tokyo in a house near Shimbashi station terminus meant that
Holtham was available for consultation on a variety of engineering
problems. But he found that delegations requiring information often
presented him with only a sketchy outline of a problem, and when he
asked for more details, found that they became suspicious and distrustful
of his motives in this curiosity. But generally life was more relaxed in
Tokyo, and he became part of a cricket team that played against
Yokohama, joined the Asiatic Society and managed to get time off to
travel.

After climbing Mount Fuji and spending a few days relaxing at
Hakone, where his favourite beer was an outrageous 60 cents a bottle,
he took a ship north in 1879 with Vice-Minister of Public Works, Yamao,
to visit the beautiful island of Kinkasan near Sendai. Further north at
Kamaishi he met the lonely British family of an engineer who was making
slow progress in building a railway line to serve a modern ironworks
there. He then proceeded overland along rough mountain tracks to
Morioka, where Yamao departed to inspect several mines further north.
Holtham turned south for Sendai, where he searched for beer and cigars,
and then started on the four-and-a-half-day journey to Tokyo by
rickshaw, horse and coach.

In 1881, his last year in Japan, he made a final three-week journey
overland from Nagasaki to Kobe. He tried hard to persuade his British
acquaintances to accompany him, but without success; so he eventually
started the mammoth trek alone. Alone, that is, except for his 'boy'
and his luggage which made up a squadron of four rickshaws hauled in
battle line. With his monocle in one eye, his parading fleet arrived at
the dirty little port of Tokitsu in as grand a style as a $550-a-month
Briton could afford, and while waiting as a western curiosity on the pier
to embark across the fiord to Omura, he was amused to see about 200
children with straw circles embedded in one eye smiling up at him!

Holtham, of course, had to have with him at all times his special
passport obtained from the British legation and signed by Sir Harry
Parkes, the Consul-General, for travel outside the Treaty Ports. At
Yamaguchi it was examined by a young policeman who tried to copy
its contents, but the lion and unicorn crest proved too difficult for his
artistic ability, and he handed it back with a sigh. 'It seemed quite
unnecessary in country districts,' reported Holtham, 'but indispensable
in the large towns.' If the foreign traveller was unable to produce his
passport when asked, he was ignominiously escorted to the nearest
Treaty Port at that time. The essence of this custom is still retained in
Japan through the Alien Registration card system.

Onward he travelled, and at Okayama was led by his 'boy' to a lodging-house that 'practised a kind of hospitality more comprehensive than suited my taste.' Another more quiet lodgings was found nearby, and by 8 am the next morning he was on the last leg of his journey, remarking that Okayama was worth 'an exploration to any one interested in temples or antiquities' but otherwise finding little else of any merit.

Chapter 25

Richard Henry Brunton — Lighthouse and Bridge Builder

NAGASAKI HAD DISAPPEARED! When dawn arrived, Henry C. St John, captain of the British naval frigate, could see no sign of the city's narrow harbour entrance. After the short 400-mile voyage from Shanghai, the officers on board were completely non-plussed about how their navigation could have been so inaccurate. The answer was that the Japanese Black Stream, a strong and erratic current that flows northwards along the east coast of Japan as far as the Kurile Islands, had moved the ship many miles off her course during the cloudy night. This was in 1864, before the coast and currents around Japan had been properly surveyed and before any lighthouse shone across her waters. Some vessels had unknowingly been carried dead to windward in heavy gales at a fair rate of knots by this dreaded current.

The frigate decided to change course and go south down the coast. Still no sign of Nagasaki. They heaved to. At that moment a small fishing-boat was spotted and the frigate sailed across to it. The men on board, seeing such a formidable sight closing in on them, hoisted all their sails, brought out their long oars and made for the coast as fast as they could. Soon they were overhauled and the fishing-boat was tied up to the frigate. All the British needed was information, but the language barrier combined with the fear of the overwhelmed fishermen made communication impossible. Nothing would induce them to climb the ladder into the frigate. A British tar was then sent down to try to carry up one of the men by force, but he resisted being manhandled. Next, a rope was lowered down in an attempt to hoist the poor man up. This failed too. Finally, a bottle of rum was lowered over the side of the frigate and the two fishermen invited to take a noggin. Almost immediately there were smiles all round and the two men carefully climbed the ladder. By repeating the word 'Nagasaki,' the men at last understood the predicament of the dark-coated officers and they piloted the frigate, with fishing-boat in tow, to the entrance of Nagasaki harbour.

They cast off just before they entered, carefully wrapped up the silver coins that the British had given them, and sailed away. The frigate had been 40 miles from its destination.

*   *   *

Captain St John has recorded other problems met by foreign ships during those years, just before the Meiji Restoration when Japan was in such turmoil. At Hakodate harbour in 1855, when Britain and Russia were at war, naval ships were instructed by the admiral of the fleet not to salute his ship in the traditional way, nor could they fire the usual blank in a musket at sunset because the Japanese authorities objected to the firing of guns by foreigners. Each Royal Navy ship, and all other foreign vessels, had to receive sentries on board to prevent anyone from going ashore and a 'yakunin,' (two-sworded government officer) was put in charge of each vessel while it was in port. Again, friendship between the yakunin and the officers developed with the help of rum, beer and wine.

The crew were permitted, under guard, to obtain fresh water from streams some way from the town, but they could not buy fresh fruit or vegetables. Such regulations and treatment, besides humiliating the British officers, meant that it was difficult for them to range far across the seas with their fifty-gun frigates and so the purpose of their mission — to sink Russian shipping — was never achieved.

After the wars were over, the regulations in Japan were relaxed and the navigational problems faced by ships as they sailed around the coasts of Japan were tackled. A recession in trade between Europe and the East caused many ships to be sold, and Japan acquired a number of large coal-burning ships. Also from 1854 several large iron-clad warships had been built in Japan, not always successfully, but it was therefore in the interest of Japanese shipping to undertake the building of lighthouses, the surveying of the coastline and ocean currents together with the placing of buoys to indicate safe channels. The Meiji Restoration gave other countries faith in the internal stability of Japan so that loans could be obtained more easily than before. Further, the western nations were putting pressure on the authorities because the lighting of the coasts was the responsibility of the Japanese government according to Article XI of the Tariff Convention of June 1866.

It was Captain St John who was given command of the surveying operation in Hokkaido using *HMS Sylvia,* a Japanese supply ship — *Keang-su* — aided in this project. Other British navy ships were employed to survey other parts of the coast, the arrangements being made through London by Sir Harry Parkes, Britain's Minister Plenipotentiary to Japan. Most of the work was completed by 1871.

In order to build lighthouses, one thing was obvious — foreign experts had to be employed. The British and French naval authorities had previously recommended which sites were most in need of lights, and they had suggested the type of apparatus required. Sir Harry had sent these suggestions to the Roju (most powerful ministers) in November 1866 and he had urged them to get started soon. The French and American ministers followed suit, and the next month the government set the wheels in motion. Eleven lights were initially agreed upon — three to be constructed by the French engineers who were in charge of the Yokosuka arsenal, and eight by British engineers. Sir Harry contacted the Board of Trade in London who commissioned Messrs D. and T. Stevenson to select personnel and construct the lighthouses.

*   *   *

It was not until 8 August 1868 that Richard Henry Brunton arrived at Yokohama to actually carry out the lighthouse construction work. Two assistants, Blundell and Mcbean, came with him and his family was to follow later. Brunton was only 27 years old, but had had 10 years construction experience in Britain on the railways and other projects. He had signed a five-year contract with the Japanese government at $450 per month which would be raised to $600 after two years. A grand reception was held on his arrival, Sir Harry interpreting for the engineer.

HMS Manila was requisitioned to undertake a preliminary inspection of the sites for the lighthouses. All operations were centred on Yokohama where offices, storehouses and workshops had been constructed. A certain Mr Saito was the government official overseeing all the work, although Brunton's contract gave him complete authority over his department. Mr Terashima, a governor of Kanagawa, showed great interest in the project and offered help to Brunton.

Despite this happy and optimistic start, many problems followed. Soon it became obvious that the programme of work was being hampered by the lack of skilled workmen. The Japanese artisans assigned to Brunton had had no experience in large building projects and could not adapt their skills to follow Brunton's instructions. He demanded that masons, plumbers, machinists and even lighthouse keepers be sent out from Britain and soon 33 British people were in Japan working for the lighthouse department. About this time Mr Saito was replaced by an 'ignorant, bumptious functionary' who refused to travel on British navy ships and he was again replaced by another — a total of 15 officials were appointed in succession over the lighthouse project during Brunton's eight years in Japan.

Blundell and Mcbean resigned the next year, complaining that their salaries of $150 per month would not allow them to live in comfort because of the high cost of western clothes and food. Immediately they were offered $300, but this did not satisfy them and they departed. However, Brunton soldiered on, although he did complain to Sir Harry:

'A man arriving in a country like this has many causes for discontent. The nature of his duties disappoints him. He is required, owing to his being the only engineer, to do trifling pieces of work which perhaps before had been given over to his juniors in the office. He is often required then to explain the minutest details to men unwilling to execute them. He has to deal with people tantalisingly slow and lazy and who are wonderfully retentive of their own system of working. All European articles of food and clothing are three times the price they are at home ...therefore a man who exchanges say, £300 a year at home for £800 a year here with the prospect of bettering himself is grievously disappointed. These things should be explained directly to anyone coming here and he should not be allowed to come out in ignorance of them.'

*   *   *

In spite of these perennial complaints, Brunton had absorbed enough Japanese tenacity of spirit to remain with his family for another seven years and see his work finished. In all, he supervised the building of thirty-six lighthouses, two lightships, thirteen buoys and three beacons, making navigation around the coasts of Japan secure and safe for the first time.

Difficulties arose over the design of the foundations of these tall lighthouses because of the frequency of earthquakes in Japan. It was feared that not only would the bright, four-wicked oil lamps be put out by a moderate quake, but that a larger quake would cause the entire structure to be reduced to rubble. Stevenson, in consultation with his team of engineers, devised 'aseismatic joints' which would provide 'a break in the continuity of the rigid parts forming the structure, so as to prevent the propagation of the (earthquake) shock.' These aseismatic joints were to be constructed as an integral part of a table on which the lighthouse was to be built. They would consist of 'spherical balls of bell-metal, working in cups of the same metal, placed between two platforms, the lower cups being fixed to the beams forming the foundation, and the upper cups being fixed to the lower beams of the superstructure, thus admitting free motion of the upper over the lower part of the building.'

Brunton did not like this idea, and while reporting to the institution of Civil Engineers in London in 1876, he politely stated — Stevenson was chairman — that 'such a contrivance is not altogether favourable.' He went on to explain that 'the pressure exerted by a gale of wind on the superstructure would give rise to a motion probably equally as distressing as a severe earthquake'! So Brunton, after studying the work of Professor Palmieri of Naples (the most experienced earthquake observer in the world) and the structure of Japanese houses, decided to make his lighthouses heavy and strong: he applied the principle of inertia that would allow the structures to stand during earthquakes. Some lighthouses were made of granite and others of stone, while the rest were constructed of bricks. Brickmaking had only recently been introduced to Japan and Brunton found them of poor quality because the burning process was not carried out properly. He preferred foreign bricks that had come into Japan as ballast for ships: there still exists to this day part of Brunton's original brickwork at the Mikomotojima lighthouse where ballast bricks were used.

*   *   *

During his stay in Japan, Brunton did more than construct lighthouses and render shipping safe. In less than a year after he stepped ashore, he was asked to construct the first telegraph line in the Far East. So he ordered the necessary wires and appliances from England, and made use of material that had been supplied by Austria after that country had been promised the concession for the erection of telegraphs in Japan, and constructed lines between the Imperial Palace and the government offices in Tokyo and other lines in Yokohama. Sir Harry had obstructed the arrival of Austrian experts to allow the British to undertake the project.

Brunton, the talented engineer, also designed drainage and road-making systems for Yokohama which were implemented in 1870 to the great delight of the community. But his ideas for lighting the settlement, for supplying pure water and providing concrete jetties in the port were rejected by the authorities because of costs. But one project that he is still remember for in Yokohama is the building of the first iron bridge in Japan. It spanned the drainage canal to join Isezakicho dori and Bashamichi dori. A replica of that bridge has just (1979) been constructed at the same spot, except that now it spans the subterranean Shuto expressway and shopping complex there. Brunton taught his Japanese mechanics to cut the iron plates, to drill holes for the rivets and put the whole thing together. By this time his opinion of Japanese artisans had become more favourable.

In March 1875, Brunton was informed that his contract was to terminate the following year. His position was taken by another. It is still not clear why this was done and many people criticised the way his contract was so suddenly terminated. Still, his work was well appreciated by certain members of the government and he was given an audience by the Emperor, a banquet at the Palace, as well as a severence bonus of £500.

Chapter 26

William H. Stone

SOON AFTER QUITE A POWERFUL EARTHQUAKE struck the Sendai area, northern Japan, in June 1978, the TV and newspapers reported 22 people dead. In Tokyo many people with close friends and relations living in Sendai became very anxious and frustrated — the telephone lines had been severed by the movement of the earth and communication with individuals was impossible. Luckily, the lines were repaired within one day and most people's minds were put at rest, but this temporary lack of telecommunications emphasised how much we all rely on the telephone and how agonising it can be when it is taken away.

Today, Japan boasts one of the best telephone systems in the world, mostly automatic, and the Japanese produce many components and even complete exchanges which are exported to other countries. But where did it all begin in Japan? Who were the pioneers who first set up the telegraphic systems, got the bells ringing so that the millions of *'Moshi, Moshi'* ('Hello') could be transmitted from place to place?

In 1853/54, the holds of the ships in Commodore Perry's squadron were crammed with presents from the American President Fillmore to Japan's Shogun. These presents consisted mainly of the then modern technological equipment, chosen to impress the Japanese government how advanced American was in these things — and one piece of equipment was a Morse Telegraphic Apparatus. Like a mid-year Santa Claus, Perry delivered it with all due ceremony to his hosts. The success of Perry in opening Japan to the world may be, in part, due to his participating in this old Japanese custom of bringing *'omeagi'* (gifts) to these shores.

However, the history of telegraphy in Japan goes back a little before Perry because Shoza Sakuma (1811 - 1864), an avid student of *'rangaku'* (Dutch Studies), had learned the theory of telegraphy from a Dutch encyclopaedia and had attempted to build an apparatus of his own in Matsushiro, Nagano Prefecture. That was in 1849, but whether he made his apparatus work or not is unknown; nonetheless, a piece of silk-coated wire used by Sakuma is preserved in the Communications Museum in Tokyo, so he at least understood the principle of insulation.

The apparatus that Perry brought was taken over by Naraikira Shimazu, Lord of Satsuma, who ordered one of his subjects, Matsuki, to study it and set up a system in his castle. According to one writer, this was 'a curiosity and not for use.' But the curiosity and fascination of Hamada Hikozo must have been immense: he was the first Japanese man to see the telegraphic system in operation in America in August 1853. This unfortunate man was shipwrecked in 1850 but rescued by an

American ship and taken to San Francisco where he became naturalised. His sponsor, a Mr Sanders, took Hamada to his home in Baltimore. When they were staying in the Metropolitan Hotel in New York, Sanders told Hamada that he was going to send a message to his brother-in-law 200 miles away and that a reply would return after 20 minutes or so. Hamada recalls in his book, *The Narrative of a Japanese,* written 40 years later:

'This I did not believe: I thought he was telling me something not true merely by way of a joke, in order to astonish me. For he perceived that many things had excited my wonder.'

Then he describes how they both went down into a basement and Mr Sanders wrote a message on a piece of paper and handed it to a man at the counter. 'The latter began to operate a piece of machinery that went on "click! click! clicking" as he so operated. I watched closely but I could observe nothing save the clicking and the man's hands in motion. Presently, the clerk from the counter brought a message undercover.' Sanders then explained to Hamada that his brother-in-law had received his message and sent a reply, but Hamada still could not believe it was true until they arrived at Baltimore station to find the brother-in-law waiting in his carriage.

*   *   *

The first telegraph line in operation in Japan was only 700 metres long. It ran between the Court of Justice in Yokohama and the office of Tomyodai. It was a French-made Breguet apparatus that had been purchased by a Britisher, Henry Brunton, and brought to Japan by his friend G.M. Gilbert. This line was for the exclusive use of government officials and began operating in 1869. On Christmas Day of that year a public service was started between Yokohama and Tokyo; however, it was not popular and many people were fearful of the strange instruments and the wires. It is recorded that on some days only two messages were sent down the wires.

When the lines began to extend over the countryside, strange things began to happen. In one locality all the unmarried girls were forced to shave their eyebrows and blacken their teeth — signs that they were married — because a rumour was started that the telegraph wires were coated with the blood of virgins. At other places the descendants of samurai always shielded their heads with folding fans when they had to pass under the wires to protect themselves from western 'devilries.' Sometimes wires and poles were torn down by mobs, especially if the shadows of the poles fell across an ancient burial ground. In Hiroshima in 1871, the quarters of the telegraphic engineers were mobbed and an instrument was stolen; then in 1873 an armed mob wrecked the telegraph office in Fukushima and three years later the telegraph office at Yokkaichi was burned down by a fanatic mob.

This antagonism, suspicion and superstition did not extend to the whole of the rural population; many people used the new-fangled service to communicate with distant friends without understanding how it worked. For example, there were some who could not understand how they could send messages and receive a written reply, yet they could not send parcels of fruit to their city-dwelling cousins! It was also reported that others stood for hours watching the wires in order to see a message go by!

*   *   *

It was into this turbulent time of ignorance, opposition and hope that many experts in telegraphy from other countries arrived in Japan. The best known was a tall Irishman, William H. Stone. He was one of the hundred or so telegraphic experts who had made the long and hazardous journey to Japan to organise the country's telecommunications services which would be absolutely essential for a country planning to become a modern industrial and military nation.

Stone was born and raised in County Sligo, just a few years before Ireland's great Potato Famine of the 1840s. He was the son of a customs officer who must have been English or of English descent, who managed to provide him with a good education in science. When he was qualified, the young Stone must have wondered which way he should go to escape from the poverty of Ireland: across the Atlantic Ocean to America where thousands upon thousands of his fellow countrymen were going every year, or to the mysterious East?

He chose the East and arrived in Japan in April 1872 to work for the Ministry of Technology (Telegraphic Dept.) at a salary of ¥350 per month. For the first two months he worked closely with Shioda Saburo who was to go on an official government mission to attend the International Telegraphic Conference in Rome. Shioda's purpose was to help Japan join other countries in the World Telegraphic Union, and after attending a similar conference in St Petersburg in 1875, the aim was finally achieved in 1879 when Japan was accepted in the International Telegraphic Treaty.

By this time, every major city in Japan was linked by telegraph wires, and undersea cables from Nagasaki to both Shanghai and Vladivostok linked Japan to the rest of the world. Stone helped in the planning of laying another cable across to Korea in 1882 and later in the laying of the Japan-USA cable that went by way of Guam.

Stone at this time had decided to devote his whole life to the progress of telegraphy in Japan. He took a Japanese wife and started a family. Some of his descendants still (1980) live in Yokohama, including one very active daughter. The government trusted him completely and he was one of the few people who could enter the telegraphic equipment room without showing a pass.

The value of the telegraph in military affairs was first appreciated in Japan during the 10-day Saga Rebellion of 1874. Eto Shimpei, a nationalistic samurai, incited his followers to attack and burn the castle in Saga and kill the government soldiers in the garrison. After initial success Shimpei expected all the clans in Kyushu to follow him, but he did not reckon with the newly-established telegraph and railways. The news soon arrived in the capital by telegraph, and orders were sent out to Okubo Toshimichi to move his troops by railway to quell the rebellion. This was easily achieved and the leaders of the rebellion were beheaded at Saga.

By the time of the Sino-Japanese War of 1894 and Russo-Japanese War of 1904, the telegraph was used even more extensively in military manoeuvres. Stone was detailed to organise and advise the military in the use of telegraphy in both these wars.

During his career in Japan, Stone was decorated by the Emperor six times for his services to the country. Three days after his death, just before his 80th birthday, the highest possible award — the Grand Cordon of the Order of the Rising Sun — was bestowed upon him by the Emperor. It was also the Emperor who authorised ¥3000 to be released from the treasury for his funeral expenses. Stone was laid to rest in the Aoyama Cemetery in Tokyo and his grave, together with a plaque describing his many achievements, is still maintained by the Communications Association of Japan.

Towards the end of the Meiji era, both the telegraph and telephone systems had developed extensively thanks to the devoted work of the foreign experts and the rapid way in which Japanese engineers learned. In fact they became, along with German beer, symbols of the Westernisation of Japan. The writer W. Petrie Watson in 'Japan: Aspects and Destinies', published in 1904, devotes a whole chapter to 'Tokyo's Automatic Telephones' in which he complains that he could not get away from signboards reading PUBLIC AUTOMATIC TELEPHONE. Practically every side-street had one and he called them 'one of the congruous incongruities of Japan' because no one seemed to use them at that time, and also other more basic developments had not taken place at the same rate as the telephone system. As an example he cites the state of the roads: 'When it rains Tokyo's principal business street is a quagmire,' and also Tokyo was 'a city in which some of its public places exhibit arc-lamps of 10,000 candle-power and in others precipitates you into hospital over a heap of shingle wanting a night-light. Its contrasts and inconsistencies are delightful until they are injurous.' Watson's final shudder comes when he describes an old, traditional tea-house at Asakusa which is surrounded by flowering trees and located next to a pond of beautiful carp — but planted right next to the tea-house was a modern Public Automatic Telephone box.

Chapter 27

Beginnings of Photography in Japan

PHOTOGRAPHY is undoubtedly a universal hobby in Japan today, and her professional photographers rank amongst the world's best. But the story of how photography was introduced into Japan is not without mystery and surprises.

In the *Asahi Shimbun* newspaper of 14 January 1978, an article in a series called *'Koko ni hajimaru'* (Here it all began) the writer gives an account of Renjo Shimooka, 'the pioneer-ancestor of photography in Japan' who was born in Shimoda in 1823. He then goes on to describe how Shimooka was possibly taught a little about photography by Henry Heusken, the ill-fated interpreter for the first American Consul. The doubt lies in the fact that Shimooka, who knew little about foreign languages, gave the name as 'Unsinn' which could possibly have been 'Heusken' but equally likely to be 'Wilson.' It is certain that Shimooka came from 'very humble origins,' yet the *Asahi* carried a picture of him with all the regalia of a samurai warrior! Still, this article states that it was in Yokohama afterwards that he struggled for years in his toilet dark-room until he finally 'discovered most of the techniques (of photography) for himself.' In other words, according to one journalist, this particular Japanese — who is famous in America amongst students of oriental photographic art — was equivalent to Niepce and Daguerre in his struggles, achievements and discoveries in photography. This mistaken notion, widespread in the Japanese educational system, that if an individual struggles, studies and experiments long enough, then he will be rewarded with success in the shape of great and famous discoveries and inventions, is reflected in this article all too clearly.

Masano Koyasu, director of the Pentax Gallery since 1972, is more realistic and logical, and in an article in *Modern Photography* in May 1976, describes a discovery that the first writer had obviously never heard of. In October 1975, a daguerreotype portrait was discovered in a treasure house in Kagoshima, Kyushu. The silver plate bore the image of Lord Nariakira Shimazu and was the evidence required to substantiate a long-established theory about the first camera imported into Japan on 1 July 1840 which was first owned by Toshinojo Uyeno of Nagasaki. Obviously it came in through the trading post in Deshima. After Uyeno had sold the camera to Lord Shimazu, this nobleman photographed himself on 1 June 1841 a mere two years after Daguerre published his discovery of the process. That is why 1 June is now designated as 'Photography Day' in Japan.

Lord Shimazu was intensely curious about western technology and it was he who bought the telegraphy apparatus that Perry donated to the nation in 1854, but both photography and telegraphy were to remain mere curiosities for several years. It was fear of the military might of the Black Ships and the realisation that Japan's feudal samurai would be inadequate against such force that caused the authorities to invite a team of 23 Dutch naval experts, under Pels Rijcken, to set up a college (Igasoki) for the study of military crafts. That was in 1854 — the very year of Perry's second visit — and in 1857 a second group of 38 scientists from Holland replaced the first. One of these is reputed to have been an Englishman who taught a course on photography, but his name is unknown. By 1862, Hokoma Uyeno, one of the first graduates of the college and son of the camera importer, opened Japan's first photography studio in Nagasaki, followed closely the same year by Shimooka in Yokohama. Both these men — Uyeno from a rich merchant family and Shimooka from a working-class background — achieved considerable success in photography during the following decades demonstrating how rapidly the traditional structure of society in Japan was changing even in these early years.

The first foreigner known to have recorded scenes in Japan by the photographic method was Eliphalet Brown Junior, who brought his camera and daguerreotype equipment with Perry's squadron on its five-month second visit in 1854. He made a series of pictures depicting many aspects of life in Japan from which lithographic plates were made to illustrate the official report of that mission. Unfortunately, all the original photographs were destroyed in a fire in Philadelphia a short time afterwards.

When the first foreigners arrived in Japan after the Treaty Ports were opened in 1859, the 'earliest European settlers in those treaty ports were usually more intent on making quick fortunes than in discovering the hidden mysteries of the interior of Japan or practising the "art-science" of photography,' according to Clarke Worswick in the *Japan Society Newsletter* for December 1979. This is not completely true, for there are two delightful ukiyo-e prints by Yoshikaza, one completed in November 1860 showing a Dutch family in Yokohama with a large 'Don Kamer' (camera) and the other completed in February 1861 showing a French couple where the man has his head partly covered by the dark cloth as he adjusts his camera on a tripod. But no more details are given, and none of their work seems to have survived. In 1861, Gower, of the British legation, published a number of photographs of Japan in London in which many people showed interest but two years later one of the finest photographers that the world has known arrived in Japan and stayed until 1884.

*   *   *

His name was Felix Beato, a one-time photographer in the Italian military, who had become a close friend of Charles Wirgman when they were both in China. These two fondly-remembered characters set up the firm of 'Beato and Wirgman, Artists and Photographers' in Yokohama in 1865 which operated for four years until Wirgman pulled out and Beato continued until 1877 on his own. Wirgman was the *Illustrated London News* reporter in Japan, but his most famous work is the production — writing, editing, publishing and printing with woodblocks — of the *Japan Punch,* a satirical review based on the famous London *Punch* magazine. In it he drew, wrote about and humoured the foreign community in Yokohama and Tokyo in the 1860s and '70s. His gravestone in the Gaijin Bochi (Foreigners' Cemetery) bears the epitaph: 'A fellow of Infinite Jest' which is fully borne out by his writings. Beato, on the other hand, determined to take his talents away from the Treaty Ports and record the scenes of feudal Japan before it changed too much from the forces of industrialisation. He realised that the unique features of this newly-opened country that had been isolated over 200 years were rapidly changing even in the countryside, or as Worswick so poetically put it: 'Medieval Japan was like an oyster — to open it was to kill it.'

During 1864/5, Beato travelled with the Swiss diplomat Aime Humbert and took many pictures which were later converted into etchings to illustrate his detailed book *Manners and Customs of the Japanese.* In it he describes a visit to Tokyo, where 'one of our party having made preparations to photograph this beautiful scene (the front of Prince Arima's palace), two officers belonging to the Prince's household came to him and begged him to discontinue his operations. Our friend requested them to go and take the orders of their master upon the subject; they went, but returned in a very few minutes, saying that the Prince absolutely forbade that any view should be taken of his palace. Beato obeyed respectfully, and ordered the 'koskei' (assistants) to take away the machine; and the officers retired perfectly satisfied, without the slightest suspicion that during their temporary absence the operator had taken two negatives.' The Japanese government guards who were accompanying this party applauded Beato's success, but even they would not agree to allowing him to photograph the sacred tombs of the Shoguns at Shiba.

The great fire that destroyed the Yokohama settlement in 1866 must have consumed much of Beato's early work, but he was not discouraged and in 1868 he published two books containing about 100 photographs each showing life in Japan. In one volume the prints were delicately hand-coloured by Japanese artists making them unique pieces of artwork combining the science of the West and the art of the East. These artists probably came from families well versed in the graphic arts, and who had been attached to a daimyo's household, but who had been rendered impecunious by the new social order that intercourse with the West had brought. The difference between their new occupation and their old one with the daimyo being that now production figures were important for their survival. No longer could they spend years on one piece of artwork for their master.

This new tradition, started by Beato, led to the production of hand-coloured postcards at the very beginning of the twentieth century. These humble ephemera are avidly collected and appreciated by a few enthusiasts today for their ukiyo-e type qualities.

*   *   *

In 1871, two Austrian barons arrived separately in Yokohama. One, Hubner, was a transient traveller who later published in his *A Ramble around the World,* a detailed account of the state of Japan that year, but the other, von Stillfried, stayed many years and was to become as influential as Beato in his photographic work. Along with a Herr Andersen, he set up a studio in Yokohama and went into business. This business was given an enormous boost when a government edict forbade ex-samurai warriors to wear their traditional top-knot hair. A great many of them, just before they obeyed the edict, went to Stillfried's studio to record their former appearance for eternity. At this time, one of Stillfried's apprentices was Kimbei Kusakabe who was later to make an important contribution to professional photography in Japan.

As in many of the undeveloped countries today, the ordinary people of Japan were at first suspicious of cameras and regarded them as one of the 'western devilries.' A belief was spread, possibly by religious leaders fearing their traditional credibility, that the evil eye of the camera could take away a piece of one's soul. But by the time of the Meiji Restoration in 1868 these illogicalities had largely disappeared and dozens of Japanese photographers had set up studios in every major city. Many of these were in the open air and consisted of nothing more than a cloth back-drop fixed to a tree. People flocked to these 'shajo', especially in the summer-time.

It was Kyuichi Uchida, a student of Uyeno in Nagasaki, who had the honour of photographing the Emperor Meiji and his Empress in 1872. Copies of these pictures were, understandably, immensely popular amongst the people, but the authorities felt that the buying and selling of images of a living god was not dignified and they passed a law to stop their circulation. But within two decades such pictures were freely sold as postcards in many different countries as well as Japan.

*   *   *

George Eastman, American founder of the Kodak company, developed and manufactured dry photographic plates in the 1880s and paved the way for universal amateur photography. Numerous books were written on the subject explaining the mysteries of this formerly specialist activity. One writer was W.K. Burton who arrived in Japan in 1887 with tremendous enthusiasm for encouraging amateur photographers. He became friendly with a rich merchant and photography fanatic called Seibei Kajima, who with other enthusiasts, started the Japanese

Photographers' Society in 1889. Kajima provided the financial backing and Burton was one of the first secretaries. At first all went well. Kajima set up Japan's first factory for making dry plates, and imported a great deal of expensive equipment which he lent to his growing circle of friends. In 1893, Japan's first international photographic exhibition was held in Tokyo. By the following year, however, Kajima's wealth appears to have gone presumably because of the great sums he had spent on his hobby and he was declared bankrupt. But the seeds had been sown and more and more Japanese found in photography an absorbing hobby, and gradually companies were set up to cater for this.

In the professional field, Japanese photography developed in its unique way, at the same time absorbing and adapting ideas from the West. In 1938, Ihei Kimura — already famous in Japan — became the first Japanese to have a picture accepted for the cover of *Life* magazine. Today, exhibitions of work by internationally renowned Japanese photographers take place annually in all the major cities of the world.

Chapter 28

Major Kinder — and Japan's First Mint

THE HISTORY OF COINAGE in Japan can be traced back to before the reign of Temmu Tenno, the 40th Emperor of 673 AD. These first coins came from China but the first coins to be manufactured in Japan date from 708 AD. Twelve sets of coins were cast over a period of twelve eras until 958 AD and are nowadays highly prized by numismatists — they are known as the Twelve Ancient Cash. Following this was a period of about six centuries when rice, silk and linen were used as currency and it was not until just before Ieyasu, first Tokugawa Shogun, came to power in 1603 that a system of coinage was widely used again in Japan. Gold alloyed with silver in the form of thin oblong plates that had been struck with mint dies made up the currency at the beginning of the Tokugawa era, but during the course of the next 270 years when this family ruled Japan, the system evolved and became more complex, laying itself open to abuse by those in control of it.

The extravagances of the court and the urgent needs of the government frequently put great strains on the finances of the country; the simplest solution was for the officials in control to reduce the proportion of precious metal in the coins and also to reduce their weight. Hence the actual value of the currency decreased over the years causing financial chaos. The situation was complicated further because each daimyo in his feudal 'han' (territory they ruled) issued his own coinage, and naturally there was a lack of standardisation. Add to this the fact that many counterfeit coins were in circulation, and it will be realised that the first foreign traders to arrive at the end of the Tokugawa era during the 1850s were faced with problems!

*   *   *

Because of her isolation from the rest of the world, Japan was not at first aware of the relative value of gold and silver as determined by the western nations. Within Japan one unit of gold could be exchanged for five units of silver, whereas in the West it required about fifteen units of silver for one of gold. Many foreign merchants noticed this discrepancy, and by importing silver coins — mostly Mexican dollars — they bought up as much gold as they could and exported it to the West at enormous profits. Within a short time these western profiteers had reduced the gold reserves of Japan by a large amount before the inexperienced government realised what was happening. This did not put the new strangers on Japan's shores in good favour.

Perhaps in retaliation for this, some Japanese merchants a few years later were found to have paid large sums of money in debased gold coins to foreign merchants. These Japanese coins were called 'nibu' and the gold content had proved to be satisfactory for a number of years of trading, in fact the coins were trusted by everyone and the value of them was indicated in the Treaties between Japan and other countries. However, there was a great outcry from the foreign merchants when it was discovered that many of them consisted of no more than an alloy of lead covered with a thin layer of gold. The government felt obliged to make up the loss to the merchants, and an artisan called Takashima was imprisoned for supplying the dies and other apparatus to the Hizen clan in Kyushu. From that time onwards the foreign merchants always employed Chinese 'shroffs' to check, by biting and other forms of testing, each coin that was passed in a transaction.

Reforms were obviously necessary if Japan was to trade satisfactorily with other countries. In early 1868 the government sponsored an official investigation of the currency situation, and later in that year decided that a new uniform coinage was required. This could only be achieved if a government mint was set up. The investigation found that the quality of domestic coins was inferior to that of other countries and recommended that the actual machinery used to mint the coins be imported.

*   *   *

Action was taken quickly, and by November 1868 the machinery had arrived in Japan. Thomas B. Glover, a merchant in Nagasaki, had purchased the British Mint in Hong Kong on behalf of the Meiji

Government for $60,000. Building work was soon under way for a mint at Osaka, supervised by the Englishman, Thomas Waters. At first all went well. The government and the foreign diplomats cooperated closely in the planning of the new currency. John Robertson, the manager of the Oriental Bank in Yokohamà, offered sound advice and warned about possible trouble that could occur, and by early December nearly everything was ready for the production and distribution of the new coinage. However, shortly after, a fire destroyed the mint and all the machinery was rendered useless.

Annoyed but undaunted, the authorities set about ordering new machinery from England through the Oriental Bank Corporation and by the autumn of 1870, less than two years after the fire, the new mint was completed. It was announced that the new currency would be based on silver and that the unit would be called the 'yen.' One silver yen would equal one silver Mexican dollar, each weighing 416 grains. The coins would be circular to conform with the practice of other countries, and not oblong as had previously been the case in Japan. From the start, almost 100 years before Britain, a decimal system for the ten auxiliary coins was adopted.

Major William Kinder had been appointed the director of this new mint in March 1870 and had supervised its construction. He had previously been the master of the Hong Kong mint. Kinder was made responsible for the supervision of all departments of the mint, and he was in charge of all the Japanese employees as well as the ten British assistants who had come out to work with him. Also he was responsible for the mint's security and was expected to draw up rules and regulations so that it ran smoothly.

The mint buildings stood in twenty acres of reclaimed swamp-land and were most impressive. The Scottish journalist, John R. Black, reminiscing a few years later, described it as being a handsome building that combined the Tuscan and Doric orders. 'Nothing like it had been attempted in Japan,' he said 'and nothing approaching to it in simplicity and solidity has since been constructed. The grounds in which it stood were neatly laid out, and houses for the European and Japanese officials were provided.' Black then described the nine separate departments. The first where the gold was melted and refined, the next where twelve furnaces could melt 70,000 ounces of silver a day, then where the metal was rolled to the required thickness, after this where the blank discs were cut, followed by the engine room: eight lever presses made the impressions with the dies, and another department contained the hardening and blanching process. Finally they were assayed and tested, and then stored. This last department had an examination room attached to it in which the workers had to deposit all their clothes before leaving!

*   *   *

On 4 April 1871, the Imperial Mint was formally opened in state in the presence of the highest ministers and the foreign diplomats. The prime minister, Sanjo Daijin, had his speech read in English by an interpreter in which he praised the cooperation of Kinder and Waters, and of the Oriental Bank Corporation. Sanjo then proceeded to the engine room where he started the machinery and the mint began production. In August the first silver yen coins went into circulation, as well as the silver 20 sen coins (100 sen = 1 yen). All seemed set for smooth financial transactions in the Treaty Ports of Japan, but it was not to be. Foreign merchants were charged 2 per cent for coinage of their silver, and as silver Mexican dollars were established currency, they continued to be used. Also, strange as it may seem, the Japanese government refused to accept their own yen in payment of certain taxes and duties!

A few weeks after the opening of the mint, further complications occurred. The government decided to change from silver to the gold standard. This was because Germany had adopted the gold standard, and other European countries as well as America were considering the change. This gave Kinder and his over-worked staff even more to do. They had to prepare new dies in order to produce gold goins. The lack of skilled workmen during the early years was a severe handicap to Kinder in smoothly operating the mint, but as the plan from the start was to train and instruct Japanese men to run things for themselves, he was reluctant to hire any more foreign craftsmen.

Business suffered at first when the change to the gold standard was introduced because the foreign diplomats and the Japanese foreign ministry continued to disagree — the foreigners insisting on a strict adherence to the Treaty agreements that stipulated silver as the basis of the currency. Goods piled up on the wharves at Yokohama and elsewhere, and Kinder reported in 1872 that the gold coinage had exceeded the demand for it. Sir Harry Parkes, the British Ambassador, was quite irritated and wrote: 'It does not now matter a bit to foreigners who works the mint nor how it is managed. Its coinage can only be used for internal purposes.'

*   *   *

During July 1872, Emperor Meiji made his first tour of the seaports in the south-west and spent three days inspecting the mint. He met Kinder and expressed his appreciation for all he had achieved. Thousands of people then showed an interest in inspecting the mint after this imperial tour, and Kinder reported that during the first six months of 1874, 19500 Japanese and 224 foreign visitors came to see it.

It was the desire of the Japanese authorities that Japanese people should run the mint, and so when Kinder's five-year contract expired in February 1875, it was not renewed. Only six westerners stayed on as advisers, and by 1880 there were only two out of a total staff of over 600.

Currency problems continued for a number of years. The government found it difficult to maintain the gold standard, and it was not until it received a substantial war indemnity in gold after the Sino-

Japanese War of 1894/5 and the passing of a new coinage law in 1897 that any progress was made. By 1905 the market value of silver had risen so much that it exceeded the face value of the yen coins, and so the government had to legislate to reduce the weights of these coins. Following these adjustments, and the introduction of free refining and coinage for gold and silver, the yen began to be appreciated as a stable currency on the international market.

Chapter 29

Petroleum and Automobiles in Japan

THE WORLDWIDE DISRUPTION caused by the rapid rise of the Japanese automobile industry has left western manufacturers in a state of amazed disbelief, and raised many cries for political intervention. But even as late as 1926, the *Pocket Guide to Japan* mentioned that: 'The rickshaw is the ordinary means of conveyance, though motor cars and taxi cabs are fast taking the place of the rickshaw, especially in the large cities.'

An unknown American imported the first automobile into Japan in 1900, it was called the Stanley Locomobile. Four years later, a Mr Yamaba of Okayama Prefecture built the first made-in-Japan automobile which was steam driven. Then in 1908, the first petrol-engine car was built from parts imported from America by Engineer Kamanosuke Ichiyama who was sponsored by a Mr Yoshida.

Developments were slow, and it was not until the early 1920s that automobiles posed a serious threat to the livelihoods of the rickshaw-pullers. It was the well-established American business house of Sale and Frazar, Ltd that became the first agency for the importation of Ford motor cars. Then, under the directorship of E.W. Frazar, the origins of this concern went back into the early days of trade between America and the Far East, when Frazar's grandfather, George, was a captain of one of the famous sailing clippers that carried tea and silk from China to Boston.

George Frazar founded the firm of Frazar and Co. in Canton in 1834, and when Hong Kong was ceded to the British government in 1842 after the Opium War, he was one of the first foreign settlers in that port. His son, Everett, was sent to Shanghai in 1856 where he established another branch of the company. Two years previously, Everett had visited Japan with the Commodore Perry squadron, but considered that trading prospects were poor at that time, and it was not until 1878 that a branch of the Frazar Company was set up in Yokohama. In 1901, Everett died, and his son E.W. Frazar, succeeded as head of the business. The following year he combined with Messrs Sale and

Company which in 1904 merged into a corporation, Sale and Frazar Ltd. The Sale Company had begun in 1879 when George Sale, an Englishman, had arrived in Japan to set up a business house.

Sale and Frazar Ltd covered a huge range of business. It was responsible for introducing the first phonograph into Japan, as well as importing the first American locomotive. It supplied the first electrical dynamo, installing the first generating plant for the Emperor's palace and for the Tokyo Electric Light Company. Then in the early 1920s, without any consumer research, it imported a number of Ford cars. These were difficult to sell, for Japan was still broadly divided into rich and poor classes, and the rich preferred the luxury of the large and expensive Buicks or Packards. The poor could hardly afford to buy bicycles. In order to overcome his dilemma, E.W. Frazar decided to start the first taxi business in Tokyo using his fleet of unsold Fords. He began with just 250 vehicles, and the business immediately began to flourish as the novel experience of riding in a car could be afforded by all at 6 *yen* per hour. Soon, he was ordering more shipments of Fords for other new taxi companies and for private buyers, and as their popularity increased it was found that there were not enough transport ships to bring them from America. So the Ford Company decided to build a car assembly factory near Yokohama in 1925, and sell their products directly to customers. This ended a lucrative part of E.W.'s business.

It seems to be a strange circle to find that the rickshaw was first constructed in Japan by an American, while the rapid decline of the rickshaw business was also caused by an American working in Japan!

*   *   *

With the introduction of the automobile, problems arose because of the state of Japan's roads. These were in an extremely poor condition because of the topographical nature of the country, and because of traditional attitudes that persisted from feudal times. One commentator explained in 1919 that: 'In old Japan the building of roads and bridges was not encouraged, particularly in the vicinity of boundaries between daimyo dominions, where access was blocked or rendered uninviting by barriers for the strict examination of travellers.' He went on to state that after the opening of the country when Japan became a unified nation, the government did undertake a road-building programme, but 'as yet this side of Japan's development has not at all kept pace with her progress in other directions, and the roads of the nation are in a poor way compared with other countries; most of them are not only ill-made but too narrow for modern vehicles.'

Englishman, W.B. Mason, author and long-term resident in Japan, wrote in the same year about touring: 'Cars are not infrequently brought by tourists themselves to Japan for touring purposes, but, taking it all together, the roads, with few exceptions, are not well adapted to them.

Roads and bridges, swept away by the floods which now and then devastate the land, are long left unrepaired, while the roads in the more hilly parts are apt to be much neglected at all times.'

The rocky mountainous backbone to the Japanese archipelago, the volcanic Japan Alps, with the numerous ridges emanating from it like huge ribs, and the steep-sided river valleys carved amongst them, all prone to landslides caused by earthquakes, was an ideal setting for containing isolated, independent communities in feudal times. But for a unified, industrial nation with a need for rapid transportation routes, the landscape presented difficult technical and financing problems. Photographs from the early age of motor cars show intrepid motorists in their vehicles being poled across wide, fast-moving rivers on flimsy wooden rafts.

The availability of petrol to run vehicles also caused problems. As today, political forces became involved in the supply of petroleum after the advent of the motor car, and whereas in the pre-automobile era, the production of petroleum within Japan from her own oilfields appeared to be catching up with demand, the predictions were all completely upset as more cars appeared on the roads as a result of increasing affluence.

* * *

It was known in Japan over 1000 years ago that crude oil or petroleum would burn, but it was not used as such for other materials were more efficient, convenient and easier to control. Its insecticide properties were soon discovered and this was its main use up to the middle of the Tokugawa era. In the early 1700s, some oil was used for illumination by the poorer sections of society, but the dangerous fumes and bad smell limited its use. Temples and shrines were lit by clean-burning vegetable wax and incense sticks were lit to obliterate the slight smell from the lanterns. By 1862, the year that Harvard professor Raphael Pumpelly, a mining engineer and geologist in the employ of the Japanese government, travelled to Hokkaido to survey for minerals, oil was used to light at least one shrine. Pumpelly recorded: 'A further ride of a few miles brought us to the large fishing village of Yamakshinai. Near this place, between the shore and the cliff, there is a marsh several acres in extent, in which numerous tepid springs bring to the surface a mineral oil of the consistency of tar. Here we found several priests, who not only used this product for light, but also in the manufacture of India ink. These old men received us hospitably, and listened with incredulous wonder to our stories of artesian borings, and flowing wells of petroleum.'

This was some time before the anti-western writer, Sada Kaiseki, wrote his essay 'Rampu Bokoku Ron' (On Oil Lamps as a National Disaster) in which he cursed oil lamps as being symbols of the evil of western culture. But the majority of Japanese were in favour of western ideas and artifacts, and many wanted to own oil lamps because of their greater safety in wooden houses.

Just after the opening of Japan, petroleum was imported in small bottles by Chinese merchants in Nagasaki as one of the curiosities of the West. Only eight cases were imported in 1869, 70 came in the next year and by 1872 the number was 3530. Russian oil was imported by the Samuel Samuel Company from 1887 to 1900, when it changed to Borneo oil because of the anti-Russian feelings that had arisen. Just before the Russo-Japanese War (1904-05), placards were displayed in some cities warning people not to use Russian oil, with the threat that one's house would be burned down if this occurred.

The American Standard Oil Company began direct sales to Japan in 1893, and also sent experts to help develop the domestic oil industry. This had previously progressed slowly because of the primitive methods of extraction used. Wells were dug by hand and the deepest did not exceed 200 metres, and the few refineries near the fields in Echigo prefecture (Niigata) output only 179,000 gallons in 1889 compared with 28 million gallons imported. But in the following three decades, several companies were carefully organised, American equipment and experts arriving to produce more efficient ways to extract the resource. A gusher drilled by the Nippon Petroleum Co. in 1891 had created a new interest in Japanese oil production prospects, and, as allowed under the 1866 treaties and a later amendment to the mining laws which permitted foreign companies to participate in mining enterprises, the Standard Oil Co. established itself in the Niigata region as the International Oil Co. It first built a large, modern refinery, and then began drilling using improved techniques unknown in Japan, finally it started negotiations with the 95 smaller producers to buy up all their production. The intention was clear — to create for themselves a monopoly in domestic production of burning oil which accounted for about 75% of the market, and by increasing the price of the oil the same company imported, for which a 20% duty was levied, an enormous profit could be made. This strategy was becoming a normal practice for large oil concerns in many countries, with disastrous results on local economies.

But in Japan this pattern was not followed. The Japanese business community had rapidly become aware of such methods of modern capitalism, and true to the old samurai spirit, the 95 smaller producers rallied to the Nippon and Hoden Oil Companies instead of the foreign intruder. The International Oil Co. failed to achieve a monopoly, and produced less than 6% of domestic output. But that was not all. Dissatisfied with the terms of the Treaty of Portsmouth as proscribed by American mediators after Japan's success in the Russo-Japanese War and disgusted with Californian legislation against Japanese immigrants, new laws were passed that withdrew the rights of foreigners to mine in Japan. So the International Oil Co. was forced to sell all its facilities in Japan to Nippon Petroleum for a mere token payment, and thus the entire production of oil in Japan became Japanese owned.

In that same year, 1907, the Toyo Line, a company operating luxury passenger ships between San Francisco and ports in the Far East decided to convert their ships to oil firing. The plan was to import crude oil from California, refine it in Yokohama and Dalny, the home ports of the fleet, and use the fuel oil to propel the ships while the lamp oil and other by-products could be sold. But there was one great complication. The imported crude oil contained a high proportion of sulphur, and Japanese refiners did not have the technology to remove it, and the plan failed. Cooperation with foreign companies seemed vital, and agreements with the Standard and Royal Dutch Oil Companies were eventually reached.

*   *   *

At midnight on 25 May 1914, the Nippon Oil Co. struck an extraordinarily large deposit near Akita. At first it gushed out at 360 gallons per minute, making its daily output over half the yearly output of 1879. Nippon Oil shares advanced by ¥22 the next day, and a great optimism pervaded Japanese business and political circles. For it seemed that Japan could become independent of imported American oil, and therefore the threat of cutting off Japan's supplies in the event of a war had disappeared. The Great Japan Petroleum Mining Co. was founded in 1916, with the proclamation that: 'Japan can be made practically independent of all foreign oilfields if her own resources are thoroughly developed.' Negotiations were started with Peru as a new supplier of oil in the hope that the shackles of dependence on American supplies could be broken.

But it was not to be. The following year domestic output dropped, demand increased with the building of more oil-fired ships, the import of automobiles, the expansion of industry and the mobilisation of the military during the Great War. New forms of military transport, including aircraft, demanded highly refined oil and so the dependence on western oil companies continued.

In 1936, the Mitsubishi Co. developed a charcoal-burning automobile in an attempt to utilise alternative energy resources. But the mould for the future had been set in oil, and when in July 1940 the United States began a policy of licensing oil shipments to Japan which were essential to keep the Japanese military machine operational, a strong reaction was inevitable.

Chapter 30

The Lindberghs and Aviation
in Japan

THE WHOLE, well-planned project seemed doomed to disaster. Not a violent, spectacular disaster, but a silly and trivial one. Colonel Charles Lindbergh's small, orange and black seaplane, *Sirius,* was drifting dangerously towards the surf and the rocky shore. The anchor rope had parted and the single engine would not start! Once in the surf the plane would turn over and its fragile plywood fuselage, wings and pontoons would become just so much driftwood on the beach. They had been forced down the previous night by thick fog and had eventually landed on the open sea on the leeward side of Ketoi, a small Japanese island to the north of Hokkaido in the chain that ran up the North Pacific to the Aleutians. Lindbergh and Anne, his wife of two years and now his radio operator, both saw the situation and raised their arms and shouted in the direction of the *Shinshiru Maru.* But the Japanese sailors had already noticed what was happening and were rowing steadily towards them.

The previous evening Anne Lindbergh had received the morse-coded message from JOC in Nemuro: 'We welcome eagerly you here tomorrow...' JOC had then requested the two-masted *Shinshiru Maru* to sail to Ketoi Island and offer assistance. The Lindberghs certainly appreciated it now as the sailors rapidly and efficiently attached a line to the *Sirius* and made it fast to their own anchor. The*Sirius* was only feet from the breaking surf, but the danger was over. The dignity and glory of the Lindberghs were saved and they could continue their flight from New York to Nanking — the first such Great Circle flight ever made.

Adventure, however, was not over for them as is recorded by Anne Lindbergh in her delightfully poetic book *North to the Orient* (Harcourt and Brace, 1935). The weather had worsened and the rain poured down that August day in 1931 as the Lindberghs slept uncomfortably in the baggage compartment of *Sirius*. The sea was growing rougher as a typhoon swirled northeast along the Pacific coast, there was a danger that the new anchor would drag. Through the noise of the early hours of the morning, Lindbergh could hear the voices of the Japanese sailors just outside the plane. Sliding back the cockpit cover, he was handed a radio message. 'The Japanese people eagerly welcome you to Japan and await your safe arrival.' He was a little angry at this disturbance. But in the morning found that the sailors had attached a two-inch hawser from their boat to the plane — the message was merely an excuse to do this. The sailors were worried about the safety of Japan's new guests.

Still the weather was too rough to clean the plugs of the engine, and so the *Shinshiru Maru* towed the *Sirius* southwards to the next island where in the calm of a bay inside an extinct volcano the maintenance work was completed. Once again they were in the air heading for the main islands of Japan, but the fog continued to cover Nemuro and they had to put down on a lake on Munashiri Island where they enjoyed the hospitality of a very poor fishing family who lived in an isolated hut by the side of the lake. Anne practised the few words of Japanese she had learned, with little success. Eventually they resorted to drawings for communication.

Within two days the Lindberghs were being paraded along the main streets of Tokyo amid cheers and flag waving. They had landed at Kasimigaura on Tokyo Bay and were met by the American ambassador and other notables. Altogether 19 days were spent in Tokyo as they were shown around all the usual tourist sites, attended receptions and parties and made speeches. Quite a contrast in sweltering Tokyo to the frozen, isolated Arctic settlements of two weeks' earlier!

The people of Osaka received them equally as warmly, and from there they visited Kyoto and Nara by car. As they were about to roar away from a wharf in Osaka, with lines of white-uniformed officials bidding them 'sayonara' with great ceremony, Lindbergh noticed that the baggage compartment was not as orderly as he had left it. He was always meticulous in stowing all the equipment — from the emergency aluminium jar of matches to the snake serum syringe, from the emergency rubber boat to the fishlines and hooks — and he knew something was amiss. He lifted the canvas flap to replace the two canteens that had been untidily left on top of the other luggage, when he noticed a human head. It was almost invisible amongst the baggage. Further investigation revealed a gray cloth suit containing the rest of the body. They had a stowaway! Lindbergh informed one of the officers outside, and the message was passed along. Soon, officers were swarming around and on the plane. They asked the stowaway to come out, with no response. Eventually, a boy of 18 in school uniform was pulled out by force and marched away with an officer holding each arm. The boy had wanted to go to America, but his plan had failed — *Sirius* was now headed for China anyway. As it finally took off from the water, a few other planes flew past in a farewell salute, for aviation was not unknown in Japan at this time. In fact, 1931 was the year that Haneda airport was opened.

*   *   *

Successful flights by balloons took place in Japan in the early Meiji era, the photographs and ukiyo-e prints show some of them in the air. But the first fixed-wing attempt at flight was not a success. In October 1910, Mr Narabara revved up the 25 H.P. engine of his heavily-built biplane but it never left the ground. However, in December of that year Lieut. Hino of the Imperial Navy flew for just over one minute in a 24 H.P.

German-built monoplane, and in the same month a French-built
'Farman' biplane flew for four minutes with Lieut. Tokugawa at the
controls. It seems that flight in Japan developed slowly at first for it had
been almost exactly seven years since the Wright brothers took off at
Kitty Hawk on the world's first powered flight in a heavier-than-air
machine. By 1905 their third plane was making 30-minute flights, and
could turn, circle and make figures of eight. Still, after 1910 in Japan
aircraft of various designs and sizes were constructed of wood, wire and
canvas with varying degrees of success and disaster in their flights. The
Japanese Imperial Army took an interest in 1911, as a report of 1919
explains:

'Aviation was not introduced into the Japanese army until 1911
when two native officers trained in France returned to organise an air
service. By 1912 two more officers were trained, and three others in
1913. Since then this service has seen much greater development. A
training ground was established at Tokorozawa near Tokyo, where some
ten flight officers are graduated every year. The army now possesses
considerably more aeroplanes and its own airship.'

*   *   *

After the end of World War I developments in aviation in Japan, as
in other countries, were rapid and diverse. The abortive attempt to
start an aerial postal service between Shibura in Tokyo and Yokohama
in 1911, with W.B. Atwater as pilot, failed because of engine trouble
after only one flight. But on 4 October 1919 a service between Amagasaki
in Hyogo and Tokyo was established. This was celebrated by a superb
postcard, some of which were carried on the first flight. Earlier in that
year the Atlantic had been crossed for the first time by air by the US
Navy Curtiss N.C. flying boat commanded by Lieut.-Com. A.C. Read.

Soon, visits to Japan by foreign aviators became frequent. British
Major S. McLaren arrived in 1925, as did Argentine Major Zanie,
followed by American Colonel Gaville in 1928. Earlier, in 1922, 29
British instructors, under Air-Commodore Semville had arrived to teach
in the Imperial Navy technical college and so aviation for military
purposes developed further.

The first passenger air service began in July 1929 on a route from
Tokyo to Osaka and on to Fukuoka. German-made Fokker Super
Universal aircraft were used which carried their six passengers at 170
km. per hour. The Tokyo — Osaka fare was 30 yen, expensive when it
is considered that the average monthly salaries of executives was then
about 50 yen.

As the years passed air services improved and expanded, and the
military became more and more powerful. A new verse was added to
the patriotic song of the naval cadets attending Etajima College where
officers were trained:

'Oh! strong ones of Etajima!
You are just like dragons who hide in a lake
Who, if a chance comes when storm clouds gather
Dash up into the sky,
To fight till we fall
Is the sincere cry of our hearts!'

After the storm clouds of the Pacific War had been blasted away, new developments in aviation in Japan took place. Jet propulsion put Tokyo within hours of America and Europe, and when, in 1958, Haneda Airport was returned to Japan by the Occupation forces a new era in passenger travel began. Unfortunately, 'bird pollution' at Haneda became a problem because the airport was next to a tidal estuary. However, the problem was solved in 1961 by hiring teams of marksmen to shoot any innocent bird in sight from the edge of the airport.

Meanwhile, Charles Lindbergh, who had flown 50 combat missions in the Pacific War, had become a director of the Wildlife Fund. This situation was a far cry from the pioneer days of aviation when Lindbergh's wife could write in 1935: 'I was conscious again of the fundamental magic of flying, a miracle that has nothing to do with any of its practical purposes — purposes of speed, accessibility, and convenience — and will not change as they change.'

After leaving Japan, Charles Lindbergh and his wife landed on Lotus Lake, Nanking, in China. The lower Yangtze River was flooded and the *Sirius* was used to help in surveying operations and in delivering medical supplies. This work being over, they flew up the Yangtze to Hankow and landed on the river near the British aircraft carrier *Hermes*. The plane was winched aboard for safety and the Lindberghs lived on the ship for a few days; this was the first time that a woman had slept on board the *Hermes*.

As the *Sirius* was being lowered back into the river, the current took it before the cable was released and it swung dangerously around. The Lindberghs leapt out into the water for their lives. The plane was badly damaged. After being rescued, Charles Lindbergh, drinking Bovril and hot brandy, supervised the rescue of *Sirius*. The flight was over and they returned to America by ship where their baby son was waiting for them. *HMS Hermes* transported the *Sirius* to Shanghai from where a merchant ship took it to the Lockheed Aircraft factory in California for repairs.

In 1933, *Sirius* made a 30,000-mile survey flight around the North Atlantic Ocean. The next year it was put into the American Museum of Natural History in New York.

Chapter 31

Thomas Glover and the Early Foreign Traders

IT WAS GENERALLY AGREED in Japan, after the first treaty was signed with America in 1854, that westerners would be welcome to trade in the Treaty Ports if some way could be found to keep opium and Christianity out of the country. However, according to one American writing in 1859:

'The first English ship which entered a port of Japan, Nagasaki, after the conclusion of the American treaty and before the English treaty was concluded, was a smuggler of opium, attempting to introduce it stealthily and fraudulently into a nation which does not use it and whose laws prohibit it. I saw that ship. The trading house owning that vessel has been known to make, as I am informed, half a million dollars a year in the Chinese opium trade, and is not content with the wages of its iniquity. It was one of the first English trading houses in China.'

The trading house referred to would seem to be Jardine, Matheson & Co., infamous for its dealings in opium at this time, which despatched the ship *Troas*, under Captain Henry Holmes, to Nagasaki in January 1859. The shipment contained sugar, velvet and 'Chinese cargo.' Previous to this, as far back as 1846, British merchants had traded indirectly with Japan from Hong Kong and other Chinese ports through Ryukyu (Okinawa).

Fortunately, no opium found its way into Japan, and subsequent ships brought more useful cargoes. In September 1859, a young Scotsman arrived in Nagasaki after a voyage from Shanghai. He was Thomas Blake Glover, aged 21, and he was to spend the rest of his life in Japan and have a great influence on the development of the country. He soon set up a trading firm in Nagasaki, T.B. Glover & Co., for importing firearms, ships and various machinery in exchange for gold, silver, raw silk, tea and marine products which he exported.

As his business grew and he leased more waterfront land, he imported a 762 mm gauge steam engine called 'The Iron Duke' which he demonstrated to an interested audience. Obviously this was an attempt to initiate a programme of railway building in Japan, but it was to take another decade before it became a reality. It may have been then that Glover realised that full-scale industrialisation of Japan, with railway tracks crossing all feudal boundaries, would not take place until after the Emperor had been restored to unite the country. For he was soon supplying arms and munitions to the pro-Imperial forces in the south, protecting many of the revolutionary samurai and helping to send young Japanese students abroad to study.

180

In 1865, against the instructions of the British consul in Yokohama, Glover arranged to supply a warship and 7300 rifles to arm the pro-Imperial rebels in Kyushu. By February 1866, the Satsuma and Choshu clans had bought 15 steamships, one sailing vessel, six steam-saw factories, machines for a dockyard and an engine shop from Glover and other foreign traders. The Satsuma daimyo (feudal lord) was always fair and honest with Glover in all their dealings and they soon became good personal friends, Glover sometimes visiting his customer at Kagoshima. Glover did do business with members of the Shogunate (military rulers), but found them less reliable as regards payment.

It was Glover who arranged the visit of the British minister, Sir Harry Parkes, and a party of British dignitaries to the daimyo of Satsuma in July 1866. It was a peace mission during which Parkes hoped to persuade the rebellious daimyo that a good understanding between the Emperor, the Shogun and all the daimyo was the best policy, and that any opposition to foreign intercourse would cause only suffering, and such opposition was, in any case, doomed to failure.

Two British naval ships, *HMS Serpent* and *HMS Salamis,* were used to transport the party to Kagoshima and then on to Iwojima. There was great interest shown in these ships by all classes of people, and thousands came to look over them. The firing of the great guns and the drills demonstrated by the marines were most impressive. Meanwhile, the foreign visitors enjoyed themselves in discussions, hunting for deer and wild boar in the woods and eating a great variety of food. The British were surprised to find a foundary next to the daimyo's palace grounds where large cannon were cast, and shot and shells manufactured, while a steam lathe was used to finish the weapons.

*   *   *

After the Meiji Restoration of 1868, business for Glover & Co. increased considerably. Early in 1868, the government sponsored an official investigation of the currency situation, and later in that year recommended that a new standard coinage be introduced. This could only be achieved if a government mint was set up, for at that time each 'han' (fief) produced its own coins which varied from place to place, and the foreign merchants would not accept them but insisted that silver Mexican dollars be used. The investigation found that the quality of domestic coins was inferior to that of other countries, and suggested that the actual machinery for minting the coins be imported. Action was taken quickly, and by November 1868 the machinery had arrived in Japan, for Glover had arranged the purchase of the British mint in Hong Kong on behalf of the Meiji government at a cost of $60,000.

Work was soon under way for the construction of suitable buildings to house the machinery and the mint in Osaka,and this was supervised by English engineer, Thomas Waters. All went well as first as the government and foreign diplomats cooperated closely in the planning

of the new currency, and by December 1869 everything was ready for
the production of the new silver coins to be called 'yen.' But then disaster
struck as a raging fire destroyed the whole mint, rendering all the
machinery useless. It took a further year before new equipment arrived
from England and was installed in a new building.

Glover's other business activities involved the purchase of the
Takashima coal mine on an island outside Nagasaki harbour, helping
to develop the Japan tea trade and the construction of the Kosuge
dockyard. As he grew older, Glover moved to Tokyo where he was an
adviser to the Mitsubishi Company. In 1908, he was awarded the Second
Order of the Rising Sun by the Meiji government for his contribution
to Japan's progress. He died on 16 December 1911 and was buried in
the International Cemetery at Sakamoto-cho in Tokyo. His fine
Victorian house at Nagasaki has been preserved as a 'cultural asset' and
is visited by thousands of tourists and school-students each year. In 1961
a metal bust of Glover was unveiled in the grounds of his house. He
was survived by his Japanese wife, Tsuruko Dankawa from Osaka, and
a son and daughter, Tomisaburo and Ohana; the son later became the
managing director of the Nagasaki Fisheries and Steamship Company.

                              *   *   *

By the end of 1861 there were 57 foreign companies in Nagasaki, and
37 of these were controlled by Britons. They formed a Chamber of
Commerce so that trading could be coordinated and made more
profitable, and they cooperated with the Governor of Nagasaki in the
running of the first municipal council which endeavoured to improve
living conditions in the city. Some foreign members were elected to
serve on this council. A foreigners' club was set up where they could
all meet after attending to business all day, as was an Episcopal Church
which they attended on Sundays. A postal system was established
between Nagasaki and Yokohama in 1862 by these merchants.

There were, however, many dishonest practices undertaken by the
foreign merchants in those early years. It all stemmed from the import
and export duties imposed by the authorities. The long-established
Chinese merchants benefited from lower duties than the westerners,
and bribery of officials made it easy for them to import goods without
paying any duty at all. The westerners were thus at a great disadvantage,
and had to resort to drastic measures. They, too, began to bribe officials.
They grossly undervalued the goods they were handling, declaring less
weights and quantities than were actually on the ships. Competition was
fierce, and the 'treasure' or gold trade had for many years been carefully
controlled by Chinese Guilds who maintained a firm monopoly despite
plans tried by Glover and others to break this monopoly.

The foreign firm that outlasted all the others in Nagasaki was Holme,
Ringer & Co. that began trading in 1868 with the assistance of Glover.
It started the whaling industry in Japan, and operated steam-driven

trawlers equipped with harpoon guns. Its other interests included tea and coal, and it was an agent for almost 100 foreign companies when it celebrated its jubilee in 1918.

*   *   *

By this time, of course, Japanese businesses were flourishing all over the country, in Taiwan and Manchuria and other parts of the vast Japanese Empire. Adopting and adapting practices from the West, many manufacturing companies expanded and were successful in exporting their goods worldwide. Opium was kept out of Japan through strict regulations, although through Empire-building in Taiwan and on the continent, the Japanese administration in these places inherited an opium problem already existing there. The strategy was to create a government opium monopoly to manufacture the drug, issue licences to habitual users who could buy it only from licensed vendors, and thus eradicate the habit. However, as an annual profit of ¥6 million was made through the monopoly, and as officials issuing licences were not always honest, there was, as one report put it 'a temptation to encourage rather than discourage the use of the drug.' But there was a general decrease in the number of users during the Japanese jurisdiction of Taiwan.

But the ideas of Christianity had eventually been allowed to enter Japan, mainly as a political move of appeasement, the missionaries being given free reign to operate as they wished. Although the religion made little impact in its organised form, some of the activities or rituals of the Christian churches were used in many Japanese companies to promote a unity of purpose and an identity of the group. For formal rituals in any sphere are the most economic means of providing social order. One of these was the creation of the famous company 'hymn' sung every morning by all company members in a sombre assembly. In translation, that of Matsushita Electric Industrial Co. is as follows:

> 'For the building of a new Japan
> Let's put our strength and mind together
> Doing our best to promote production
> Sending our goods to the people of the world,
> Endlessly and continuously,
> Like water from a gushing fountain.
> Grow, industry, grow, grow!
> Harmony and sincerity:
> Matsushita Electric!'

While the company hymn of Suntory Ltd., producers and exporters of alcoholic beverages, is translated as:

'What a manly name "Red Light" is!
Shaking the axis of the earth,
The sun rises with a roar at dawn,
Like our company, beloved company,
With its bright future rising!'

Such propaganda devices, probably adopted, as noted above, from Christian ritual, have proved to be effective tools in post-war Japanese industry. The impact of Japanese products worldwide have increased standards of living, and provided a richer spiritual and wider educational base for a large proportion of mankind. Somehow, Karl Marx's pronouncement, written in the cloistered dignity among the privileged users of the Reading Room in the British Museum, about the connection between opium and religion, takes on a new dimension in the history of Japanese trade.

Chapter 32

Westernisation of the Japanese Legal System

IN THE DECADE before the Meiji Restoration of 1868, when the Emperor once again became the figurehead of the Japanese government, hundreds of Europeans and Americans visited Japan. Most of them were confined to the narrow limits of the Treaty Ports and saw very little of the country just as today foreign seamen are confined to the 50-mile radius of their ships. Members of the diplomatic corps, however, were permitted to travel around under the protection and surveillance of government '*yakunin.*' One of these was Aime Humbert, the Minister Plenipotentiary of the Swiss Republic, who was resident in Japan from 1863-64. His vivid descriptions of the Japanese legal processes, in which the sword and the bamboo stave played important roles, make it easy to understand why western governments insisted on 'extra-territoriality' in their treaties. As J.E. de Becker later said: 'It would have been positively criminal for the Foreign Powers to have placed their nationals at the mercy of the ignorant, untrained, brutal Japanese judges of those early days, when the grossest forms of torture were freely employed as officially recognised part and parcel of judicial proceedings.'

'The repression of common offences,' states Humbert, 'is marked from beginning to end by ferocity.' He then proceeds to describe how the police fall upon suspected persons like vultures on their prey, and that in the eyes of a Japanese judge, every accused man is guilty. The confession of guilt — a requisite under ancient Chinese Law — was extracted from the accused by a rain of blows on his shoulders with a bamboo stave. If this failed, he was compelled to kneel on a framework of hard wood and great slabs of stone were placed on his bended legs until they went red with the pressure of his blood and until the pain produced the replies that the judge wanted to hear.

The prisons were just as bad as the ones in Europe at that time — as the one preserved at Meijimura shows — but prisoners were not permitted to shave or comb their hair, or even allowed to speak. The only time that they could utter a sound was when a fellow prisoner was led out to execution. But the actual terms of imprisonment did not last long, except for the accused persons awaiting trial, for the main part of the punishment for misdemeanours and petty offences consisted of flogging or branding with a red-hot lancet. A 'totting-up' system operated whereby more than 24 brands meant death.

The execution of lesser criminals took place within the prison compound. Decapitation was the usual method and the severed heads were displayed in public for 24 hours afterwards; this was the penalty for such crimes as murder, treason, rape, forgery and even adultery and sale of children. For more serious crimes, crucifixion or death-by-fire were carried out in public after the condemned man had been paraded around the town on a horse with banners proclaiming his crime and announcing the execution. Attempts were made to make the punishment fit the crime, therefore the arsonist who tried three times to burn down the foreign settlement in Yokohama was put to the flames. Because iron chains were not used in Japan at that time, the straw ropes binding him were covered with wet earth to prevent them from burning through.

The noble classes were not subjected to such forms of justice. For their crimes against the state or against a stronger rival family, they were banished to an off-shore island like Hachijojima or Sadoshima or else they were expected to commit 'seppuku' or 'harakiri' (self-disembowelment). This mode of suicide fascinated foreign observers from the start, and it was explained that boys of noble birth were taught by their teachers of swordsmanship that the short sword correctly inserted brought instant and painless death. Unfortunately, it was impossible to confirm such assurances, but up until the end of World War II, this method continued to be used, unofficially according to the books, for satisfying feelings of guilt. Even today in 'Yakuza' (gangster) circles, the self-amputation of the small finger on the right hand serves as an instrument of justice.

* * *

When the new foreign consulates were built in the Treaty Ports, a small prison was often included in the structure. A policeman and jailer were members of the consular staff and a room was selected where a court of justice could be held, with the ambassador or consul as the judge. Each diplomatic corps was responsible for dealing with the illegal acts of their own nationals under the law of their own land. This was the nature of extra-territoriality, and it was a source of considerable embarrassment and irritation to the Japanese government.

When Michael Moss, a Yokohama merchant, was returning to the settlement after illegally shooting game in Kanagawa in November 1860, a group of Japanese policemen tried to arrest him and his servant — for the killing of birds by firearms was forbidden within a distance of 50 *ri* of the Shogun's palace. Moss's gun went off, perhaps intentionally or perhaps by accident, and one policeman was severely injured. Under Japanese law Moss would certainly have been decapitated, but the British consul, Vyse, merely fined him $1000 and deported him. This was one of the first cases that caused a great deal of friction and hard feeling between the Japanese and foreigners under extra-territoriality. But what could be done to ameliorate the situation?

The answer was to adapt certain aspects of western law into the Japanese system so that extra-territoriality could cease. But unlike the introduction of purely scientific or technological achievements from the West, such as the building of railways, lighthouses, the production of beer, etc. where techniques and processes could be adopted wholesale, western law could not be imported and absorbed in quite the same way. The law of any country is irretrievably bound into the social customs, and way of life of its people; evidently, the social customs, structure of society and so many aspects of life were completely different in Japan from that in the West. Change in this respect, therefore, was no easy task. In fact, it was probably the most difficult task that the Meiji rulers attempted. Indeed, success for Japan as far as western democratic and legal traditions were concerned, came only in 1898 after about 40 years of painstaking research and debate had been undertaken.

It was also necessary to consider the fact that Japanese society at this time was changing dramatically due to the changing economic situation. Industry brought wealth to the energetic ex-samurai and trade brought wealth to the formerly low-status merchant class. The new capitalism meant that individuals, by their own efforts and risks, could accumulate wealth and it would have been grossly unjust to insist that the male head of the house *(koseki)* to which that individual traditionally belonged, possessed all the fruit of that individual's efforts. Also the head of the house did not want to be held responsible for any debts of enterprising members of his house. Although today this feudal structure has not disappeared completely — an individual's *'koseki'* (family register) is still an important document in education, job-applications, etc. and the ceremonies relating to Shinto ancestor-worship occur universally — the importance of the individual and his rights were recognised at this time. At first, the problem lay in the Japanese language. There were no Chinese ideograms (characters) for 'rights,' 'property,' 'compensation,' etc. Even the ideogram for 'law' *(ho)* —

composed of three parts meaning 'water,' 'an animal that can distinguish the just from the unjust' and 'the act of disappearing' — did not convey exactly the same meaning as 'law' was understood in Europe. 'Ho' was generally interpreted as those arbitrary edicts proclaimed by the ruling class. It was at first to the energetic and brilliant scholar Rinsho Mitsukuri that the government looked to translate the French Civil Code into Japanese. He began in 1869 with little knowledge of legal science, no dictionary and no French lawyer to consult. But he succeeded and his work was recognised by Shimpei Eto, the Minister of Justice. What Mitsukuri did was to invent new ideograms for certain terms and concepts — which was done with the aid of a Chinese translation of an English text on International Law. Professor Yosiyuki Noda of the Faculty of Law of Gakushuin University in *Introduction to Japanese Law* (1976) says that Mitsukuri 'was like an architect who had to begin by making his own bricks.'

Mitsukuri took five years to complete his work; Eto was keen to get this Japanised French code adopted, but it was not to be. However, the translations did influence Japanese justice and an urgent need was identified to formulate some kind of Civil Code. Eto set up a committee to draft another one,but shortly after this, in 1874, he was executed for leading an insurrection against the government — a government unwilling to allow universal individual liberty.

*   *   *

It soon became apparent to the Japanese side that cooperation with foreign experts who had had direct experience of western law was required. Attempts to revise the unequal treaties began almost as soon as they had been signed. In 1871, for example, the American, Erastus Peshine Smith, began to work for the Japanese Foreign Ministry. He was an adviser on International Law and his energy and enthusiasm impressed many high officials. He identified himself absolutely with Japan's interests during his five years' employment and was responsible for three major treaty revision drafts, but the frivolous behaviour of this 60-year-old Harvard graduate, especially with respect to his Japanese mistresses, caused some concern in certain circles along the way.

In 1872, Georges Bousquet, a French lawyer, arrived to establish a special School of French Law, to lecture and to advise the Justice Ministry. But of all the 3000 or so *'oyatoi gaikokujin'* (honorable foreign menials) employed by the Japanese government at the time, the one who had most influence must have been Professor Emile Gustav Boissonade de Fontarabie of the Faculty of Law in Paris. He arrived in 1873 at the age of 48 and he was over 70 when he left. By that time he had been instrumental in helping to effect changes in the whole legal system of Japan. His salary was a fantastic $1300 per month and in addition he received another $1200 per month in gold. He was employed by both the Justice Ministry and Privy Council simultaneously, and later by the Cabinet.

One day, soon after he arrived, he was disturbed in his work in the Justice Ministry building as he was reading through a draft dealing with civil rights. Screams of terror were coming from downstairs, and he went to investigate. Down in a dark cellar of the building he found officers of the law torturing an unfortunate suspect. Boissonade became very angry at this barbaric procedure and immediately threatened to resign his post. He was eventually pacified after a promise was made that torture in criminal procedures would soon become illegal. In 1876, torture did become illegal.

By 1877, Boissonade finished drafting a penal code and a criminal procedure code which, after translation, was submitted to the legislature for modification. They were adopted and promulgated in 1880 to come into force in 1882. These were the first modern codes of law to operate in Japan, and Boissonade's penal code continued until 1908. Next, Boissonade set about drafting a civil code as applied to property, leaving that as applied to family and succession law in the hands of Japanese draftsmen for they were more closely associated with the traditional mores of the people. It took 10 years to complete this task and, together with the sections worked out by the Japanese experts, it was to come into force in 1894. However, things did not go smoothly for there was great opposition to Boissonade's work: Japanese lawyers were divided into two camps and articles and polemics circulated, some supporting and some condemning Boissonade's civil code. Part of the reason for this was that students of English Law had become a strong faction in Japan at the Law Faculty in the University of Tokyo and they objected to the overall French character of the code. In 1892, the Imperial Diet, taking advantage of these arguments, voted to postpone it for they were showing a growing interest in the German and Prussian systems.

*   *   *

In the early years of the Meiji era many translations of the classics of European thought had appeared in Japan. The works of J.S. Mill, J. Bentham, J.J. Rousseau, etc. were well known to Japanese intellectuals and influenced their thinking. A number of Japanese judges had studied French and English Law and, despite their freedom within the old system, they tried to make their decisions according to it. Liberal groups flourished but found it impossible to gain any real political power. The government, appearing to bend to the liberals, drew up a constitution but instead of being based on the French model as expected, it followed the model of the absolutist Prussian Empire. The tragedy with this choice was that the armed forces became independent of the civil ministers and had direct access to the Emperor.

A greater interest was now shown in the German legal system, and in 1878 Hermann Roesler came to work for the Foreign Ministry as a legal adviser on International Law and the Constitution. He was followed by Albert Mosse, Julius Scriba, Karl Rudolph, Hermann Techov — all

German lawyers — as well as Ottmar von Mohl, a Prussian Court chamberlain who advised on Japanese Imperial Court Etiquette and on the police system. Later, in 1885, Wilhelm Haehn, a Prussian, was hired to train Japanese police. He helped to train the chief officers at the training institute in Tokyo and then travelled all over Japan to inspect and report upon the police stations. He pointed out that it was inefficient to send groups of constables from central or branch stations to patrol large areas, and suggested that small sub-stations should be set up to control each small district. In 1888, the 'koban' (small policebox) system was begun.

Another Prussian, Otto Rudorff, in 1887, began drawing up the law on the organisation of the courts. Mosse, Roesler, Boissonade and the Englishman, William Kirkwood, all assisted in this and the results of their work became law in 1890. This bill governed the court system until radical reforms were made during the Occupation after World War II. On all these teams, of course, were many Japanese experts (several had studied law in Europe), who endeavoured to modify each point so that it could be applied to Japanese society. They also tried to ensure that the legal system came under the general policies of the government; this had changed from the pre-Meiji 'western techniques, oriental morality' to 'rich country and strong military.'

*   *   *

So after much struggle and argument, Japan emerged towards the end of the nineteenth century with a Constitution — though one based heavily on the idea of the divinity of the Emperor — and with the codification of laws governing all aspects of life. Professor Noda comments that 'although Japan succeeded in faithfully and skilfully imitating the French and German legal systems, its own culture could not help but give an original character to the system.' A great deal of admiration was shown for this rapid achievement both in Japan and abroad, and extra-territoriality ceased forever after 1892. Soon afterwards, Dr J.E. de Becker arrived in Yokohama, learned Japanese and took on the task of translating all the legal codes into English. He became a naturalised Japanese and practised law in Yokohama and Kobe. His son was also a lawyer in Japan and continued his father's work.

In 1917, de Becker in an article commented that in the criminal courts 'the trial is not by jury, but is before three or five judges,' and he adds that 'this is probably a better tribunal than a jury would be so far as foreigners, at any rate, are concerned.' Still, he did criticise some aspects of the legal system and suggested further reforms, adding that 'the courts have shown themselves particularly careful in foreign criminal cases.' Even today, it seems, foreigners are dealt with especially carefully and a special prison for them exists in Yokosuka, near the American naval base south of Yokohama. The old complaint is still heard concerning the painfully slow rate at which proceedings progress, and the immense waste of time involved before a decision is finally handed down. In times when inflation is high, this would appear to make any legal process in the civil courts a situation where justice itself is a secondary consideration. This is probably one reason why private courts abound in Japan, making the statistics show that law-breaking is minimal. For as Professor Noda points out: 'To an honourable Japanese the law is something that is undesirable, even detestable, something to keep as far away from as possible. To never use the law, or be involved with the law, is the normal hope of honourable people.' Compared to the enormous amount of money, time and energy wasted in some countries where litigation is a common sport, this attitude is not without its own merits.

PART IV

Images of Japan
Transmitted to the West

REGULAR PASSENGER STEAMSHIP SERVICES to the Treaty Ports of Japan were established soon after the Meiji Restoration, and a considerable number of the rich, globe-trotting tourists who visited the country were so impressed that they later published books that described their experiences during their short stay. Most of these proved to be shallow and patronising, over-indulging in words like 'quaint,' and 'doll-like.' But from their writings readers in the West formed an impression of life in Japan.

A few of these books still hold interest if only to relate how tourists were treated by the Japanese at the time, while others give detailed descriptions of activities long since past. Some writers, however, who only knew Japan second-hand by reading such accounts, did create popular works of fiction in the West that either idealised or distorted the nature of the country beyond all recognition. This sometimes led to peculiar behaviour by western tourists arriving for the first time, and necessitated the printing of strict warnings in the front of many tourist guide-books giving advice on the proper treatment of ordinary women in Japan and how to behave in traditional homes and hotels. There were, of course, a number of scholarly and factual works produced by western residents in Japan that were written with insight and understanding, but these were outnumbered by the sensational pulp publications.

The phenomenon of fanatical collecting and sending of picture post-cards in Europe during the first two decades of this century was also reflected in Japan. Millions of Japanese postcards were produced and found their way to Europe, thus adding information and creating their own image of the country. Many of those that have survived are proving to be useful historical reference material.

Chapter 33

A Victorian Family Meets Japan

THE TIME-BALL fell and the noon-day gun crashed and echoed across Yokohama Port on the edge of Tokyo Bay. It was Monday, 29 January 1877, and those people who had clocks and watches checked them as usual. The owners of such instruments were proud of their affluence. Almost all the foreign merchants from Europe and America possessed a pocket-watch on a silver chain, and many of the rising merchant class amongst the Japanese were also acquiring such symbols of affluence. But out in the harbour a glimpse of real affluence had just arrived.

The private yacht *Sunbeam* had just dropped anchor amongst the large men-of-war ships of the various western nations. With the memory of the dreaded 'Black Ships' of the early 1850s fading, this strange new 'White Ship' posed many questions. If this vessel was not a man-of-war or a merchant ship, what was she? Why were these English people, men, women and children, sailing this sleek, 100 foot, three-masted, gaff-rigged, screw-assisted schooner around the world? What purpose did they have for risking the elements of the ocean during the winter in such a vessel?

The answer was that Mr Thomas Brassey, a British Member of Parliament and owner of the vessel, was taking his wife and their four children on a pleasure and educational cruise around the world. Commander Brown and Captain Lecky, both ex-Royal Navy, were taking care of most of the sailing and navigation with the assistance of a 23-man crew. Also on board were nine stewards, cooks, maids and nurses to serve every need of the Victorian family, as well as a qualified surgeon and the Hon. A.Y. Bingham who had been commissioned to provide sketches for illustrating Mrs Brassey's book which was due to be published once the voyage was over. Altogether there were 43 people on board '*Sunbeam*'; in addition, there were the family pets: two dogs, a cat and three caged birds. This did not include a number of exotic animals bought in Hawaii a few weeks earlier; unfortunately, many of these had died in mid-Pacific because of the coldness of the winter.

Thomas Brassey's family pedigree, according to *Burke's Peerage, Baronetage, and Knightage,* could be traced back to 1613. Although by profession he was a Barrister-at-Law, he had been a liberal M.P. for Hastings and was later to be created a Baron and then an Earl. He had been educated at Oxford and Dublin before being called to the Bar at Lincoln's Inn in 1866.

From the carved wooden angel that was the ship's figurehead, back to the ensign on the stern, the ship was most impressive. The brilliant white of the hull was superb at a distance, but once on board it was the varnished and polished woodwork with the shiny brass fittings that caught the eye. Inside the navigation room one was impressed by the latest aids to navigation and also by such luxurious details as the velvet curtains that could be drawn on runners, the carpeted floor and the velvet-covered stools with gold tassles hanging around their perimeters. Each piece of wood in the ship was carefully carved and fashioned in the Victorian style according to the detailed design of Mr St Clare Byrne of Liverpool. Indeed, the ship had been constructed using the finest wood available and fitted out without regard to costs.

It had not been all plain sailing in their circumnavigation of the globe, for they had experienced many misfortunes and adventures. There were four fires on *Sunbeam* while they were at sea, there had been a case of smallpox on board amongst the crew, and once they had rescued 15 shipwrecked seamen and takem then to safety. The voyage around Cape Horn was not easy and one of the children had nearly been swept overboard, some of the other children had become rather sick and in Tahiti some of the crew had been involved with drugs. However, the more pleasant and interesting aspects of the voyage more than made up for these hardships and they arrived in Yokohama Bay with a couple of spars lashed to the decks after a storm in mid-Pacific.

As soon as they had dropped anchor, they were surrounded by a swarm of small boats full of people who wanted to come on board. Many of them succeeded despite the efforts of two crew members to keep them off by force. Both Japanese and foreigners were curious about *Sunbeam* and her passengers and soon there were several newspaper reporters on board asking questions about the voyage.

*   *   *

Once on shore, using a rickshaw that Mrs Brassey compared to a Hansom cab, the Brasseys' visit went immediately to the British Consul and then on to the recently-opened Post Office. An international telegram awaiting their arrival contained the sad news that Mr Brassey's father had died on 3 January. Thomas Brassey, senior (1802-1877) had been born a member of the landed gentry in England but had thrown all his energy into the spirit of the times by organising and building railways not only in Britain, but throughout the world. He was a close friend of George Stephenson and he himself was almost as famous as Stephenson at the time. His work in France, Holland, Italy, Prussia, Spain and Canada was well appreciated and at one time he commanded a workforce of 75,000 men.

The Japanese winter of 1877 was particularly hard and the day after *Sunbeam* arrived the whole of the Kanto Plain was covered in snow, but this did not stop the Brasseys from seeing as much of Japan as they could. In Yokohama the British Consul acted as guide and interpreter, and in Tokyo the British Ambassador, Sir Harry Parkes, took them on sightseeing trips while his wife helped with the purchase of souvenirs. The British Embassy at this time was located inside the walls of the Imperial Palace which Mrs Brassey described as 'a nice red brick house, built in the centre of a garden, so as to be as secure as possible from fire and attack.' On the return journey to Yokohama, she complained of the cold omnibus-like railway carriages and the even colder rickshaw ride to the Grand Hotel, but she praised the roaring fire inside and the excellent dinner that warmed and comforted them.

Out in the town of Yokohama Mrs Brassey browsed in the famous 'curio shops' where 'the inhabitants are wonderfully clever at making all sorts of curiosities.' She mentions 'antique bronzes' and 'old china' in particular. She goes on to explain that 'they scrape, crack, chip, mend and colour the various articles, cover them with dust, partially clean them, and imitate the marks and signatures of celebrated makers.' But she found the lacquerwork 'respectable-looking' and mentioned that genuine antiques from the temples and from the large houses of 'reduced daimyos' could be found in some shops.

*   *   *

The Brasseys were in Japan for less than one month but they certainly saw a great deal, and descriptions of 12-course meals show that they lived in grand style. Despite this short stay, Mrs Brassey's book *A Voyage in the Sumbeam: Our Home on the ocean for 11 months* is valuable because she quotes conversations that she had with Sir Harry Parkes and other residents, and she was invited to many significant functions. Her description of the opening of the Kobe to Kyoto railway by Emperor Meiji is full of detail and humour — as when the nervous Governor of Kobe read an address in his ill-fitting European dress. 'His knees shook, his hands trembled, and his whole body vibrated to such an extent that his cocked hat fell and rolled on the floor of the dais.'

In Osaka the party visited the Imperial Mint, but Mrs Brassey did not think it worth while to describe it because 'it is arranged on exactly the same principle as the one in London.' The old streets of Osaka which they visited that afternoon had interest because of the famous waxworks and theatres. She describes an incident that occurred the previous year when one play was produced that depicted the 'cruel and unprovoked assassination of a French officer and two Frenchmen.' The English and French Consuls objected to the Governor of Osaka who promised to stop the play and remove the obnoxious posters advertising it. Nothing happened, and in the meantime some officers and crew from a visiting ship went to see the play and almost created a riot. The consuls and governor were called for, and this time the management were forced to close the production by a detail of Japanese soldiers.

As they were preparing to leave their moorings at Kobe a few days

later and sail through the Inland Sea, they were warned by the Chief
of Police that rebels from Kyushu were in the hills. It was not clear
whether they wanted to attack the foreign settlement or capture the
Emperor in Osaka during his expected visit. Quickly they fetched the
children who were at a local circus and set sail.

                              *   *   *

On departing, Mrs Brassey recorded some recommendations about
travelling in Japan, saying that 'no one should come to Japan in the
winter because it is not at its best, and the scanty protection afforded
by houses and carriages makes travelling a penance rather than a
pleasure.' Then comes the comment, made 100 years ago, that 'travellers
who wish to see Japan should do so at once for the country is changing
every day, and in three years more,' she prophesies, 'it will be so
Europeanised that little will be left worth seeing; or a violent anti-foreign
feeling may have taken place, and then the ports will be closed more
strictly than they were even before the execution of the first treaty.
Nothing that we can give them do they really want; their exports are
not large; and they have learned nearly all they care to know from the
foreigner.' This last parting observation, she declares, is confirmed by
'European engineers of Japanese vessels (who) all agree that the natives
learn to imitate anything they see done with wonderful quickness,' and
these engineers also 'aver that in a few years there will not be a single
foreigner employed in Japan.'

     With such a poignant sayonara Anna Brassey turned her thoughts
towards China as *Sunbeam* fought through the waves. Her views were
issued from the luxurious cabin in that ship that she had grown to accept
as part of her home, as part of old England. Ten years later in September
1887, while cruising in *Sunbeam* off Port Darwin, she died and was
buried at sea.

Chapter 34

Coal and Coaling

AS THE PROCESS of modernisation got under way, Nabeshima Kanso
(1814 — 1871), daimyo of the Saga clan, became personally very
interested in western industries. He knew that if he could exploit the
coal resources at the Takashima coal mine, on Takashima Island which
was about 16 km. off Nagasaki harbour, he could use the profit from
the enterprise to build superior defences for Nagasaki. As it happened

Nabeshima was friendly with the British merchant, Thomas B. Glover (see pp 180-184), and in May 1868 they signed a contract whereby they would jointly expand the coal mines at Takashima. Glover's company would provide the capital for this development, and the profits would be shared equally. The next month, an English mining engineer, Mr Morris, was hired to advise on how the mines should be operated, and some months later two English working miners arrived to assist. Modern mining equipment was ordered, and for the first time in Japan steam-driven machinery was used to raise coal from a mine. Steam winches were used to lift the coal up the shaft, and steam pumps kept the mine dry. Also, special safety lamps were used by miners to prevent explosions, and a small railway hauled the coal to ships at the pier.

A member of the Saga clan was production manager of the mine, and Glover's company marketed the coal. In December 1868, the British Engineer responsible for the erection of lighthouses around Japan, Henry Brunton (see pp 154-158), visited the mine and reported that about 300 men raised 200 tons of coal daily. It was good bituminous coal, which was better than Welsh coal for fuelling ships. Some coal was imported from England at this time and sold for $7.50 a ton, while the Takashima coal sold at $4.50 a ton, so the future of the industry looked bright. However, in general, the longer a mine is worked, the more difficult it becomes to obtain coal and by 1870 only 90 tons a day were being raised. But the situation improved when two more foreign engineers arrived, and production increased. In 1873 the Meiji government took control of the mine, and Glover and Company received $400,000 as interest. Then, after only 10 months, it was bought as a private venture by Goto Shojiro who owned it until 1881 when it was purchased by Iwasaki Yataro.

Shortly after, the mines were taken over by the Mitsubishi Company, that had also built a dry-dock in Nagasaki. But disaster struck in 1885 when there was a great cholera epidemic, and the village of miners of the island nearly all died. Nagasaki harbour was almost deserted, and the American and English mission stations there were closed as the missionaries all fled to the mountains. Of the whole foreign population of Nagasaki only the Catholic priests and nuns remained although the governor tried to persuade them to leave also.

Miss Eliza Scidmore, an American who was resident in Japan for many years and who wrote a book *Jinrikisha Days in Japan,* came into Nagasaki harbour by ship during the cholera epidemic, and wrote:

'On our way to China we touched at Nagasaki while the epidemic was at its height, but no passenger was allowed to go ashore, and all day we kept to the decks that were saturated with carbolic acid. It took six hours to coal the ship, and from noon to sundown we beheld a water carnival. As the first coal-barge from Takashima drew near, a man in airy summer costume — which consisted of a rope around his waist — jumped over the side and swam to the stern of our steamer. When he came dripping up the gangway the steerage steward gave him a carbolic spraying with his bucket and brush. The barge was hauled up alongside and made fast, and our consignment of coal was passed from hand to hand along a line of chanting men and women. At the end of each hour there was a breathing spell. Many of the women were young and pretty, and some of them had brought their children, who, throwing back the empty baskets and helping to pass them along the line, thus began their lives of toil and earned a few pennies. The passengers threw to the grimy children all the small Japanese coins they possessed, and when the ship swung loose and started away their cheerful little 'sayonaras' long rang after us.'

*   *   *

In October 1907, Marie Stopes, an English lady who was spending 18 months in Japan to search for and study fossils, visited Takashima mine and recorded how it had expanded:

'I reached Nagasaki and found Mr G - (the half-Japanese son of a Scotsman and an important person here) most kind. He arranged for a delightful steam-launch all to myself to take me to Takashima, a small island which exists for, and is entirely populated by, the coal-mining people, to whom it belongs.

'The mine was the first opened in Japan, and was for some time owned by Mr G-'s father; it is the most completely arranged I have yet seen, probably owing to its age, but is rather dangerous to work, as it goes miles under the sea, and there is a large quantity of gas. Last year (1906) 300 men were killed in it — I was on the very spot where the engineer was found dead.

'There is another little island very near to it, with a coast-line of only 4000 feet and a population of 2500! It also has a mine which is entirely under the sea. As well as working huge quantities, the quality of this coal is the best the Japanese have. They must use salt water, of course, so they combine their engine work with salt making, and thus make a lot of money, as well as provide their thousands of people with distilled water for domestic purposes. It was very funny to go only a couple of yards from the black coal sacks to the great room filled with snowy salt.'

The lives of coal miners in Japan at the time of Marie Stopes' visit was tough and miserable, as it was in many other countries. The miners would bring their wives and families to the site of the mine and live in small thatched huts provided by the mining company, while the unmarried men lived in dormitories. Food was provided by the company, but the miners had to pay for it. Maximum wages for men was 78 sen per day, for women 60 sen per day, and children 20 sen per day in 1918, and in this year there were 56 boys and 34 girls less than 12 years old working underground in coal mines in Japan. Children of both sexes under 15 years old working in the coal industry totalled 4975. The total number of adults, both men and women, working underground in Japan's coal mines was 142,000, and the annual output of coal about 20 million tons. The Japanese miner at this time was considered by many to be careless, and accidents were frequent and disastrous due to fires caused by the misuse of explosives. But as they had to work for up to 11 hours daily, and for 27 days per month, such accidents are not surprising. It is also not surprising that the mining companies had agents in the cities to try to secure workers for the mines, for most people did not care for the life underground in the black coal.

The great steamships that crossed the oceans and circled the globe, transporting manufactured goods, passengers and mail, and allowing industry to expand, were all powered by coal at the beginning of this century. It was the age of the 'globe-trotter,' thousands of people from Europe and America wanted to 'see the world' by travelling between countries on the massive and impressive steamships.

*   *   *

Arriving by ship for the first time in Japan was a slow, but exciting, process during the Meiji era. The coal-powered engines made the entire ship vibrate, and there was great excitement on board when land was first sighted. At first, there was just a thin, grey line, but as the hours passed, mountains could be made out, then rice paddies, then trees and houses. Finally, people could be seen on shore as the ship slowly and gracefully slid into port.

Those ships that came across the Pacific Ocean from America put into Yokohama first, then steamed on to Kobe and Nagasaki where the coal holds were replenished. Coming from the West, the ships put first into Nagasaki and coal was taken on before rounding the coast to Yokohama.

The coal that was mined in Kyushu was of very high quality and well liked by the ships' engineers. The tourist on board was also fascinated by the way the coal was taken aboard and deposited in the coal holds. Hundreds of people, both men and women, took part in this operation and the muscles of these workers strained as the coal holds were slowly filled; their small loin-cloths and head-bands were the only protection they had from the sun in summer. Charles T. Waters, author of the book called *A Holiday in Japan,* described what he saw in 1902.

'We were surrounded by coal-barges carrying large gangs of Japanese girls. Planks were put to our sides, on which lines of the little coal-porters were ranged side by side. They were quaint little figures in their Japanese dress, with cloths bound round their heads, as they passed the coal from hand to hand in small baskets with amazing rapidity. So regular was the combined movement that the whole had the appearance of a huge piece of machinery at work. The coaling was continued for hours and how the girls' small arms bore the constant strain was a wonder to me. In this manner, we are told, ships have been loaded at the rate of over five tons of coal a minute.'

A more detailed and graphic description of this scene is given by James A.B. Scherer in his book *Japan Today* of 1904. Although he saw the scene many times in Nagasaki, he prefers to quote Bishop Potter who earlier wrote in his book *The East of Today and Tomorrow:*

'If I were asked to say of all that I saw in Japan, what that is that lives most vividly in my memory, I should probably shock my artistic reader by saying that it was the loading of a steamship at Nagasaki with coal. The huge vessel, the *Empress of Japan,* was one morning, soon after its arrival at Nagasaki, suddenly festooned — I can use no other word — from stem to stern on each side with a series of hanging platforms, the broadest nearest the base and diminishing as they rose, strung together with ropes, and ascending from the sampans, or huge boats in which the coal had been brought alongside the steamer, until the highest and narrowest platform was just below the particular port-hole through which it was received into the ship. There were, in each case, all along the sides of the ship, some four or five of these platforms, one above another, on each of which stood a young girl. On board the sampans men were busy filling a long line of baskets holding, I should think, each about two buckets of coal, and these were passed up from the sampans in a continuous and unbroken line until they reached their destination, each young girl, as she stood on her particular platform, passing, or rather almost throwing, these huge basketfuls of coal to the girl above her, and so on to the end. The rapidity, skill, and above all, the rhythmic precision with which, for hours, this really tremendous task was performed was an achievement which might well fill an American athlete with envy and dismay. As I moved to and fro on the deck above them, watching this unique scene, I took out my watch to time these girls, and again and again I counted sixty-nine baskets — they never fell below sixty — passed on board in this way in a single minute.

'The task — I ought rather to call it an art, so neatly, simply and gracefully was it done — was this: the young girl stooped to her companion below her, seized from her uplifted hands a huge basket of coal, and then, shooting her lithe arms upward, tossed it laughingly to the girls above her in the ever-ascending chain. And all the while there was heard, as one passed along from one to another of these chains of living elevators, a clear, rhythmical sound, which I supposed at first to have been produced by some by-stander striking the metal string of something like a mandolin, but which I discovered after a little was a series of notes produced by the lips of these young coal-heavers themselves — distinct, precise, melodious and stimulating. And at this task these girls continued, uninterruptedly and blithely, from ten o'clock in the morning until four o'clock in the afternoon, putting on board in that time more than one thousand tons of coal. I am quite free to say that I do not believe that there is another body of work-folk in the world who could have performed the same task in the same time and with the same ease.'

Such sights of manual labour had almost disappeared from America and Europe at this time, except perhaps during fruit-picking time or the harvest season in the countryside. It was not long after this that ships were loaded in Japan by special machines and the scenes of hand-loading that had impressed so many foreigners in the past ceased for ever.

Chapter 35

Pierre Loti and Clive Holland

MARCO POLO made his historic travels in Asia in 1271 and brought back stories to Europe about the people and different countries of the Far East, including descriptions of Japan and the Japanese. He never actually reached Japan. His reports were based on conversations with other travellers who had visited the country, but they were the first reports in the West about the existence of Japan. Today television, radio, films, books and magazines can give anyone in any part of the world a fairly accurate insight into many aspects of life, on many different levels, of any country. No so even a mere 80 years ago. Written reports were still the chief means of communication along with photographs, pictures as well as novels and theatrical productions supposedly set in other countries. These were the means that people formed their impressions of other countries in the cities of Europe and America at the turn of the century. In England, the Gilbert and Sullivan musical comedy *The Mikado* (the performance of which in Japan was banned until 1946) and another musical called *The Geisha* were very popular for a time, while in France the novels of Pierre Loti, especially *Madame Chrysantheme* published in 1887, helped create impressions and opinions of Japan and of Japanese women for a vast number of people.

Pierre Loti was the pseudonym of Louis Marie Julien Viaud. He was born in 1850 and his family were Huguenots. At the age of 17 he entered the French navy and soon rose to the rank of captain. For nearly a year he was stationed at Nagasaki where he wrote his autobiographical work *Madame Chrysantheme* which tells how he arranged to buy a temporary wife for the duration and how he moved into a small house and lived with her up on the hills surrounding Nagasaki harbour. Finally, he recounts his feelings as he sails away — without her. The fresh and humorous descriptions of minute details of Japanese customs and of the various artifacts used in Japan at that time, as well as the impressionistic landscape descriptions of Nagasaki give the book some literary merit. 'Then there is the little silver pipe that must absolutely be smoked before going to sleep; this is one of the customs which most provokes me, but has to be borne. Chrysantheme, like a gypsy, squats before a particular square box, made of red wood, which contains a little tobacco jar, a little porcelain stove full of hot embers, and finally a little bamboo pot serving at the same time as ash-tray and spitoon.' Such smoking accoutrements can now be found in many antique shops in Japan.

*   *   *

Later in the book Loti describes a mild brush with the officers of the law that visited the people who had arranged his temporary marriage and accommodation. 'The Japanese police agents had called and threatened them with the law for letting rooms outside of the European concession to a Frenchman morganatically married to a Japanese; and the terror of being prosecuted brought them to me, with a thousand apologies, but with the humble request that I should leave.' However, after explaining to the authorities in person, he was allowed to continue.

Basil Hall Chamberlain, in his book *Things Japanese,* remarks with indignation that 'as for Pierre Loti's books the resident community has less respect for them than the public at home: his inaccuracy and superficiality go against the grain. Nevertheless, the illustrations to his "Madame Chrysantheme" are very pretty...though the volume can in no wise be recommended either to misses or missionaries.' Chamberlain comes down firmly on the side of the moralists, although how he can claim to know about the inaccuracies in Loti's book without actually having associated with a similar temporary-wife remains a mystery.

H.B. Montgomery commenting in 1908 in his *The Empire of the Far East* states: 'There can be no question that a large number of European people have formed their estimate of Japanese women either from a visit to a comic opera such as "The Geisha", or from a perusal of a book like Pierre Loti's fascinating work "Madame Chrysantheme.' This is in effect the story of a liaison between a man and a Japanese girl of the lower classes, with, of course, a large amount of local colouring, and rendered generally charming by the writer's brilliant literary style. Unfortunately, that large number of Europeans who have never visited Japan have taken the French academician's study of a girl of a certain class as a life picture of the typical Japanese woman who is, accordingly, shown to be more or less, to use an accepted euphemism, a person of easy virtue. Nothing could, of course, be more erroneous, no conclusion further from the truth.'

Despite these criticisms, Loti's book sold well and was translated into many languages, including Japanese. Some people even claim that his portrayal of Madame Chrysantheme as being a kitten-like woman of 'easy virtue' was directly responsible for the increase in tourism in Japan following its publication! Be that as it may, it certainly did provoke a reaction — or perhaps a polarisation of reactions — and his book seems to have been the inspiration for Puccini's opera *Madame Butterfly*.

*   *   *

The publication of books, both factual accounts and fictional novels set in Japan, were very numerous in Europe at this time. One extremely popular writer in England, who wrote seven books on Japan — three novels, two factual accounts and two plays — was Clive Holland, M.B.E. He was the son of the Mayor of Bournemouth and, typical of a certain class of privileged persons from wealthy families in England, he was educated privately at the exclusive Mill School in London after which he trained for the law. If Madame Chrysantheme typified Japanese women for Europeans, so Clive Holland would have typified an English gentleman for Japanese! However, the practice of law did not satisfy Holland for his heart was in writing, and so he went into journalism in Fleet Street and by 1893 he was freelancing for several important publications. Before this, at the age of 22, he had had his first book published and had contributed many articles to boys' papers even while he was still at college. Altogether he published over 50 books and in 1895 his most popular book came out. It was a short novel called *My Japanese Wife*. It had gone through 21 editions by 1933 and sold an astounding 435,000 copies.

Like Loti's book, it was set in Nagasaki. Like Loti's book, it was written in the first person singular. Like Loti's book, it concerned a foreign man who meets a Japanese girl. But she was called Miss Hyacinth, and the foreign man was English not French. Like in Loti's book, they both live together high on the hills surrounding Nagasaki harbour in a Japanese house. However, unlike Loti's book, the Englishman, Cyril, first falls in love with and marries his Miss Hyacinth before they start to live together! It is made quite clear on the first page of this novel that Cyril takes his Japanese wife back to England with him where they live — presumely happily — together in a solid brick house, as opposed to the house with paper walls in Nagasaki. He states that he is writing his account of his adventures in Japan at his desk in his dull English study, while Miss Hyacinth leans over him while dressed in an apricot kimono of silk that has a magenta obi made of satin.

*   *   *

All of Holland's books on Japan were published between 1895 and 1908. But until 1912 he lived in the pleasant English seaside resort of Bournemouth, although it is true that he did visit many European countries as a lecturer and journalist, but, as his eldest son relates 'he never went outside Europe.' One enthusiastic newspaper reporter in a short article on Holland in a local paper said: 'His travels took him to Japan, and he has never since been able to escape from the lure and fascination of that country.' But his eldest son corrects this statement by saying that 'the journalist who wrote this article has allowed his imagination to run away with him. My father never visited Japan.'

On knowing about Holland's lack of first-hand knowledge of Japan, a careful reading of his novels reveals certain flaws. Odd details appear strange. For example, the Japanese do not eat by impaling morsels of food on chipsticks — they are not used like primitive, spearlike forks!

Nor is dog meat found on the dinner table in Japan! Not even in the *'henamono'* (strange food restaurant) where unlikely insects and the even more unlikely parts of certain animals are served up. The dog is a sacred animal in Japan, a god, and is never eaten. Holland was obviously confusing Japan with China where dog meat used to be eaten.

The publication figures of *My Japanese Wife* indicate that while this book was in print, the moralists were winning — at least in England! Holland's ingenuity at making minor moral adjustments to Loti's story opened a market that *did* include 'misses and missionaries'! However, the tempo of the times has now changed and it is Loti who is still read and not Holland — Loti's authenticity created a minor classic, but Holland's fabrication has now very little interest. For several years Holland was the editor of the *British Congregationalist* and one suspects that he felt that he had a moral mission in writing his own version of *Madame Chrysantheme*.

What, then, can we make of Holland's books on Japan? Did he capitalise on the mysteries of the Far East that were far beyond the reach of most of his millions of readers? Should we disregard him as being a fraud? Perhaps the novels should be read as quaint moral tales by a British congregationalist who was outraged by the promiscuous Frenchman, Loti, who, incidentally obtained his pseudonym from a young Tahitian girl as described in a previous work called *Le mariage de Loti*. But in another book *Old and New Japan*, Holland gives a reasonably detailed history of Japan from the time of Emperor Temmu up to 1907 when it was published. In the final chapter he tries to predict, as so many other writers were then trying to predict, the future of Japan. When discussing the future military ventures of Japan, he states: 'A breach of amicable relations with the United States...seems to provide the most probable point of friction.' This was 33 years before Pearl Harbor. Indeed, this final chapter is still worthy of study because of his objective perception of problems that Japan was facing, and still faces:

'In some departments of public life, especially that of education, she has attempted too much. The endeavour to force the knowledge of another language upon the masses of Japanese students and school children, was found to have detrimental and even disastrous effects; and we are bound to record this although the language most taught was English. The attempt to teach the nation English wholesale was unsuccessful and involved a very considerable waste of time, and an immense waste of money.'

*   *   *

Clive Holland is interesting to Japanophiles because of the impression of Japan he created in Europe through his popular books and because of his accurate predictions and perceptive comments — not for first-hand information concerning Meiji-era Japan. This professional writer created, in the days before our present information explosion, an image of Japan that was probably accepted by the majority of his hundreds of thousands of readers, and the image still persists. He did not create great literature like some of his personal friends that included Zola, Thomas Hardy and R.L. Stevenson. During both World Wars he did propaganda work for the allies, and he received many medals and honours from several governments. So he was very much a man of his age.

At the height of the popularity of his books on Japan, Holland was invited to a reception given by the Japanese Ambassador in London. The ambassador asked him, naturally, how long he had lived in Japan, and when told he had never been there, the ambassador looked surprised and is quoted as saying: 'I cannot believe you! How could you know the colour of the road along which you and your Japanese wife walked? Or what the flowers were that grew in the crevices of the stone bridges?' Holland merely gave an inscrutable smile.

In 1901 an illustrated novel called *Mousme* by Clive Holland was published. Some of the illustrations consisted of buxom English women dressed in kimonos and obis, for it seems that Japanese women were few and far between in London at that time. However, in the spring of 1914, his son recounts, an old friend brought a young Japanese lady to see him on a few occasions. Holland was always a keen photographer and, as the cherry trees in his English garden were in bloom, he asked the lady if she would bring her kimono, etc. on the next visit so that he could take a picture of her. This she did, and the results were so good that one of the pictures was later used on the cover of the paperback edition of *My Japanese Wife*. This lady whom he met six years after he wrote his last book on Japan was the only other living contact Holland had with that country.

Chapter 36

Western Haute Couture Reaches Japan

THE TWO TALL YOUNG WOMEN looked at each other in horror. They had been in Tokyo only a few weeks as tourists, and this was their first party in a Japanese home. But now the meal was ready and it was time to sit on the small cushions so neatly arranged on the floor around the low table. The smiling Tomita family used friendly hand movements to invite tham to sit as guests of honour for the meal, but a cold chill of apprehension seared through both of the fashionable ladies. It was November 1888, and both were dressed in the latest fashions from Victorian England: tight corsets with bone stays, plentiful underwear with a network of straps and laces, a large bustle exaggerating their *derrieres,* and long petticoats all covered with flounced silk dresses.

They hesitated. Surely one of the gazing men in the family would glimpse a sexy ankle, perhaps even a frilly piece of petticoat under the dress! Still they stood transfixed in silence. But realising that no further ceremony could proceed without their sitting, they both slowly subsided over the small cushions with unearthly groans from the noise of straining fabric coming from their clothes. Miss Love whispered to Miss Duncan: 'I shall never get up again without a derrick!' Then, suddenly there was the bitter sound of parting laces and seams, and the tearing of material deep inside. The meal was then taken in good-humoured friendship tinged with slight embarrassment as Miss Love's attire continued to creak under the strain of the unaccustomed sitting position.

Yet, strangely, during the 1880s more and more high-class Japanese ladies were acquiring and wearing such western dress and forsaking their comfortable traditional kimono. This produced an angry outcry from western women. The local English-language newspapers recommended that women continue to wear the traditional garb, resident foreign women tried to persuade their Japanese friends not to buy expensive fashionable wear from the West, and American supporters of women's liberation in these early days of the movement spoke out publicly against the dangers to health that tight lacing and torture-chamber corsets could bring.

The blame for Japan's adoption of painful and inelegant European dress lay with the early Meiji government of 1873 that insisted all officials should wear contemporary western clothes. Although this directive only applied to civil servants and bureaucrats, it started a movement towards the adoption of suits, shirts and ties, and patent-leather shoes, by other men in the private sector. Having no word for 'suit', one was derived from English; the new word was 'saburo' from 'Saville Row' — London's most famous street of high-class tailors.

*   *   *

The trend was slower at first for women, but when the Imperial Court ladies ordered fashionable gowns from Berlin in 1886, and the Empress and her entourage appeared in public in their new German dresses, the mould was set. Tottering on unstable high-heeled shoes seemed not to matter, the Empress had set a precedent and all ladies who considered they had class felt obliged to follow.

At a bazaar held in Tokyo, Misses Love and Duncan observed the parade of high-class society in their European dress. They recognised styles from Paris, some from London's Oxford Street, a few from the Bowery and others from 'Tokyo dressmakers inspired by vague European ideals.' As the eastern dragon is supposed to be a representation of a lion that the Chinese artist never saw, so these latter dresses were dragons of the fashion world, remarked Miss Duncan. But she was amazed that most Japanese ladies wore the cramped foreign bodice and multitudinous skirts with no sign of suffering on their faces as they peered out from the bonnets tied under their chins. Remembering her previous experience, she wondered what techniques they would adopt for sitting on *tatami,* and was amused that Japanese ladies were doing exactly what western women were trying to undo. Then she noticed one lady perfectly dressed in authentic European costume, everything exact from the hat-pin to the glove buttons, with the tallest bonnet-bows and the highest heels. But every time she met an acquaintance she automatically bowed profusely, causing the bustle and puffed skirt to bob around comically. She climbed the staircase of the hall and as she entered the doorway of the first room, she paused to bend down and removed her shoes!

One suspects the truth of the latter incident as being a figment of a western satirist's imagination, for these young ladies spent hours studying western manners, ways and etiquette before becoming confident enough to appear in public in western attire. But a British professor at Imperial University, B.H. Chamberlain, did comment that: 'No caricature could do justice to the bad figures, the ill-fitting garments, the screeching colours, that ran riot between 1886 and 1889. Since then there has been a slight wave of reaction.' Chamberlain then makes the observation that Japanese women in European dress seemed to be treated with more respect by their husbands than when they wore traditional costumes. She was ushered through a doorway first by her husband when in western dress, but had to follow respectfully behind him when in kimono. He considered this 'mighty moral effect' to be for the better.

*   *   *

A special place was built in Tokyo where western-orientated Japanese could meet wearing their western clothes and practice western manners and customs. It was financed by the government and opened in 1883. Its name was the 'Rokumeikan,' meaning 'Deer Cry Pavilion,' and was a huge building where many aspects of western social intercourse and activity could be undertaken: dancing waltzes, playing games of billiards, dice or cards, sampling French food and drinking American cocktails or German beer. Designed by British architect, Josiah Conder, who worked 10 years for the Public Works Ministry and constructed many prominent buildings in metropolitan Tokyo, it cost ¥18,000 and stood near Hibiya Park.

Concerts, balls and bazaars were held there and westerners invited to attend these functions for the promotion of international communication. Count Mayada, son of the Prince of Kaga, escorted English globe-trotter Herbert Roberts there in October 1884 for lunch. Roberts precociously named it 'The English Club' as well as the 'Rokumeikgwon' or 'Bird Hotel,' but gave no other details. However it attracted many ukiyo-e artists and western-style painters who produced dozens of detailed pictures of the interior, exterior and occupants of the building.

Miss Clara Whitney, daughter of an American teacher of business administration in Tokyo, recorded the fancy-dress ball given by Count Inoue on 12 November 1884 when 1500 invitations were sent out. 'Nearly everyone was there,' she noted. Another grand ball was given in 1887 by the prime minister, Count Ito, who arrived dressed as a Venetian' nobleman, while under the crystal chandeliers danced the cream of the international community dressed as pirates, fairy-queens and insects. Perhaps on this occasion the cocktails were too powerful, for it developed into a melee of blasphemy and indecency, and a scandal involving Ito and a certain woman followed. Somehow the circumstances had allowed the thin veil of etiquette to be broken, and no more masquerade balls were held there.

Mrs Fraser, wife of the British minister in Tokyo, in October 1889 worked hard to decorate the Rokumeikan, or Nobles' Club as she called it, in preparation for a charity concert in aid of the Lepers' Hospital at Gotemba on the lower slopes of Mount Fuji, founded and run by the French missionary, Father Testevuide. The concert, a variety show of singers and musicians performing among the palm branches and potted plants, was a great success, with a handsome sum raised for the charity.

*   *   *

Initially, the Rokumeikan had a definite political function. It was another demonstration for showing that Japanese could behave in a 'civilised' way in order to have the unequal treaties revised. It was part of the quest for national equality. The government felt some of its citizens needed to put on the airs and graces of privileged Europeans, and follow the strange and complex behaviour patterns native to European courts to help achieve its aim. In 1884, the old daimyo status system was replaced by a peerage system based on the one in Prussia. An unexpected result, however, was the semi-liberation of women and the rise of the famous 'strong Meiji Woman.' She came out of the home to help organise fairs and bazaars, she created new businesses in western clothes manufacture and in hairdressing, for each of these businesses for the traditional styles were controlled by men. This was a practical move for, as today, a visit to a western-style hairdresser or dressmaker cost much less than to the Japanese-style counterparts. Furthermore, in order to pursue their national cause, women insisted on adopting western dress styles in schools and colleges, on learning a foreign language, on taking lessons in western dancing and playing western musical instruments, and on being granted extra rights. One right allowed men to enter their college dormitories for the first time!

After 1890, the popularity of the Rokumeikan declined, probably because the novelty of western ways in high society was wearing thin as they became more familiar. An earthquake in 1893 damaged the structure badly, and money was not forthcoming for the extensive repairs. A few members of the Japanese nobility then decided to adapt a smaller pavilion nearby in the grounds in which to continue the social activities. This was Japanese-style and proved to be just as successful on a more intimate scale, and with a more relaxed atmosphere than the formal grandeur of the Rokumeikan.

Only a foolish man would try to unravel the reasons behind fashions in clothes, or try to explain the social, religious, technical and geographical forces that produced the various forms of traditional costumes around the world. But it was unfortunate that some upper class Japanese women decided to turn to western fashions at a time when it was at its most hideous and impractical. However, the phenomenon did provide them with an opportunity to challenge their traditional role revolving entirely around the home. The Rokumeikan led to the rise of numerous other similar clubs for other classes, thus creating a richer social life throughout society.

Chapter 37

Japanese Picture Postcards

HOW CAN a thin, rectàngular piece of pasteboard, less than 100 years old and of which many thousands were produced, be sold at auction for over $800? The answer is that on one side of the pasteboard is printed a scene — perhaps an early balloon post of 1903 — and on the other is the postal address of someone together with a brief message and along with a postage stamp cancelled with a special strike that was only used on that particular occasion. With the destruction of most of the postcards from the so-called 'Golden Age' (1895 — 1918), when about 900 million were sent annually through the post in Britain alone and a considerably greater number not mailed, such ephemera have become rare collectors items and fetch high prices.

In Japan today a wide range of postcards is on sale. Not only common topographical views on card, but wooden versions which have decorations burnt into them by the Ainu in Hokkaido can be purchased and in some places one can find a machine dispensing 'Record Postcards,' where the purchaser can record his voice on a small plastic disc set into the picture on the card. Prismatic illusion cards abound, whereby a beautiful young woman is seen either clothed or nude depending on the angle the card is held, and similar cards giving a three-dimensional effect can be found. Such novelties are not found in many countries these days, but during the Golden Age the range of postcards was even wider. There were 'hold-to-the-light' postcards which revealed a surprising new scene when light was transmitted through the card, there were superbly embossed postcards depicting such things as coins and stamps, there were cards prepared for special events such as the visit of a foreign dignitary to Tokyo or of a foreign warship to Yokohama or Kobe and there were cards, all different, that were hand-painted in lacquer-paint showing traditional landscapes of Japan and left unsigned by the street-artist.

* * *

Japan joined the Universal Postal Union in 1877, just 23 years after Commodore Perry arrived in his armed Black Ships to try to persuade the Japanese rulers to open their shores to modern trade and leave feudalism behind. The first Japanese postcards, which were plain, were issued by the Post Office in 1873. This was only four years after the very first postcards were issued in Austria in 1869.

These earlier plain postcards were issued by official government agencies — the Post Offices — and most details are known about them. However, the origin of the picture postcard is not so clear. They were produced commercially by private companies and records have disappeared. They first appeared in Germany in the 1880s soon after touring became popular with the growth of railways and steamship services. These were called 'Gruss aus' (greetings from) cards and were beautifully printed showing three or four coloured sketches of the tourist spot being visited. A small, blank area was always left on the picture side so that the tourist could send a brief message to his stay-at-home friends, for the other side of the card was to be exclusively used for the mailing address — this was a Post Office regulation until about 1900. Britain allowed commercially produced picture postcards to be sent through the post on 1 September 1894 at half the cost of a letter. By this time the tour agents, notably Thomas Cook, had extended their activities to the Far East. Round-the-world tours became popular with the richer sections of the population in Europe and America, and one port-of-call that was especially looked forward to was Yokohama. These 'globe-trotters' as they were called were not really welcomed by the foreign residents in business in Yokohama and the other Treaty Ports at first, but slowly attitudes changed and excellent hotels and other facilities were built to accommodate them during their short visits.

Not only hotels, but whole streets of shops came into being to tempt the tourists to part with their money — especially Benten dori and Motomachi dori along with Isezakicho dori which also provided theatrical entertainments. Several shops in these streets sold postcards showing scenes of Yokohama as it was then, as well as cards showing Japanese men and women in traditional dress and many illustrated the traditional life and customs of old Japan. Street-singers, jugglers and acrobats, rickshaw pullers and farmers, fishermen and villagers making *mochi* — all found their places on postcards as well as the shrines and temples and that all-important cone of lava called Mt Fuji. To contain such a collection of cards, there were unique hand-made albums on sale. The covers were made of lacquered wood decorated with pieces of ivory and the pages were silk-covered and hand-painted, the whole thing being neatly bound.

*   *   *

A few enterprising foreigners in Yokohama went into publishing postcards. One was Karl Lewis who was established at 136D Honmura. This was on the edge of China Town and stood next to the Chinese consulate at that time. His cards showed tinted scenes from 'A Bird-store, Tokio' (No 2070) to stirring battle scenes, 'Forcing the Russians to Retreat' (No. 636), of the Russo-Japanese War of 1904/5. Another publisher called Mayes issued rather poor, hand-tinted postcards in a series called 'Japanese Geisha.' Then there were the photographers of A. Farsari and Co. located at 32 Yokohama just behind the Oriental Hotel, where the New Grand Hotel now stands. This company specialised in producing postcards for hotels and other businesses, and many of their cards show interior scenes.

The majority of picture postcard publishers within Japan at this time were Japanese if the proportion of surviving cards is anything to go by. Some were published by Ogawa of Yokohama, by the Akasawa Fine Art Co. of Minamoitamachi, Yokohama, by Yamakashoten of Tokyo and numerous other companies. Unfortunately, the vast majority of them bear only the inscription 'Made in Japan,' with no hint of the publisher. Many Japanese companies published postcards showing scenes in China, notably Shanghai, and in Korea to which countries they were exported. During this Golden Age, the inscription, 'Made in Japan,' was a sign of quality for they were superbly printed from excellent photographs or drawings and coloured by hand in this pre-colour film era. One company that excelled above all others was 'Tonboya' of Isezakicho, Yokohama that used the dragonfly as its trademark. All their cards were numbered and prefixed with the letter of the city depicted — 'Y' for Yokohama, 'K' for Kobe, etc. — and it seems that several hundred of each place were published.

After 1 October 1903, postcards from Japan to Europe were marked either 'Via Siberia' or 'Via America' for by that year the Trans-Siberian railway had been completed and a mail service installed. A steamer left Nagasaki with the mail and took two days before it arrived in Shanghai, a further two days of steaming took it to Dalni (then called Dairen). The mail was then transferred to the train which took it to the edge of Lake Baikal where, depending on the season, it was either taken across by boat or sledge. Another train took it to Moscow and from there it was sorted for its correct destination in Europe. It took only about 17 days this way, whereas the America route took about 33 days. A surcharge was levied on letters and packages going via Siberia, but the postage for postcards was the same for both routes — 4 sen. Both the

Russo-Japanese War (1904-5) and World War I (1914-18) disrupted this service.

*   *   *

Far exceeding the number of picture postcards of Japan published in Japan, were the number of picture postcards of Japan published in Britain and other European countries. This may sound like a strange statement, but it is true because of the so-called 'postcard mania' in Europe during the Golden Age. At this time in Europe, the humble picture postcard was a major force in education, if we regard education in its broadest sense. Today we have TV, movies, video-recorders and other electronic devices for visual communication; at the turn of the century there were none of these. The most prolific visual aid to education and the fastest means of visual communication was the picture postcard. Events were recorded and distributed on postcards sometimes within 48 hours. They recorded everything. From the face of the King to the face of the farmer, from palaces to slums, from philosophers to freaks, from the wonders of science to the mysteries of nature. It is only now being recognised how much is owed to these early picture postcard companies for recording all aspects of the past. Newspapers then contained little in the way of illustrations and almost every event, important or trivial, was documentated visually by means of the picture postcard.

Events during the Russo-Japanese war were recorded and published on postcards soon after they occurred. Hundreds of them were issued. Not only photographs and drawings of the actual fighting, but also propaganda and political cards were issued — one series of political cartoons being entitled 'Jap the Giant Killer.' All the top echelons of the army and navy found their likenesses on postcards, and it was at this time that Japan's first 'pin-up' postcards were issued for the troops fighting abroad. The funeral of the Emporer Meiji was recorded on a series of postcards, and so were the floods in Tokyo a few years later. Also there was the terrible destruction of the Tokyo/Yokohama area during the great earthquake and fire of 1923 which was celebrated in postcards afterwards, but by this time the quality of printing for picture postcards had so deteriorated that not many collectors are interested in them; by then the Golden Age was over.

Mr P.T. Andrews of Alton in Hampshire was responsible for importing thousands of Japanese postcards into England where they found their way into collections. But the majority of Japanese cards circulating in Britain at the turn of the century were actually published in Britain by the famous postcard companies of the time. They were issued in series of 6 or 12 cards with titles like: 'Life in Japan.' 'Japanese at Home,' 'Old Japan,' 'Queer Things about Japan,' 'The Real Japan,' etc. A few specialist books on postcards give details. These cards were usually printed in Germany or Saxony where techniques were most advanced. So today we can find many cards in Europe showing scenes of Japan, like the one showing shell pickers at Mississippi Bay, Yokohama, that was posted by a Mr R. in central London to a Miss C. a few miles away at Kingston-on-Thames on 8 October 1903 which he complains is 'the rottenest, muddiest, gloomiest, beastliest day of the whole blooming year' but goes on to comment that 'the beautiful translucent water of this picture invites delicious paddling.'

*   *   *

So instead of watching a TV programme about Japan, our grandfathers in Europe would adjust the kerosene lamp and show their children and friends their collection of picture postcards of Japan. There was no commentary, nor explanation — just the photographic or artistic representation of the scene. One wonders what they thought of what they saw. Some of the comments written on the cards from this time are quite amusing, others are quite embarrassing to repeat today.

Occasionally, a publisher allowed their artists to indulge in fantasy about the Orient. Misch and Stocks in their series entitled 'The Far East' published one card showing a woman with Japanese features wearing a cross between a kimono and a colourful evening dress, carrying a cross between an umbrella and a parasol and with a most peculiar hair-style. She leads a strange dragon-like creature on a leash, while behind her stands a man with an extra-long pigtail that vaguely resembles a Chinese man. The caption reads: 'Oh golly-wolly! Ain't she just? Kissee---Kissee!'

In London at this time there was one Japanese artist living and working. His name was Yoshio Markino, and in 1905 he worked for postcard publishers Delittle, Fenwick and Co. of York. It was Markino that made sure that the cards of Japan published by this company did not stray into the realms of fantasy. Markino seemed to have relished living in London as his book *A Japanese Artist in London* shows; his other book: *My Idealed John Bullesses* describes the many young English women that he met, including the suffragette, Mrs Pankhurst, with whom he had much sympathy.

'Picture postcard mania' did not infect Japan during the Golden Age and not many postcards of this time survive in Japan today. Add to this the fact that a Japanese home is not so durable or as large as a European house or apartment where there is space and relative safety from fire to keep collections of things. It is to the avid and maniacal collectors of Europe, where a collection of 50,000 cards was not unusual, that we must give thanks for preserving such ephemera concerning Japan! The top dealers and auctioneers of Golden Age postcards in Europe nowadays report that over the last few years there has been an influx of Japanese customers attending their sales, so many of these interesting and fascinating pieces of pasteboard of the late Meiji era appear to be finding their way back to their place of origin.

PART V

Equality at Last — Reactions and Consequences

BY 1900 the industrialisation of Japan was almost complete, and the country could boast a modern army and navy. The government no longer employed a legion of foreign 'experts' in its schools, colleges and service industries, although several were retained as advisers. However, a great many foreign-run businesses flourished in the cities, and the population level of westerners remained steady. But new laws had been passed that restricted their activities, giving Japanese businessmen a definite advantage.

In manufacturing, Japan now faced the same problems as European nations, especially Britain, and these centred around the supply of raw materials and other resources. So, following the strategies of some European nations, Japan, in the name of national defence and security, began a series of Empire-building adventures into the less industrialised lands nearby. The reactions of the established western powers in the same area were an essential consideration of these exercises, and so a series of pacts and military manoeuvres followed. The economic and idealistic climate of the time, coupled with a resentment against American treatment of Japanese who were trying to settle on the West Coast, eventually led to a brilliant attack on the US Pacific fleet at Pearl Harbor in December 1941.

213

Chapter 38

Hirobumi Ito — Japan's First Prime Minister

DISREGARDING THE LAW of the Tokugawa government, five disguised Japanese men sailed away from Yokohama on 12 May 1863 bound for Europe. Among the group was 23 year-old Shunsuke Ito, later to be renamed Hirobumi Ito, who the previous year was one of a larger group who had set fire to the British legation building at Shinagawa in an act of anti-western hatred.

Yet the group that sailed from Yokohama were not trying to escape punishment for anti-western crimes. Rather, their passage had been arranged with the clandestine help of a Briton named Mr Gower who was an employee of the respectable British trading company, Glover and Co. Ito and his associates were from fairly rich families, and Ito himself was carrying US$ 8000 on his person when they slipped into Yokohama. These ex-samurai then bought outfits of second-hand sailors' clothes, had their 'top-knots' cut off, and posed as Portuguese sailors. Before departing they took a last supper in a seaman's eating house, making signs and grunts to order their food, for they dare not speak Japanese to the serving boys as that would give them away. As they ate, each heard clearly as the serving boys remarked how strange these 'foreign' men looked in their ill-fitting clothes, adding that their faces looked remarkably Japanese! Foreign persons were then a novelty in Yokohama and such commentary was normal. Ito, meanwhile, kept calm and cool, well aware that his newly purchased leather shoes were many sizes too big, and that he would have to walk with care, not shuffling as if wearing 'geta.'

At the appointed hour, 2 am., the five emerged from the shadows to follow a courier from the ship. As they passed the custom house with its vigilant guards, they tried to imitate the speech patterns of Europeans in a gibberish of sounds improvised to fool them. At the ship's gang-plank trouble immediately arose and their careful plans seemed doomed. The captain, either a righteous man or one dissatisfied with his bribe, refused to allow them on board, claiming that he knew it was against Japanese law for Japanese to travel to foreign countries. Gower pleaded, but to no avail. One of the group then drew a knife and threatened to commit *harakiri* there and then on the dockside. Gower explained his words to the captain, who knew about this determined and sensational act and so began to take them seriously. They could board, he agreed, provided they stowed themselves in a tiny hole behind the engine room until the vessel was clear of Tokyo Bay. Mutual understanding had been reached, and the five sailed on the tide before dawn.

*   *   *

As the ship drew into Shanghai, Ito had his first close view of western naval vessels bristling with guns. He remembered his youth when he was training to be a samurai warrior for the Choshu clan at the village of Miyata, near Uraga. In 1854, just 13 years old, he had been prepared to fight the foreign intrusion of Commodore Perry and his 'Black Ship' squadron, sword in hand and raging with indignation! But the naval ships in Shanghai with their flags from so many European nations fluttering above polished cannon and well-drilled obedient crews, made Ito realise what an ineffective weapon his sword would have been.

This view in Shanghai showed him and his compatriots how right they were in their strategy. They just had to visit the West themselves in order to assess how strong Europe really was and thereby formulate a sensible policy for Japan which would dictate the way she responded to the intrusions by America and the major European countries.

It was obvious that the policy of isolation, effective over the last 220 years, could no longer be maintained. To prevent Japan being permanently disadvantaged it was now essential that she face up to integration with the outside world — at least to a certain extent. Knowledge of these other countries and their peoples, therefore, was urgently needed. European countries then having the most influence over world affairs, it was natural that Ito along with Monta Inouye, Yozo Hameo, Yakichi Nomura and Endo should go there for information.

During his early military career, Ito had been selected from other Choshu samurai to go to Nagasaki to learn western military and technical methods from a team of Dutch officers stationed there. The dramatic and bustling scene at Shanghai brought home to him the meaning and significance behind his earlier lessons as the hardware gleamed in actuality in the springtime sunlight of the harbour.

From Shanghai the men split into two groups, Ito and Inouye travelling on a separate ship. During the four-and-a-half month voyage they held endless discussions, but both agreed that Japan must become an open country, and the careful handling of affairs at home was necessary to achieve this without chaos, war or colonisation.

*   *   *

Once in London, Ito began to study science under Dr Williamson, a professor of chemistry, as well as to avidly study and observe various British institutions in operation. But after only six months away, in March 1864, he received a message from Japan informing him that Choshu samurai had bought modern guns and fired on French, Dutch and US warships from shore batteries on the Shimonoseki Straits between Honshu and Kyushu. Retaliation seemed inevitable. At once

Ito and Inouye left London for Japan to try to stop their clan from meeting the western military in a direct conflict, for there was no chance of success. Arriving in Yokohama on 10 June, they were smuggled shore by a Mr Harris, of Glover and Co., again disguised as Portuguese seamen and hidden at first in an English boarding house.

Ito's mission was to rescue his clan from disaster by initiating some negotiations so that a compromise could be reached. He met Sir Rutherford Alcock of the British Legation and requested a delay for the intended bombardment of Shimonoseki. Twelve days were granted, and Ito and Inouye provided with a ship to take them to Yamaguchi, the main town of Choshu. The Choshu daimyo granted them an interview in which they explained the danger, describing the fire-power of the 18 warships being prepared in Yokohama harbour which could cause immense destruction. The daimyo listened carefully and discussed the whole matter, but finally refused to consider a peaceful solution. Meanwhile, a plot had been hatched to kill Ito and Inouye as traitors to their clan, but the daimyo managed to prevent this.

When the 12 days of grace ended, Ito and Inouye reported to Ernest Satow, secretary of the British Legation, on the failure of their mission, and the bombardment began. Accurately placed exploding shells completely devastated the shore batteries, killing many men. The daimyo was advised by his military strategists, Takasugi and Shimizu, to sign a truce and allow Commodore Shishido, Ito and Inouye to negotiate peace terms. Ito's capacity was that of interpreter, but he was also the author of the agreement that Satow and Shishido signed. In it the Choshu clan promised to treat all foreign ships passing through the Shimonoseki Straits fairly and kindly, and to supply water, provisions and fuel when requested. Also it agreed not to rebuild the shore batteries and forts, and to indemnify the foreign powers for the expenses of the bombardment amounting to $3 million. Such loss of face and capital annoyed the Shogun who sent troops against the Choshu clan, but these were defeated and Shogun Iemochi died. He was succeeded by Hitotsubashi, the last Tokugawa Shogun, who realised the real military strength of western powers that could be united against Japan: a poor feudal nation divided and almost fragmented by internal strife.

A decree from the Imperial Court of Kyoto, prompted by the daimyo of Choshu and Satsuma, to abolish the shogunate was reluctantly agreed to by Hitotsubashi. Those daimyo who supported the Shogun, but who could not agree to the abolition of his powers, resisted by force. Systematically, one by one, they were defeated in bloody battles: at Fushimi, near Kyoto (January 1868), at Ueno, Tokyo (July 1868), at Aizu (November 1868) and lastly at Hakodate (June 1869). Fortunately, the 'Japanese Revolution or Civil War' was over quickly with relatively few deaths. Most of the men of power now appreciated the wisdom of Ito, which had been learned during his illegal travels, and adapted their thinking along these lines. The myopic policy of isolation was hopeless because of western steamships and other technical developments, and a new vision involving cooperation with foreign powers in the name of the Emperor who had been restored to a position of importance was formulated, expressed by the popular slogan *'Fukoku Kyohei!'* ('Rich country, strong military!'). The Emperor and his household were transferred from Kyoto to Edo (Tokyo) and established in the castle there in 1869, while a flurry of anxious reorganisation got under way to replace old feudal institutions with modern ones.

* * *

A new age had begun in Japan — the Meiji era — and Hirobumi Ito was lionised now for his understanding of the West, becoming a doyen of Meiji politics. He was appointed a *'sanjo'* (councillor) in the new government even before the fighting had ended, becoming a justice for the Foreign Bureau and of Osaka City. Later, he was also a governor of Hyogo Prefecture around Kobe. He helped to plan the first railway line in Japan, which was to run from Tokyo to Yokohama, negotiating the loan from Britain and consulting with foreign engineers.

But the reorganisation of the government took first priority, involving the creation of many new (western-style) departments. Similarly, reforms in taxation, currency and coinage, and in banking were essential. From 1868 to 1870, Ito was a valuable member of the Iwakura mission that visited Europe to investigate methods among such institutions there. While early in 1871, Ito made another fact-finding tour to the US where other institutions and business methods were studied. On his return he was made head of the new government mint at Osaka and vice-minister of Public Works. He was just 30 years old.

By 1877, only eight years after the last internal battle, the new government had a system of railways, telegraphs, a postal system, a modest modern military, and a standardised monetary system in operation. So when the Satsuma clan rebelled that year it was soon quashed, using these new facilities, although the cost of the operation was high and caused serious inflation. But it did finally establish the new Imperial government beyond any doubt.

In the 1870s it was generally agreed that a constitutional government was a necessity in order to win the respect of all the western powers. Once again, it was Ito on another team of investigators who left Japan to study this aspect of government in Europe. Working under Professor Gneist of Berlin University and Professor Stein in Austria, Ito returned, having helped appoint a small team of highly-paid foreign experts on law to accompany him to Japan as advisers, with new knowledge to prepare the country for the Imperial Edict of 1881 which pronounced that a constitution be promulgated in Japan, and be enforced by 1890.

The task of drafting the constitution fell on Ito and his team in 1883, and by the end of the decade it, and the associated civil code, was complete. It became the basis of the fundamental law of Japan in 1889, and the new Diet was set up in 1890 to administer it. It was a great

success, admired by all western nations, and eventually caused the end
of extra-territoriality (whereby all foreign residents were unaffected by
Japanese laws) in the Treaty Ports. Now each and every resident would
be under the new Japanese laws, and Japan at last would have complete
sovereignty over all her territories and all people residing there.

*   *   *

Over the decade many of the old leaders in the government from the
progressive Choshu, Satsuma, Tosa and Hizen clans had died, leaving
as their successors those dynamic and energetic ex-samurai who had
prepared so much of the groundwork from their overseas experience.
Ito was the brightest star among them, and was later designated the
'Father of the Constitution' although it was very much a team effort
involving many dedicated foreign experts. But Ito's real strength lay in
his diplomacy both at home and abroad; he acted as a wedge between
the various clans who tried to individually dominate the government
rather than pool resources and cooperate with each other. For it still
was clan identity and allegiance that controlled the lives of many of the
new generation of leaders. Indeed today in many parts of the world, we
still observe ancient clan adhesion, perhaps reflecting a nostalgia for an
earlier 'Golden Age'. In present-day Japan, the company has replaced
the clan or tribe, with perhaps 'old boy' college and university networks
complicating matters further. In Britain, the four principal regions, (five
if Cornwall is included) of England, Scotland, Wales and Ireland still
induce partisan feelings that are often expressed in violence, although
here one should add that football team identification coupled with 1930s
racist themes (a sad product of Darwinism) has again complicated clear
thinking. In other parts of the world — Africa, Israel, the Gulf — even
America — the clans war as they did in Ito's Japan a century ago! But
Japan outgrew her clan system, or tribalism, under Ito, and the August
1945 experience caused her to seek a new mature relationship with the
rest of the world. The 'chosen clan' concept has been replaced by 'the
chosen race' concept which in turn has been replaced by an 'international'
concept. Many Japanese are now impatient for the rest of the world to
catch up with the latest philosophy based upon economic reality!

Because of Ito's diplomatic and less partisan stance, he was selected
as the first Prime Minister of Japan in December 1885 at the age of 46.
He breathed a sigh of relief as his rival, Okuma, from the Hizen clan
was forced to resign. Okuma had moved too fast in trying to have Japan
adopt wholesale the British parliamentary system, to be administered
by members of his own clan.

During the two years and four months of his premiership, Ito
established his position in politics. Cooperating closely with Yamagata
of Choshu and Matsukata of Satsuma, he precipitated the final fall of
autocratic government in Japan. He encouraged men from all clans to
rise to power, paving the way for real unity. However, because Ito failed
to obtain rapid revision of the treaties with foreign nations to establish

equality of Japan with the West, he had to resign. But for the following decade he remained a dominant force behind the scenes in Japanese politics as a *'genro'* or elder statesman. The oligarchs or genro made their opinions felt in all cabinet ministries, manipulating those who ran the departments in name only, and able to move slowly and leisurely but effectively. They influenced the evolution of Tokyo University which was designed to educate the cleverer men from all clans for future position in the civil service and higher bureaucracy, and this still continues.

Anti-foreign passions ran high from 1887 onwards, after two years of 'foreign-mania' when western-style dress, music, dancing, athletics and velocipede riding were all the rage. There were many murderous attacks on both foreigners and Japanese statesmen related to the slowness of treaty revision. Many prominent foreigners in Yokohama protested in public meetings against the imminent loss of their 'treaty rights,' and their houses had to be protected day and night by special police against incendiary and personal attacks.

But the 'genro' worked steadily for a satisfactory solution, trying to reach a compromise between *Taito joyaku kaisei* (Treaty revision on an equal footing) sought by many Japanese, and 'No unconditional revision' of the foreign community. In 1894 there was a breakthrough. The British government, impressed by the carefully composed Constitution, the way that the governing institutions were evolving, and by the terms of the new treaties and legal codes, relinquished extra-territoriality when these became effective in 1899. All other countries followed the British lead, so by 1911 the confidence of Japan was restored by her complete autonomy.

*   *   *

Even before this, the new-found confidence and dignity had begun to express itself in unfortunate western ways. Having adapted a Constitution along with laws and technical developments after a long, determined and intelligent struggle so that they served well the unique needs of Japanese society, Japan then unintelligently and greedily tried to impose such systems on her neighbouring countries, notably Korea and Taiwan, disregarding the unique nature of those countries. This was following western imperial nations too closely and too far, and was eventually doomed to disaster. Believing unscientific propaganda from the West, that undeveloped nations were composed of people who were less than human, but who could be 'civilised' by force, Japan disregarded her own lessons and proudly began flag-waving imperial expansion.

In 1876 Korea was virtually a closed and mysterious land as Japan had been before 1853 and the forceful intrusion of Commodore Perry's fleet. In that year Japan sent a Perry-type fleet to Korea to force an opening of the country by the signing of a treaty. Thus began a process of colonisation of the Korean population whose unique traditions, like

Japan's, had evolved over more than 1000 years in their own independent ways. Once entrenched, Korean traditions were largely disregarded and Japanese rule was imposed oppressively, leading to a deep resentment and hatred, which even today has its overtones. This imposition led to two major wars: in 1895 with China and during 1904/5 with Russia who also had imperialistic designs on the 'Land of the Morning Calm' (Korea). Resorting to ancient mystical and magical beliefs with respect to the naming of parts of the real world, the Japanese rulers even renamed each Korean town and village in their own style. Thus the capital, Seoul, became Keijo.

Ito, having satisfied himself that the government was running smoothly, moved more into international politics and was a major adviser in the formulation of the Anglo-Japanese Alliance of 1902. Then, after negotiating with the Russian authorities after their defeat in 1905, in that year became Resident General of Korea.

However, during this later period of his life, Ito tended to spend more time with his family at their Oiso residence on Odawara Bay called 'Sorokaku' (Villa of the Blue Waves). It was a western-style house where his wife, Umeko Kida, whom he had married in 1866 when she was 17 years old, presided over all with the grace and dignity of a Tokyo society lady. His three sons, one adopted, and two daughters appreciated the presence of their father, who now had been made a Count. Advice to his eldest son, Bunkicki, included loyalty to the Emperor, sincerity and honesty with oneself, not to hurry or force events and to observe everything happening in the West as westerners, Ito claimed, still had more foresight than orientals.

Mary, wife of British Ambassador Sir Hugh Fraser, met the Ito family on several occasions, describing the Count as 'having the cleverest face I have ever seen; it is not noble or elevated in any way, which is not strange perhaps, since he did not originally belong to the higher class of Japanese, but for sheer intelligence and power I have seen few to beat it,' and, 'He is a very astute yet broad thinker, determined and ruthless, and had absolute control of personal emotions and ambitions' yet he could attain 'any object which he considered important enough to desire.'

In Korea many of his duties were purely ceremonial where the genial 65-year-old statesman, who had an honorary degree from Yale University and a reputation for heavy drinking, in full uniform decked with medals, spent his time inspecting various groups of people and their projects.

It was on 26 October 1909 that he arrived at Harbin railway station to review part of the Russian army in the capacity of Honorary Commander. As he stepped from the special train to be greeted by Russian officers and other foreign dignitaries, three loud shots rang out behind him in quick succession. Ito clutched his neck and felt blood, collapsing to the ground. Panic reigned as the assassin, a Korean malcontent called An' Chung-Keun, was overpowered, and the wounded

Ito was attended by the few medical facilities available. Within 30 minutes he was dead.

His elaborate state funeral in Tokyo on 4 November 1909 was attended by thousands who knew him through his earlier achievements and adventures, and he was finally buried at Yadane Cemetery near the Memorial Hall of the Constitution at Omori. A set of black-and-white postcards of his funeral was later issued. His assassin, one of a group of 14 each determined to kill Ito at Harbin that day, was executed on 25 March 1910.

Chapter 39

The Anglo-Japanese Alliance

TWO MEN WERE SEATED solemnly at the polished table in the large government office. The weak daylight of the London winter filtered through the high window as they checked the six articles in the document before them. The pens had been prepared with just sufficient ink for their signatures, and in turn they appended their names and titles to the document, which then constituted a legal international agreement between the governments of Britain and Japan. It was the occasion of the signing of the first Anglo-Japanese Alliance on 30 January 1902, a quiet affair that was not made public until 12 February when Prime Minister Katsura announced its completion to the House of Peers in Tokyo, and newspapers reported on it in Japan the following day. It was not mentioned in the London *Times* until 21 February, but its consequences were to affect the lives of thousands of people in China, Korea and Russia.

Sitting on one side of the document was the Marquis of Lansdowne, His Brittanic Majesty's Principal Secretary of State for Foreign Affairs. He had been born Henry Charles Keith Petty-Fitzmaurice in Lansdowne House, Berkeley Square, in 1845. After an undistinguished career at Eton and Oxford University, where several private tutors aided his slow progress in learning, he found himself in 1866, on the death of his father, one of the largest landowners in Britain and a member of the House of Lords. The inheritance of his land in Ireland and England could be traced back to the Norman Conquest in 1066, and the rents paid by the tenants were responsible for the immense capital of the family.

For 15 years Lansdowne was a liberal M.P. under Gladstone, then in 1883 he was appointed Governor-General of Canada, and afterwards he became Viceroy of India. In 1895 he had returned to Britain to hold the position of First Secretary of State for War. It was also in 1895 that his mother, Emily Jane Mercer Elphinstone de Flahault, died and he inherited further large estates in Scotland. The Boer War in South Africa soon followed Lansdowne's appointment, and he came under harsh criticism for the mistakes and failures of the army in the early part of the mêlée, when two small republics with economies based in agriculture, out-manoeuvred the trained British militia. In 1901 he was transferred from the War Office to the Foreign Office.

It was because of the British army's pathetic escapades in South Africa, together with the rapid increase in strength of Germany and America, that Baron Komura, the Japanese Foreign Minister, suggested at the time: 'Since there are grounds for believing that Britain has already passed her zenith and will to some extent decline, it would be best to fix a time-limit for any British treaty.'

This advice had been considered, and when Baron Tadasu Hayashi, Envoy Extraordinary and Minister Plenipotentiary of His Majesty the Emperor of Japan, the other signatory, sat next to Lansdowne, he could see that the alliance was, according to Article VI, to last only five years. Born in 1850 in a long-established samurai family, Hayashi's early education had centred around military training. In 1868, he had fought under Admiral Enomoto in the capture of Hakodate city, on the remote north island of Hokkaido, in an attempt to re-establish rule by the Shogun in Japan. This attempted coup had soon been defeated as Imperial forces arrived, but Hayashi and others involved in the anti-Imperial operation were not killed or imprisoned, and many of them were given positions of power and leadership in the new regime. At the age of 23, Hayashi was appointed to a government position in the Ministry of Public Works and was responsible for the administration of the first engineering college in Tokyo. Afterwards, he entered wider administrative departments, and was appointed governor of a prefecture in the south of Japan. Later, he joined the diplomatic corps, and was posted to China. During the Sino-Japanese War in 1895, he returned to Japan to become Vice-Minister of Foreign Affairs, and was made a Baron in that same year. After a few years as Japanese ambassador in Russia, he arrived in Britain to become the ambassador in London.

*   *   *

In all the preliminary negotiations in preparation for the signing of the alliance, there were no consultations at all with the King and Court in Korea or with the Chinese imperial administration, even though the results of it would directly affect their sovereign lands and people. This, of course, was because the military forces of these two powers did not have the strength to resist the 'open door' policy as laid down, and backed by force, by western powers and Japan. This policy as formulated by John Hay, the American Secretary of State, during the time when American influence and control had stretched into the Pacific from Hawaii to Guam and the Philippines, stated that all nations must have equal and unrestricted opportunities to trade with China and, by implication, neighbouring Korea. In reality, this policy, seen in the West as benevolent and fair-minded Uncle Sam helping his 'little brown brothers' in militarily weak places around the Pacific, meant that western nations could help themselves as best they could to the resources in the area.

This led to the nationalistic Chinese Boxer uprising in 1900, where fairly well organised gangs killed and destroyed many westerners in the foreign settlements around China, under the condoning eyes of the Chinese authorities who did little to control them. In Peking the western embassies were fired upon and besieged, defended only by a small international force directed by the Japanese Major Shiba, who later was regarded as a hero. They held out until an allied force could be assembled and a rescue mission mounted. The defeat of the Boxer movement soon followed this, and those members who were caught were put to death by being suspended by their jaws in special death-cages. A huge indemnity was demanded from the Chinese government by the powers that had suffered in the troubles, and this weakened the economy of China even more.

Although Russian troops had taken part in the suppression of the Boxer rebels, the politicians of that country refused to accept the 'open door' policy and demanded that a vast area of north-east China be their exclusive domain with no interference from other western powers. This frightened the Japanese and British authorities when the precise nature of the demands were made known. Japan feared that she would be excluded from exploiting the resources of Korea, while Britain feared that her naval supremacy in the Far East would be threatened if more ships were not sent there. The Boer War had put a strain on British military resources, and the Russian threat to the north of British India was now real. So an alliance with Japan seemed appropriate and useful, for the British and Japanese warships could join and cooperate during any incident or threat, making it unnecessary to expand the British fleet in the area. This would save money for the Admiralty, but end Britain's long period of 'splendid isolation' based on gunboat diplomacy.

The history of the development of the Japanese navy and its close ties with the Royal Navy had some bearing on the decision to form an alliance with Japan. Before 1860, the Japanese had no navy, indeed the laws of the shogunate forbade the building of large ocean-going ships of any kind. But in the 1860s, several French dock- and ship-building experts had been hired to undertake and instruct in the construction of iron naval vessels at Yokosuka in Tokyo Bay. But in the actual use and organisation of these warships, the Japanese had looked to Britain. British instructors from the Royal Navy had been continually employed by the Japanese government to train officers and sailors. Some Japanese cadets came to Britain to learn about everything from battle tactics to signalling and from gunnery to feeding the crew — all the skills required to allow the government to maintain aggressive policies around the world. Battleships and cruisers were annually supplied to Japan from British shipyards, and Etajima, the top naval academy near Hiroshima, was based on the one at Dartmouth. Even English words and expressions were absorbed into the vocabulary of all Japanese seamen and used for issuing orders and giving commands.

So there was an intimate and well-established connection between the Royal and Imperial Japanese Navies, and the British Admiralty felt a certain trust in the ability and loyalty of the Imperial Navy which was favourable for the alliance. A further advantage for Britain was that the obsolete dockyards and coaling facilities at Hong Kong, requiring a huge expenditure for improvements, need no longer be used as much and could be updated at a slower rate, for an alliance would make the efficient facilities in Japan available to the British China squadron.

*   *   *

As soon as the alliance was made public, Union Jacks appeared on the streets in Japan's cities and towns, hung out with the Japanese flag, decorating all public buildings. Celebration postcards appeared in the racks in shops both in Britain and Japan. One set of six cards called 'Alliance Geisha Dance' showed young kimonoed girls in various wooden poses in a tatami-floored studio holding the flags of both nations, and a British-made set of cards showed two young boys, one English and the other Japanese, playing seriously with the model of a cannon.

In the Imperial Hotel, Tokyo, a meeting to celebrate the alliance was held on 8 March 1902, organised by the Tokyo Chamber of Commerce and the Commercial and Industrial Club. The British Ambassador, Sir Claude MacDonald, was an honoured guest. It was in Japan, more than in Britain, that the alliance was strongly welcomed and appreciated, for it proved in the minds of the people that the 30-year struggle to metamorphose from feudalism to industrialism had been successfully completed. The indignity suffered when Commodore Perry had arrived on the shores of Japan to force the signing of the unequal treaties could be forgotten, and Japan could now be proud to be an equal with a prominent western power.

But what was the real significance of the alliance in terms of the political and economic backdrop of the Far East at the time? Article II stated that if either Japan or Britain should become involved in a war through 'defending their interests' in China or Korea, then the other power should remain neutral and try to prevent other powers from joining in hostilities against its ally. But, according to Article III, if a second power should join the first in a war against one of the allies, then the other would come to its aid. In other words, it was a careful preparation for a war between Japan and Russia, with Britain playing the role of an umpire who keeps intruders off the pitch! It gave Japan *carte blanche* to exploit Korea and expand her political influence and industrial installations — mines, timber works, etc. — on continental

Asia. This was in direct conflict with the interests of Russian entrepreneurs who had built similar installations in south Manchuria a short distance away along the extensions of the trans-Siberian railway.

There had been much opposition to the Anglo-Japanese alliance within Japan during the preceding decade, for many believed, like former Prime Minister Ito, that an agreeable settlement could be reached by negotiating directly with Russia. As late as autumn 1901, Ito had gone to America and then to St Petersburg in an attempt to obtain a last-minute agreement with Russia, but without success. The new Japanese Prime Minister, Marshal Yamagata, was a believer in the use of military force to 'solve the Korean question.'

Within three months of the signing of the alliance, pressure was put on Russia to withdraw all her troops from Manchuria by September 1903, and an agreement was signed with China. In July 1903, Japan opened direct negotiations with Russia and demanded that all troops (except a few to guard the railways from gangs of bandits) withdraw and that the administration of Manchuria be returned to the Chinese. After some delay, Russia agreed to the demands in January 1904, but took no action. On 6 February Japan severed diplomatic relations with Russia, then the Japanese navy delivered a surprise attack on the Russian fleet anchored in Port Arthur on the night of 8 February, and declared war on 10 February. By attacking before declaring war, the Japanese military had broken the accepted international code, but the press in Britain praised the surprise attack as brilliant military strategy. And so began another bloody war fought for imperialistic ends in which 165,000 men were killed or wounded. This event was also celebrated by the publication of postcards, and the Japanese victory in 1905 by the displaying of flags.

The Anglo-Japanese alliance was also renewed, in modified form, in 1905, and then again in 1911. But when the second renewal terminated in 1921, it was not revived for the situation in the Far East had changed after the Great War, despite the efforts of the Prince of Wales.

Chapter 40

The 1910 White City Exhibition

THERE WERE SAMURAI WARRIORS striding around the streets of London. A short distance away Japanese experts demonstrated the martial arts of judo, kendo and akido; sumo wrestlers performed twice a day in an authentic ring of clay, while in the small wooden houses with their sliding doors (*shoji*) there were kimonoed men practising the ancient Japanese art of forming vessels in bronze. There was a stand displaying the products of Daisuke Akiba, rickshaw maker, but no rickshaws were to be seen carrying portly English businessmen along the streets as there had been two years previously in the 'Colonial' section of the Franco-British exhibition. Japan was no colony, in fact she had colonies of her own at this time, and no Japanese man was going to degrade himself by pulling Englishmen around in rickshaws on this magnificent and splendid occasion.

It was the 1910 Japan-British Exhibition and Japan had come to Britain to show off. The relationship between Britain and her empire and Japan and her empire had never been better. For just over half a century Japan had been emulating the west — using, developing and producing the fruits of western science and know-how. Now was the time to show her self-confidence and maturity in the modern world. The name of the Pacific archipelago had even been changed to *Dai Nippon* (Great Japan) in the quest to become equivalent to an 'eastern Great Britain.'

                         *   *   *

The most prominent feature of the exhibition was called the 'Flip-Flap'. It was a unique piece of British engineering that enabled visitors to transfer from one side of the site to the other, getting a panoramic bird's-eye view of the whole exhibition at the same time, with the minimum of effort. The Eiffel Tower had been built for an exhibition in Paris a decade before, and the British had thought hard about constructing something even more impressive in terms of large-scale engineering. They came up with the Flip-Flap. It consisted of two huge, crane-like structures both hinged at one end to the same place on the ground that moved simultaneously through 180 degrees from horizontal positions. On the end of each was a three-storied steel conveyance in which people could be transferred in a huge arc that took them far above the exhibition and gave them a grand view.

On the day of the opening, Saturday, 14 May 1910 *The Times* enthused at the whole enterprise after remarking on the incredible boldness of Mr Kiralfy who designed and built the main structures on the site for the 1908 Franco-British Exhibition. 'The assemblage of palaces, domes and minarets' were all in a brilliant white (which gave rise to the still-used name of 'White City') but even though they had braved the 'British skies and London chimneys' for two years, their effect was 'to make the most of the sunshine and give a London summer twice its value amidst the shadowless reflections.' In other words, the bold use of white in the middle of smoke-polluted London, though seeming to be madness, was a great success.

The business of organising the exhibition had begun in March 1908 when the Imperial Diet had granted 1.8 million yen for it, and Prince Fushima was appointed its Honorary President. Baron Oura, the Minister of Agriculture and Commerce, was made president and Baron Matsudaira made Vice-President, and soon a committee of over sixty officials was formed to administer the exhibitors. All the public corporations in Japan were contacted as well as public manufacturing industries, and also private companies. Soon a total of 1318 exhibitors had submitted 32,867 exhibits for possible display in London. Only 19,943 of the exhibit proposals were eventually accepted.

*   *   *

By 1910, Japan had had considerable experience in contributing to international exhibitions. The first one had been the 1873 exhibition in Vienna and in the following year exhibits valued at 8,982 yen were shown in London. In the years that followed, Japan contributed to 36 other exhibitions before 1910, and these were held all over Europe, North America and Russia. However, the 242,700 square feet (22983 m^2) allocated to Japan in the 1910 London exhibition was the greatest area ever — more than double the area she had had in the St Louis Exposition of 1904. But so many new developments had taken place in Japan that there was no problem in filling such a vast area. As the detailed souvenir book by Mochizuki pointed out: 'The Japanese department will set forth most graphically not only the civilisation of Japan, the development of industry and the natural resources, but in order to show the steps taken in the progress of Japanese civilisation, historical outlines of education, army and navy, communications and other institutions together with ancient fine arts.' It was to be very comprehensive. 'A miniature Japan both past and present will be built up in London,' commented Mochizuki.

Characteristically, the Japanese section was all set up and ready two weeks before the opening date. *The Times* commented on 28 April that 'The Emperor and the Government of Japan have made a supreme effort by means of this exhibition to familiarise the western mind with their country both as it is and as it was.' He went on to describe the 'magnificent Romon, or gateway of the Kasuga Shrine at Nara which has been reproduced at the Wood Lane entrance' (now in Kew Gardens) and the 'platform where the famous Noh dance will be performed,' the two large Japanese gardens with 'their lakes, rockeries, and islands crowned with quaint pavilions' and the model of Osaka City 'with 50,000 separate houses spread out before the spectator.'

The day before the opening, Halley's Comet had appeared in the skies, and only one event dampened the gaiety of the occasion. This was the death of King Edward VII a few days before on 6 May. A Japanese resident of London, Satori Kato, in a letter to *The Times,* apologised about the actions of his countrymen and wished to 'exonerate Japan from a most astounding blunder' in opening the exhibition during a time of national mourning. However, as usual, the British compromised by opening it on the appointed day, but by postponing the fireworks and the special illuminations until after the King's funeral.

The British summer weather of 1910 was kind and thousands flocked

to the exhibition, watched the sporting activities, rode the Flip-Flap and
posted postcards of the displays on the site so that they would be franked
with a special mark. People were impressed, and much business was
arranged as the post-exhibition trade figures show. The artists of Europe
that came were inspired by the artwork they saw which added to the
influence of Japanese art on the 'art nouveau' movement. Exactly how
much this exhibition and others preceding it influenced the course of
movements in art, in thinking and in the way that Europeans lived is
difficult to assess, but certainly it ran deep.

*   *   *

The Edwardian age that had just ended was an era of optimism in both
Britain and Japan. The rational future that such writers as H.G. Wells
and G.B. Shaw were outlining and popularising seemed to be bright and
peaceful. But Masaharu Shinohara from Fukui prefecture went a little
too far in his optimism. An article in Mochizuki's souvenir book is
entitled 'Discovery of the Means for Triumph over Death' which
describes a liniment that Shinohara was selling at his store in Tokyo.
'After long tedious study and experiment, he finally succeeded in
discovering the means for curing the origin of diseases,' it was claimed.
'By annointing the particular parts of the body' this liniment cured the
origins of 'cancers, T.B., rheumatism, syphilis, leprosy, bites, itches,
contusions, scalds, burns, frostbite, etc.' It seems that Mr Shinohara
was taken to court both in Tokyo and Kyoto for deceiving the public,
but it was proved to the courts that his liniment was quite effective, and
the cases were dropped. It is not clear whether this product was exhibited
in London, and no records can be found that describe the reaction of
the British public to it.

Chapter 41

Prince Hirohito's Visit to Britain

WHY DID the Japanese Crown Prince Hirohito,the late Emperor, visit
Britain in 1921, and what did he do? He arrived at the Royal Navy base
of Portsmouth on board the Japanese battleship *Katori* which was
accompanied by the *Kashima,* and escorted by several British destroyers.
The Prince was accompanied by his brother, Prince Kan-in, and both
had suites of assistants and advisers. Royal salutes were fired as the
Prince of Wales boarded the *Katori,* a ship built in England in 1905, to
welcome the visitors. Within a few hours, on 9 May 1921, they were all
on shore to be greeted by Baron Gonsuke Hayashi, the Japanese
ambassador, and a host of military dignitaries. A special train took them

to Victoria Station, London, where King George V welcomed them. The Dukes of York and Connaught paid their respects, and the Earl of Chesterfield, Master of the Royal Horse, conducted the Prince to a carriage. The procession of six carriages and two motorcars then drove to Buckingham Palace along a route lined with cheering citizens protected by rows of armed troops.

The visit had been timed to coincide with discussions in the British government about the renewal of the Anglo-Japanese alliance that had first been signed in 1902, and then renewed in 1911. This equal military alliance, the first of its kind for Japan, had been effective for almost 20 years. But since the end of the Great War, international attitudes had changed in the West. The early post-war years had inspired an optimistic idealism, and there was strong belief in the rationalisation of military power through the League of Nations. The old imperialistic concepts in the Anglo-Japanese alliance were becoming outdated.

Powerful sections of public opinion in both Japan and Britain opposed a renewal of the alliance. In Japan, businessmen and army officers doubted if it would be beneficial, and in Britain, brutal events in Korea by the Japanese colonial regime had made many people suspicious and resentful of Japan's ambitions. This suspicion was reinforced by reports from expatriate British businessmen operating in the Treaty Ports of China, who were finding that lucrative trading was being adversely affected by intrigues by the Japanese military.

Another factor, probably a more important one, was that British overseas power was crumbling, and since the Great War the United States had emerged as the dominating world force. Very few Japanese realised the extent to which the United States had displaced Britain as the leading power on the international scene, yet it was obvious to every British soldier who had survived the Great War. These came from every British village, and almost all individual families, and they knew that without the intervention of the United States the map of Europe would have been completely different.

Nevertheless, a message arrived from Tokyo: 'Gratified at the safe arrival of Prince Hirohito. It must be remembered that his peaceful, pleasant journey was due to the fact that his route was almost entirely within the Dominions of Great Britain, and for this all Japan is extremely grateful.'

The day after his arrival, the Prince visited Windsor Castle by train where he inspected St George's Chapel, and then proceeded to Frogmore where he laid a floral wreath on the tomb of Queen Victoria. The next day the crowds cheered as his party went in procession to the City of London to be received by the Lord Mayor and the Sheriffs at the Guildhall. After a luncheon at the Mansion House, the Band of the Coldstream Guards played for the party, which included a selection from the current musical comedy showing in London, Chu Chin Chow.

The following week the newspapers reported the Prince's daily activities that ranged from a visit to the Houses of Parliament followed

by an hour in the National Portrait Gallery, to watching air displays at
Kenley Aerodrome followed by a visit to the Greenwich Observatory.
At Aldershot the Prince participated in a regimental review and watched
a gymnastic display, then drove to Farnborough for another air display,
followed by an inspection of cadets of the Royal Military College at
Sandhurst. All these visits to government establishments in the
countryside of England during the daytime, were interspersed with
various receptions in London during the evening where the Prince met
all the important political figures of the day. 'Prince Hirohito's Busy
Day' ran the headlines in the newspapers, while on other pages of the
same newspapers were advertisements for the Save the Children Fund,
appealing for help to save starving British children. 'British Children in
dire WANT this Whitsuntide' headed one such appeal that described the
unemployment in Britain that was leading to starvation in some sectors
of the population. Most stone-masons, however, were fully employed
as they chiselled the names of each conscripted soldier who had died in
the Great War to be placed on the war memorials that were to be erected
in every village.

                          *   *   *

On 18 May 1921, the Prince travelled to Cambridge University where
he was awarded an honorary degree, and listened to a lecture by Dr
Tanner of St John's College on: 'The Relationship between the Crown
and the people of England.' Then, after a brief visit to Ely Cathedral,
he went by train to Edinburgh, Scotland. Here he stayed in Holyrood
House, and from there took a special train to see the new Forth Bridge,
toured the dockyards on the River Forth, and embarked on a destroyer
which took him around the estuary to inspect *H.M.S. Hood.*

    Back in Edinburgh, the Prince, in the uniform of a British General,
inspected some Scottish Boy Scouts in King's Park, and then presented
£100 as a gift to the poor of the city.

    On the return journey to London, the Prince's itinerary took him
to Eton School. As he entered the School Yard, 1000 assembled boys
heard the acting captain of the school, H.G. Babington-Smith, cry out
in Japanese: 'Long life to his Highness the Crown Prince — Banzai!'
After inspecting the school buildings, the Prince promised to present
some Japanese books to the library.

    It was a quiet departure from London for the Prince on 29 May
after his three-week stay. There was no pomp and ceremony as the
King, the Prince of Wales and Duke of York bade him farewell at
Victoria Station. There were no ceremonies at Portsmouth either,
although he did meet some Boy Scouts and Girl Guides, while the
Secretary of State for War, Sir Laming Worthington-Evans, made him
an honorary general in the British army. Then the *Katori* slipped out
of Portsmouth harbour at 5.30 a.m. on 30 May, bound for France.

In December 1921, the British government had decided against renewing the Anglo-Japanese alliance. A new kind of agreement was thought necessary, more in line with the spirit of the League of Nations, and on 13 December, under pressure from the new might of the United States, the Four-Power Treaty was signed in Washington. This was a broader-based grouping of the United States, Britain, Japan and France, and involved agreements on rights in the Pacific Ocean region.

However, in Japan many people thought it was a treacherous step on the part of Britain away from Japan, and many blamed the intimidation of the United States. The preliminary talks between Britain's Prime Minister Balfour and the United States' Secretary of State Hughes had taken place in secret without the knowledge of the Japanese ministers, and this had given rise to distrust in some quarters in Japan for the old ally. Prince Hirohito's busy tour of Britain had not generated the required enthusiasm for the old alliance to be renewed.

Chapter 42

Prince Edward's Tour of Japan

THE WHIRLWIND TOUR of Japan by Britain's heir to the throne, Edward, the Prince of Wales, in 1922 raised eyebrows, created excitement with its unpredictability and had, in retrospect, ominous and foreboding elements. In the year before the Great Kanto Earthquake that destroyed Yokohama and much of Tokyo, the largest earthquake for 28 years occurred and part of the famous Imperial Hotel in Tokyo went up in flames as the Prince attended a concert party nearby along with an audience of 20,000 people. He was the last prominent guest of the old Yokohama foreign community, attending functions at the Gaiety Theatre, the United Club and Christchurch before they were obliterated. Little did the members of The Bluffers Jazz Band or the Bijou Players realise at the Royal Ball — 'the triumph of the social season' — held at the Gaiety, that the next year their theatre would be no more and many of their lives would end. Nor did the hearty members of the United Club, as they rendered 'For He's a Jolly Good Fellow!' for the Prince, know that their premises would be completely destroyed. And no observer or journalist, writing cosy copy on the Prince's habits, could prophesy that the Prince, on becoming King Edward VIII, would abdicate after 11 months for the love of a divorced woman.

A great-grandson of Queen Victoria and born seven years before her death, Prince Edward was the eldest son of King George V who became heir to the British throne after the death, at the age of 28 years, of his elder brother Albert Edward, Duke of Clarence, in 1892. The Duke of Clarence, rakish and snide, was officially reported to have died in agony from pneumonia, but it was afterwards speculated that syphilis of the brain was the real cause of death and that perhaps he was the undiscovered murderer, called Jack the Ripper, of several London prostitutes in 1888.

After a strict upbringing and education, in which a cruel nursemaid and harsh and fault-finding father made their impression, Prince Edward did some training with the Navy and then spent some time at Oxford University. The brutality of corporal punishment for naval cadets guilty of petty misdemeanours had a traumatic effect on the teenage prince who, along with all his peers, was forced to witness the floggings.

In his early twenties, Prince Edward saw military action on continental Europe during World War I, although he was continually being protected from real danger. Returning to England in February 1919, plans were made by the government for him to travel to several Commonwealth and other allied countries to thank them for their efforts in achieving a 'British victory' in the war, and to try to weld chains of friendship with Britain. By August he was leaving for Canada and the United States, where his personal human qualities and friendly manner endeared him as 'The Democratic Prince.' Early the next spring, another long tour of duty took him to New Zealand and Australia, stopping off at Fiji and Barbados to perform rounds of additional ceremonials.

Then, after a few months resting in England, he left again in November 1921 on board *HMS Renown* to visit India where he was to inaugurate new reforms, followed by tours to Ceylon (Sri Lanka), Malaya, Hong Kong and Japan.

*   *   *

Arriving at Yokohama on 12 April 1922 amid the roar of naval guns, displays of flags and decorations, daylight fireworks and military bands, the Prince was greeted by Prince Higashi Fushima as airplanes soared overhead. Then representatives of the British and Indian communities were introduced. Soon followed by his 500 pieces of luggage, he travelled by special train to Tokyo Station where a procession of horse-drawn carriages took him to the Imperial Palace in the company of Prince Regent Hirohito. The Emperor himself was ill. A massive replica of London's Tower Bridge across a wide thoroughfare was the special feature of the decorated streets through which the Prince, wearing Guards uniform with tall busby, passed amid the cheering crowds.

In the full programme of the following four weeks, the Prince surprised the public and annoyed many officials on account of his casual and unpredictable behaviour. 'Prince breaks many Formality Rules' ran headlines in *The Japan Advertiser,* and during his first public function at 9.30 the next morning at the Imperial University, he spoke informally and sincerely to the 5000 students, ignoring his prepared speech. This was a great departure from accepted pre-war regal behaviour. But after the formal part of his visit, where he met and bestowed medals and other honours upon various officials and dignitaries, unveiled plaques to the war-dead and attended theatre performances, embassy balls and industrial concerns, he relaxed even more. In his frequent unprecedented 'walkabouts' he was the first royal personage to stop to talk with children or groups of spectators, once requesting a light for his cigarette from those in the crowd, and breaking many old rules confining princely conduct.

On his side-trip to the shrines of Nikko, the Prince wore 'a walking suit of knickers, leggings and a cap, and carried a stout cane. The members of his suite were also dressed informally. But among the Japanese reporters and photographers could be seen morning coats and top hats!' A Rolls-Royce carried him part of the way up the steep road to Lake Chuzenji in the mountains, then he decided to walk up the final section. He stuffed his cap into a pocket and strode up through the trees so fast that the rest of the party had to run to keep up. When he arrived in front of the Kegon waterfall that drains the lake, he decided to experience rickshaw-pulling and instructed the portly Admiral Halsey to be his passenger. Running in the shafts at a brisk pace towards the main road, one of the wheels caught in a culvert, spilling out the admiral and bending the wheel beyond repair. Laughing that it was 'easily the most amazing experience of the trip,' the prince insisted that Mr Fair, the photographer in the party, take his picture between the shafts of the rickshaw.

It should be remembered that at the time, royal families in Europe felt far from secure. Just four years after the Russian Revolution, when the Romanov family had all been executed by the Bolsheviks, and the Hapsburg and Hohenzollern royal families disposed of, it was felt that the British monarchy was far from stable in view of the discontent of thousands of ex-military men living in poor conditions on inadequate pensions in Britain. The 28-year-old Prince's more humane attitude to all around him was perhaps a defence mechanism responding to his fear and insecurity based on an inner struggle to find his real place and function in the world.

*   *   *

Coincident with and connected to Prince Edward's visit was 'The British Civilisation Exhibition' held in Tokyo. In it, British life, achievements and history were illustrated, but the special influence of Britain upon Japan was stressed. The entrance was decorated with British war posters — 'Come and do your bit: Enlist Today!' was one message, and a prominent exhibit was a piece of wood described as being a fragment of the Japanese warship, *Kenko,* which was sold to the Satsuma clan in the early 1860s. Previously named *HMS Beagle,* the three-masted sailing ship had taken Charles Darwin around the world on his epic voyage of evolutionary discovery, and also seen military action in the Crimean War. As well as explaining British sports, religions, coinage, childrens' games and industry, the exhibition was also concerned with the lives of the early British settlers, diplomats and employees in the Treaty Ports. This included unflattering Japanese prints of *Eikokojin* (Englishmen), and sketches of Japanese people by Charles Wirgman, reporter for the *Illustrated London News*.

The prince mentioned the British-Japanese connection in a speech in Tokyo, where after commenting on the rapid progress of Japan over the 40 years since feudalism ended in which 'some of my own countrymen have been able to contribute,' and on the long-lasting Anglo-Japanese Alliance that had just been terminated, he added that 'if you have learned from us, we also learnt and still hope to learn from you, and in the realms of art you are exercising an influence which promises to be both healthful and enduring.'

The progress of *Ei Kotaishi Denka* (Prince from the West, as he was known in Japanese) was recorded on movie film by Major Distin Maddick whose cameras rolled at every formal and informal occasion during the visit. Much of the footage, however, was lost in the fire at the Imperial Hotel, as were the belongings of 36 members of the *Renown's* band and all the decorations and presents due for distribution by the Prince of Wales. Souvenir postcards were a feature of this visit and several superbly designed, coloured and embossed ones were issued by the Tokyo Design Printing Co. Ltd. Considering the late date, when the popularity of the humble postcard was declining in Europe after its Golden Age that ended with the Great War, they were excellent productions. In Yokohama, postcards were used as instruments of friendship when middle-school students hand-painted 7000 of them to send to the officers and men of the cruisers *Renown* and *Durban*.

On his return to Tokyo from Nikko, Prince Edward took part in a duck hunt in the grounds of the Hama Detached Palace as a guest of Prince Regent Hirohito, and watched sumo wrestling before spending a few days at Hakone. Here he made efforts to keep out of the public gaze by slipping out of the kitchen door of the Fujiya Hotel to walk alone in the hills, and to ride in the electric railway cars, second class, to Yumoto. Again the adjective 'democratic' was flourished in the newspaper reports.

His itinerary then took him to Kyoto where a great lantern parade accompanied his visit to the Meiji tomb and many other national shrines. Again, in his free time the prince walked incognito around the streets in his grey suit and black derby hat. There were official functions to attend, like the Municipal Reception at the Town Hall, and arranged trips to Lake Biwa, where he left his party to visit some fishermen by launch to learn their methods of fishing, and to the cormorant fishing at Gifu, but by now the prince was more famed for his inconspicuous solitary rambles. 'Geisha on Look-out for H.R.H. Incognito' one newspaper proclaimed, adding that every male westerner in Kyoto had been accosted by young ladies believing him to be the Prince of Wales.

Before departing from Kōbe in early May, the Prince attended a special Royal Ball given by the resident Britons at the Oriental Hotel. Among the 600 guests was the young Mr H.S. Williams, the writer on Japanese history. The officers and men of the British naval cruisers were all entertained at Kobe's Shurakukan theatre before they left with their royal passenger for the Philippines, British North Borneo and Penang. The prince disembarked at Suez to visit King Fuad in Cairo, and returned to England on 20 June after a strenuous eight-month tour that had caused much controversy and consternation among the upper echelons of the court, but which had spread more goodwill than any previous royal tour.

Chapter 43

Occupation

THE VOICE OF EMPEROR HIROHITO came over the radio. It sounded weak and exhausted against the background static from the hot vacuum tubes. It informed the Japanese people that the war was ended, that Japan had surrendered, and that they had to bear the unbearable. It was the first political action that an Emperor of Japan had initiated for centuries, and the first time ever that one had made direct contact with the people.

In the heat of that day, 14 August 1945, the tired, undernourished population was momentarily stunned to inactive silence. All around the country the desolate urban landscapes portrayed the results of militarism: ruined buildings everywhere, nothing growing, rats thriving, dirty black radioactive rain over two major cities where dying civilians and military men alike lay screaming in relentless agony, huddled groups of ragged people, mostly children and the aged, sleeping under broken walls, and everyone infused with intense psychological confusion. In Yokohama, at the Naval Interrogation Centre, Lieutenant Lewis Bush, hungry and dirty after years of captivity, smiled as his warden bowed and said: 'Well, now I am your prisoner! What are your orders!' Thinking quickly, he ordered all the other foreign prisoners to fall in and march to the local bathhouse. As they scrubbed off the grime from their light-coloured skins, a crowd gathered to watch them, and cheers were heard all around.

But elsewhere the relief at the ending of hostilities was mixed with fear. What now? The propaganda of the military machine had sown hatred of westerners in so many minds. Lies of enormous and fantastic proportions had been circulated to ensure that soldiers and arms manufacturers dedicated their lives to the war effort. Now the conquerors

were coming, would they rape and pillage, murder and torture as they
had been told? Many young women were sent to hide in the countryside
as a first precaution. The rest waited in the remains of their homes,
hungry, tired and afraid.

As the first wave of US marines landed on the coast outside
Nagasaki, no one could be seen. The jeeps and trucks moved into the
villages where houses were still standing. Still no one. Then a child's
face appeared peeping around a corner, then another. Soon dozens of
childrens' faces appeared at doorways and windows. Some of the foot
soldiers, armed to the teeth with all manner of destructive devices, held
out bars of chocolate to the shy, but curious, children. Unaffected by
the propaganda, but knowing they were hungry, the youngsters emerged
timidly and surrounded the soldiers. Instantly, they forgot their worn-out
clothes and began to chatter animatedly, tearing off the wrappers and
nibbling at the chocolate, too young to know how to behave according
to ancient Japanese etiquette when receiving gifts from strangers. The
older folk, spying from the shadows inside their houses, saw that the
dreaded Americans were not bayoneting the children as they had been
warned, and they, too, nervously emerged onto the streets. The seven-
year American Occupation of Japan had begun well. It was to be a
unique experience in world history, for most previous occupation had
involved the conquerors wildly destroying the ways and institutions of
the conquered, taking away the riches and resources, and imposing their
own ideas. Never before had one modern nation tried to reform another
by suggesting changes within it, nor was a defeated nation to receive so
much financial aid from its conquerors.

*   *   *

It was to be a revolutionary new approach to occupation that began in
the autumn of 1945 when American troops under the guidance of General
Douglas MacArthur entered Japan with a specific programme to reform
the country. Each member of his forces was regarded as a diplomat
hoping to bring a marriage of American and Japanese ways. However,
the majority of the GIs were not really suited to achieve this subtle
objective. Nevertheless, major changes were effected during Occupation
years, and these were far more radical and rapid than those that followed
the Meiji Restoration. Long-established institutions were reformed or
abandoned, and attitudes changed throughout the population despite
the fact that there was just one American present for 31,000 Japanese
citizens.

With MacArther established as the Supreme Commander for the
Allied Powers (SCAP), Japan virtually had two emperors. After
organising the demilitarisation of the country, involving the destruction
of research cyclotrons in university physics departments and the
repatriation of over six million Japanese soldiers from abroad, SCAP
made it publicly known that Emperor Hirohito was no longer to be

regarded as a divine being. This was announced on 1 January 1946 by
the Emperor himself, and he thus became a mere symbol of the Japanese
state. That year he emerged into the community on walk-abouts, meeting
ordinary people and showing interest in the reconstruction work.
Meanwhile, MacArthur became more and more of a recluse, seldom
appearing in public.

The state religion of Shinto, held responsible for aggressive
fanaticism, was to get no further aid from the government, and all ultra-
nationalistic organisations disbanded. Then came the war trials and the
purge. Seven former leaders were hanged, including Tojo who was Prime
Minister during the war years, and all former military officers and police
were banned from government service or any position of responsibility.
About 200,0000 people were purged, including many teachers. Members
of the great trading families, the zaibatsu, were purged and their vast
concentrations of wealth transferred into government hands by capital
levies. The nobility, a hangover from feudalism and perhaps encouraged
by British influence in the Meiji era, was abolished apart from the
Emperor and his immediate family, and all titles were officially dropped.
The education system was revised, but since Meiji times it had always
been universal and of high quality. The revision entailed the rewriting
of textbooks to eliminate all militaristic and nationalistic notions, and
making opportunities at university level more egalitarian.

*   *   *

These sweeping reforms were all imposed by SCAP but all were
administered by a functioning Japanese government. The unjust situation
of tenant farmers was changed. Absentee land ownership was abolished,
and within a decade almost all farmers owned the land they cultivated.
The greatest and most far-reaching task, however, was the writing and
adoption of a new constitution. This amended the 1889 constitution,
and in it the Emperor lost his divinity, and government similar to the
British parliamentary system was re-established. The concept of
'fundamental human rights' of the individual, quite alien to Japan before
this, was described, and by it women could vote for the first time and
had equal rights in marriage. Women organised themselves into groups
to discuss their new rights. Some told their group how they had daringly
left their homes alone to attend movies or cabarets — unheard of before
the war. In Osaka the first Union of Women's Hairdressers was formed
to breakaway from'the tyrannical male leaders of the Barbers' Union
and their old, unhealthy hair-styles.' At election times women kept their
places in queues of voters, not giving way to men. In city streets modern
wives walked next to their husbands instead of several places behind,
and they did not carry all the shopping. Young people, too, attempted
to absorb the spirit of the times; one youngster entered the office of his
town mayor without knocking, saying: 'Hello! I no longer have to bow
to you. We are now equal!' School children began to argue more with

teachers, and appeared less docile and disciplined. The most popular word current during the Occupation was *democrashi*. Democracy, too, was a brand new concept and was often misinterpreted; it was vaguely associated with everything American: electrical household gadgets, large cars, cocktail parties and Christmas presents.

Although it was called an 'allied occupation,' the personnel were almost entirely American. Two international committees were set up to advise MacArthur, one of them representing the 13 countries that had fought Japan, but these had little influence. British and Australian forces were stationed in remoter parts of the country and were largely uninvolved with political affairs. In any event, it might well have been considered hypocritical for Britain to have helped implement such reforms given the fact that the nobility, absentee landlords and a state-supported religion were firmly entrenched in her own semi-feudal social structure!

*   *   *

Post-war Japan had thousands of orphans, many of them vagrants who lived by their wits on the streets. Older girls drifted into prostitution to survive, boys tended towards thieving. Others collected cigarette butts by following Americans around, and selling the tobacco, and home-made shoe-shine stands appeared everywhere. Many orphans were repatriated from China and Taiwan, some carrying boxes of the ashes of their parents, suffering from disease and malnutrition, with no relatives to go to in Japan.

The police set up a special Youth Crime Section in Tokyo, and reformatories were built to house the new species of delinquent until they could be adopted into a family. Some Americans used their own initiative to help alleviate the problem, including Roxane Lambie from Detroit, a Red Cross club worker in Yokohama. She fed and bathed hundreds of homeless children, giving them new clothes after burning their lice-ridden rags, then taking them to local orphanages. Many ran away, unable to live a regimented life, preferring the freedom of the streets. Tokyo's 2000 homeless gathered at night in and around Ueno Station. Fires burned on the streets, fuelled by stolen grave markers, and the huddled crowds ate scraps taken from garbage. Many died after eating food containing poison, put out by householders to try to control the rats.

Rationing had immediately been introduced, and a black-market flourished. Prices of consumer goods were fixed by the authorities but seldom adhered to, and a 'New Yen Zaibatsu' arose among those controlling the goods. The newly-liberated farmer-owners did especially well. But the most propitious of all were the American occupationeers. Bartering food, cigarettes, soap and clothes, they accumulated ancient samurai swords, pearls, silk and treasures of all description. The entrances of the bases were constantly surrounded by wily Japanese dealers ready to fall in step with the serviceman with cartons of cigarettes under his tunic. Many stuffed an empty carton with newspaper, and made quick exchanges with more gullible dealers! But the penalty for such black-marketeering was four years' hard labour, and many Americans served this.

An early SCAP directive allowed all inmates of 'geisha houses' to break the contracts of bondage that kept them constantly in debt to their masters. In feudal times, the old system had operated efficiently, but now a new order had arrived. Yet thousands of women became prostitutes through economic necessity, their services being paid for in cigaretes, soap or food — equivalent to about ¥30. Many were free-lance street-walkers while others entered large brothels set up to please American customers. Just outside of Tokyo, on the road to Chiba, the huge 'Willow Run' contained 3000 girls, and jeeps and staff-cars continually lined the road outside. Official signs of 'Off Limits!' and 'V.D' did not deter many. Indeed some ordinary Japanese storekeepers noticed that the 'V.D.' signs seemed to attract American servicemen, and they too erected 'V.D.' signs over their shops.

Unwanted babies were everywhere — floating in canals, dumped amongst garbage or left outside houses. In a Yokohama bathhouse, a mother left her GI baby in a basket outside. Another similar mother arrived with her baby, the child of a negro soldier, and switched babies. After her bath, the first mother's screaming could be heard along the whole street as she vainly searched for her own child.

But even if an American serviceman established a steady relationship with a Japanese girl, regulations prevented them from marrying, and the Oriental Exclusion Act stopped any Japanese entering the USA. Since the intrusion of the West in 1853, when Perry's sailors swam ashore to fraternise with Japanese girls, the unfortunate children of 'mixed blood' had always been deprived. Such was the unjust nature of state nationalism. The most pathetic case, not uncommon during the Occupation, was described by Miss Lucy Crockett as she sat on a train at Kobe. Two Japanese girls, probably pregnant, tearfully waved goodbye to their GI boyfriends who were homeward bound. One sobbing girl shouted: 'When you come back?' and the reply came: 'Come back? Why, when you ****** Japs bomb Pearl Harbor again! We'll be back!' So much for military diplomacy.

But as the years slowly went by, more order came to Japan. Tokyo's Ginza street, at first a line of burned-out shells, became lined with tiny wood-and-cloth stalls selling all kinds of wares for black-market yen. Behind them the gutted department stores were reconstructed, one becoming the main PX, and more and more Japanese-produced goods appeared in them, showing that the wheels of industry were beginning to turn again. By the end of the Occupation, American and European missionaries had arrived to try to fill the spiritual gap, left by the devastation of war, with Christianity. Christmas, celebrated by the occupationeers with great relish, appealed to the Japanese, especially its commercial aspects. One enterprising department store displayed a life-size Santa Claus in its main window — the bearded, red and white figure was nailed to a cross.

On 8 September 1951, Japan signed a Peace Treaty with 48 nations, but excluding Russia and Communist China, in San Francisco. The following April the Occupation ended, and Japan once again became independent. A year later Yokohama celebrated the centenary of the arrival of Commodore Perry.

References/Bibliography

'A.M.' (PROF. JAMES MURDOCH) *From Australia and Japan* 1892

BARR, PAT *The Coming of the Barbarians* (Macmillan 1967)

BARR, PAT *The Deer Cry Pavilion* (Macmillan 1968)

BEAUCHAMP, EDWARD R. *An American Teacher in Early Meiji Japan* (U. of Hawaii 1976)

BIRD, ISABELLA L. *Unbeaten Tracks in Japan* (Murray 1880)

BLACK, J.R. *Young Japan* (Baker, Pratt 1883)

BLUM, PAUL *Yokohama in 1872* (ASOJ 1963)

BRASSEY, Mrs. A. *A Voyage in the Sunbeam* (Longmans, Green & Co. 1879)

BRINKLEY, CAPT. F. & BARON KIKUCHI, *A History of the Japanese People* (Encyclopaedia Britannica 1914)

CAMPBELL DAVIDSON, A.M. *Present-day Japan* (Fisher Unwin 1904)

CARY, OTIS *A History of Christianity in Japan* (Revell 1909)

CHAMBERLAIN, B.H. & MASON, W.B. *Murray's Handbook for Japan* (John Murray 1907)

CHAMBERLAIN, B.H. *Things Japanese* (1891)

CROCKETT, L.H. *Popcorn on the Ginza* (Gollancz 1949)

DE BECKER, J.E. *The Nightless City* 1899

DEL MAR, WALTER *Around the World Through Japan* (Black 1904)

DOI, TAKEO *The Anatomy of Dependence* (Kodansha 1973)

DYER, HENRY *Dai Nipon* (Blackie 1904)

ETHERTON, COL. P.T. & HESSELL TILTMAN, H. *Japan: Mistress of the Pacific* (Jarrolds 1934)

FAULDS, HENRY *Nine Years in Nipon* (Gardener 1885)

FOX, GRACE *Britain and Japan 1858-1883* (OUP 1969)

FUJIMOTO, T. *The Nightside of Japan* 1914

FUJIMOTO, T. *The Story of the Geisha Girl* 1917

GOODMAN, GRANT JOHN *The Dutch Impact on Japan 1640-1853* (E.J. Brill 1967)

GRIFFIS, W.E. *The Mikado's Empire* (Harper 1900)

GRIFFIS, W.E. *Verbeck of Japan* (Revell 1900)

HOLLAND, CLIVE *Old and New Japan* (Dent 1907)

HOLLAND, CLIVE *My Japanese Wife* 1895

HOLTHAM, EDMUND G. *Eight Years in Japan 1873-1881* (Kegan, Paul & Trench 1883)

HUBNER, LE BARON DE *A Ramble Round the World 1871* (Macmillan 1884)

HUMBERT, AIME *Manners and Customs of the Japanese* (Bentley 1874)

JONES, HAZEL, J. *The Meiji Government and Foreign Employees 1868-1900* (Doctoral Thesis, U. of Michigan 1967, unpub.)

JONES, HAZEL, J. *Live Machines: Hired Foreigners & Meiji Japan* (Paul Norbury 1980)

KNOX, G.W. *Imperial Japan* (Newnes 1905)

MORTON-CAMERON, W.H. (Compiler) *Present-day Impressions of Japan* (Globe 1919)

NAKAYAMA, SHIGERU *A History of Japanese Astronomy* (Harvard U. 1969)

OLIPHANT, LAURENCE *Narrative of the Earl of Elgin's Mission to China and Japan* (1859)

PAPINOT, E. *Historical and Geographical Dictionary of Japan* (Kelly and Walsh 1910)

PORTER, R.F. *Japan the New World Power* (OUP 1915)

POTTER, BISHOP *The East of Today and Tomorrow* 1900

REISCHAUER, EDWIN O. *Japan: the Story of a Nation* (Tuttle 1976)

ROGERS, P.O. *The First Englishman in Japan* (Harvill Press 1956)

SCHERER, JAMES A.B. *Japan Today* (Lippincott 1904)

SCIDMORE, E.H. *Jinrikisha Days in Japan* (Harper 1892)

STORRY, RICHARD *Japan and the Decline of the West in Asia 1894-1943* (Macmillan 1979)

ST. JOHN, CAPT. H.C. *Wild Coasts of Nipon* (David Douglas 1880)

SUGIMOTO, M. & SWAIN, D.L. *Science and Culture in Traditional Japan 600-1854* (MIT Press 1978)

TOFFLER, ALVIN *The Third Wave* (Pan 1980)

VOYCE, REV. A.H. *Sunrise in the East* (Polwinkle 1975)

WARREN CLARKE, E. *Life and Adventure in Japan* 1878

WHITNEY, CLARA *Clara's Diary* (Kodansha 1979)

WILLIAMS, HAROLD S. *Shades of the Past: Tales of the Foreign Settlements in Japan* (Tuttle 1958)

WILLIAM, HAROLD S. *Foreigners in Mikadoland* (Tuttle 1963)

In Japanese

Kune Fune Kitaru (Sekai Bunkasha 1977)

Nishi-E Bakumatsu no Rekishi — Meiji Konishi Shiro 1977

Showa Jidoshashi (Nihonjin to kuruma no 100 nen) (Mainichi Shimbun 1979)

Meiji, Taisho Zushi (Tokyo) Chikuma Shobo (Showhan Dai Isatsu Hako 1978)

Meiji, Taisho Zushi (Yokohama, Kobe) Chikuma Shobo (Showhan Dai Isatsu Hako 1978)

Newspapers:
Japan Herald (1861-2), *Japan Weekly Mail* (1871-4), *Japan Weekly Times* (1902-9), *Japan Advertiser* May 1922, *The Japan Times, Godey's Lady's Book and Magazine* (1859-70).

Index

243